P9-BTX-963

Prison Reform and
State Elites

Prison Reform and State Elites

by
Richard A. Berk
Peter H. Rossi

Ballinger Publishing Company ● Cambridge, Massachusetts
A Subsidiary of J.B. Lippincott Company

CARNEGIE LIBRARY
LIVINGSTONE COLLEGE
SALISBURY, N. C. 28144

This book is printed on recycled paper.

Copyright © 1977 by Ballinger Publishing Company. All rights re-
served. No part of this publication may be reproduced, stored in a re-
trieval system, or transmitted in any form or by any means, electronic
mechanical photocopy, recording or otherwise, without the prior written
consent of the publisher.

International Standard Book Number: 0-88410-214-9

Library of Congress Catalog Card Number: 76-212 40

Printed in the United States of America

Library of Congress Cataloging in Publication Data

Berk, Richard A
  Prison reform and State elites.

  Includes bibliographical references.
  1. Corrections—Florida. 2. Corrections—Illinois.
3. Corrections—Washington (State) 4. Elite (Social
sciences) I. Rossi, Peter Henry, 1921-   joint
author. II. Title.
HV9304.B46   365′.7′0973   76-21240
ISBN 0-88410-214-9

365.7
B 512

Dedication

To Edmund Dantes,
Count of Monte Cristo,
who first aroused our interest
in prison reform.

12.60

2-13-78

BET

105494

Contents

List of Tables

Acknowledgments

Many persons contributed their time and talents to the research reported in this volume. First of all, we are grateful for the help provided by the men and women of Florida, Illinois, and Washington who gave freely of their time and thoughts in answering our queries. We hope their willingness to spend up to two hours with our interviewers is justified by the ways in which we have summarized their remarks.

Second, the staff of NICJLE helped us from straying off the main topic and constantly fed ideas into the design of the study. Without their help, our study would not be as sharply focussed.

Third, the staff of Audits and Surveys, Inc., particularly Dexter Neadle and Nagesh Gupta, ably undertook the main task of fielding the study and collecting all but a handful of the interviews reported here.

Finally, in each of three universities we were supported by staffs who made it possible to complete the study and this book. The field work on the study was conducted while Peter Rossi was research director of the Center for Metropolitan Planning and Research of Johns Hopkins University. This manuscript was completed at the Social and Demographic Research Institute of the University of Massachusetts. The Center for Urban Affairs at Northwestern University, home-base institution of Richard Berk, participated in all of the phases of the research.

At Hopkins, Sally G. Zulver was primarily responsible for producing our list of respondents. These efforts were seriously complicated by reluctant bureaucrats, scattered information, and state governments reorganizing after recent elections. Her tenacity, charm, and intelligence managed nevertheless to win the day. Lawrence Kaagan played a similar role at Northwestern with comparable skill, a sophisticated understanding of local politicians, and a sense of humor that kept us all from taking ourselves too seriously.

From the design stages onward, we were also able to rely on the considerable data-processing skills of Northwestern's Richard Hay and Geoffrey Gilbert; Hopkins' Christine Bose and Emily Waite, and Thomas Laurent of the University of Massachusetts. While intense exposure to computer hardware over long periods seems to produce a chronic degeneration of the neural centers responsible for getting work done on time, Hay, Gilbert, Bose, Waite, and Laurent somehow met our demanding schedule with both efficiency and good spirits.

In addition, Thomas Laurent participated so extensively in the analysis presented in chapter 6 that he should be considered a coauthor of that chapter.

Shirley Sult and Barbara Lansky typed innumerable drafts of the questionnaires, memoranda, and a preliminary report while Rossi was at Johns Hopkins. At Northwestern, Deborah Lubeck, Diane LeFavor, and Marcey Friedman handled the clerical tasks with equal skill. Finally, drafts of this manuscript were typed at the University of Massachusetts by Laura Martin and Marcia Alves. Clearly, we have been blessed with unusually fine assistance in all phases of this research.

The work reported here is another product of an enduring close collaboration between the two authors, a cooperative enterprise that manages to persist as mutually fruitful despite the distances between Amherst, Massachusetts, Evanston, Illinois, and Baltimore, Maryland. Thus, while we may secretly disagree about who deserves more credit for this study's merits, we jointly acknowledge responsibility for its faults.

July 1976

Richard A. Berk
Peter H. Rossi

✳ *Chapter 1*

Research Goals and Procedures

Although this is neither the best of times nor the worst of times, it is certainly a period of widespread dissatisfaction with many fundamental American institutions. Private enterprise is being challenged as both ambiguously private and avariciously enterprising. Oligopolistic markets are criticized as hardly markets at all, while corporate elite and federal regulators, incestuously coupled, attempt to maintain the fiction of open competition. Hence, unemployment, inflation, inefficiency, and environmental pollution are all readily laid at the doorstep of corporate America.[1]

Unfortunately, performance in the public sector seems no more heartening. The "welfare mess" stumbles along with little sign of concrete remediation. Schools seem less and less able to teach even survival skills, while surprisingly high infant mortality rates signal that nutrition and medical care are inadequate despite massive governmental subsidies.

And then there is crime. What Ralph Nader has called "crime in the suites" has ravaged not only executive board rooms, but all levels of governmental activity. At the same time, its out-of-doors cousin has made people fearful of fully utilizing their neighborhoods, parks, and shops. Police departments by themselves seem largely incapable of dealing with these realities, and recent revelations of rampant corruption and serious civil-liberties infringements have added still more fuel to popular anxieties.

While criticisms of law enforcement personnel seem most immediately directed at police, the entire criminal justice bureaucracy is under attack. Prosecutors are deemed both inefficient and biased, public defenders are blamed for selling out, and judges are denounced both for summary justice and unwarranted delays.

It is partly in this context of widespread disillusionment with a variety of large-scale efforts that one can begin to understand current dissatisfactions with state correctional systems. If we take as their primary goal the sequestering of convicted felons from society, they are probably doing an adequate (though perhaps not cost-effective) job. However, if we ask for something more from our prisons, they obviously fall far short of expectations.

By and large, there is no evidence that prisons "rehabilitate."[2] Even if they did, the cost in tax dollars is rapidly becoming prohibitive.[3] Similarly, there is no evidence that by itself, the threat of lengthy sentences deters would-be offenders.[4] In contrast, prisons clearly foster oppositional communities, demean and demoralize inmates, and ultimately release embittered men and women who may be even worse off than when they entered.[5] Finally, there are now also signs that prisons are failing even in the limited goal of incarceration. Prison riots over the past few years are ample testimony that many institutions are unable to control their inmates.

Although we may be quickly reaching consensus on corrections failures, debates continue on appropriate remedies. One side adamantly adheres to the earlier optimism of such thinkers as Karl Menninger[6] and would hold with Vernon Fox that "corrections is intended to be a people-changing process. The current lack of professional personnel and resources make people-changing almost impossible. . . . The crux of prison reform lies in its personnel."[7] In other words, were the "therapeutic community" fully achieved, rehabilitation would be easily realized.

A second position contends that the potential for rehabilitation has been vastly overstated both in the numbers needing help and in the possibilities for meaningful change. Moreover, this view typically argues that it is naïve to attempt rehabilitation within the confines of traditional prisons when adjustment must ultimately occur elsewhere. Thus, there is a call for far less incarceration, with various kinds of community-based alternatives the most popular substitute. These "alternatives beyond prison walls" coupled with innovative nonclinical programs within prisons would promise not only reduced recidivism, but lower costs.[8]

A third side attacks rehabilitation even more fundamentally. They begin by noting the inevitable contradictions within the "forced treatment" implied by imprisonment,[9] and some even challenge the concept of rehabilitation altogether. It is not at all clear, they argue, that inmates are in any sense "sick," and even if they were, change must necessarily be self-motivated. In short, they propose that corrections systems completely drop any pretense of rehabilitation.[10] Some would also contend that, therefore, detention and deterrence are the only legitimate prison goals.

In summary, virtually all of the historical trends noted by such authors as Leon Radzinowicz are alive and kicking today.[11] It is true that across the country proponents of rehabilitation are on the defensive, but despite the heroic efforts of reformers like Jerome Miller, their programs remain largely intact.[12] Nevertheless, it is also fair to say that there seems to have been a significant decline in popular expectations for prisons. This may be part of an overall disillusionment with American institutions; nevertheless, there appears to be sufficient unrest about correction policies and programs to suggest the possibility of important changes in the near future.

PURPOSE OF THIS STUDY

The signs and portents of change in state prisons formed the background of the larger study of which the present research was designed to be a part. The overall purpose of the aborted larger effort was to gauge the receptivity to reforms in adult corrections among persons who were potentially instrumental in initiating, approving, and carrying out programs within state corrections systems. It was to be, therefore, a study of "elites," in the technical sense of persons occupying positions of power and influence. It was also to be a study of "opinion" in the sense of being concerned with the manner in which members of state elites might evaluate a hypothetical set of changes in state prisons for adults.

The original study was designed to be policy relevant. First, the reforms considered were among the more important proposed by the National Advisory Commission on Criminal Justice Standards and Goals and hence had a reasonable chance of being seriously considered over the following years.[13] Second, the study was designed to plumb elite opinions in some depth, being concerned not only with reactions to global descriptions of the proposed changes, but with rather specific reforms as well. Third, the study attempted to weight opinions by the influence of their proponents. While it may be technically true that all are equal before law, it is also true that few are equal in making it. Finally, where possible, we planned to extract the practical implications of our findings for strategies of corrections reform. In short, policy-makers were seen as a critical audience for our efforts.

Although these were the overall goals of the total study, this book is confined to the results of a fairly elaborate prototype study conducted in three states: Florida, Illinois, and Washington. We are all too aware of the limitations of our sample of states and our samples of elites within each. *We must therefore caution the reader that these results are limited in their generality.* Perhaps the most important message of this research is its technical feasibility.

THE RELATIONSHIP BETWEEN THE LARGER STUDY AND THE PILOT PROJECT

We began this project with the aspirations described above. To fulfill these it was necessary to obtain a reasonable sample of states and, within each of the sample states, reasonable samples of persons occupying the relevant elite positions. The details of our projected study are given in the next section.

The larger study was never completed. This book reports only on the results for a far smaller feasibility effort conducted in three states. Here it was hoped that two important questions might be effectively addressed. First, was it possible to interview the busy men and women who constituted the elites of state corrections, obtaining reasonable responses without arousing antagonism? Second, would results obtainable yield information of value in formulating strategies for changing state corrections systems?

We completed the pilot project in the late winter of 1973 and presented our report to the staff of the National Institute of Criminal Justice and Law Enforcement. The preliminary report, upon which the present manuscript is partially based, showed, we thought, that it was possible to affirmatively answer both of the questions that had prompted the pilot project.

Our own optimism was not matched by the staff of NICJLE. For reasons we were never able to fully understand, plans to proceed with the larger study were cancelled. A subsequent small grant from the NICJLE made it possible to prepare this book.

RATIONALE OF THE RESEARCH

The basic design features of this study rest upon a view of political decision-making whose content dictated in very broad terms the kinds of persons to be interviewed and the kinds of measures to be gathered. To begin, our perspective is particularly appropriate for short-term rather than long-term concerns; in predicting what may occur within the next year or so. It rests upon the simple assumption that, at any given time, those formally or customarily authorized and required to make political decisions are of primary interest in the projection of which decisions are likely to be made in the immediate future.[14] In other words, whatever the ultimate sources of changes in our legal structure, the agendas of formal decision-makers are the ones immediately under consideration and, hence, are most likely to affect local penal codes or administrative procedures. There are obviously no changes in state law without the action of state legislatures, and there are no fundamental alterations in formal administrative procedures without the cooperation of corrections personnel.

Hence, our study of potential penal reform is centered on decision-makers. Of course, it is easy enough to locate through state constitutions and enabling statutes those positions in a political structure with the formal power to make a difference. But decision-making extends beyond these structures to include an amorphous group who attempt to influence official decision-makers and to whom the latter may look for advice and guidance in formulating legislation. Indeed, the full model includes "partisans," defined as positions within organizations that one can reasonably expect would have a stake in the corrections system of their states. For example, in any study of corrections reform, one might include such partisans are the state courts, lower-level corrections and parole officials, such private associations as the American Civil Liberties Union, and associations of ex-prisoners. The particular decision-makers and partisans in this study are described in detail later in this chapter.

Decision-makers and potential partisans were to be interviewed to estimate the extent to which certain types of prison reforms would find relatively friendly or hostile receptions. In order to measure this receptivity, each interview contained questions covering:

1. assessment of the adequacy of each state's adult prison system;
2. assessment of the relative importance of specific decision-makers and partisans in the decision-making usually surrounding corrections legislation;
3. approval-disapproval of alternative corrections "futures," i.e., brief descriptions of alternative ways in which corrections systems might be changed;
4. priorities given to overall goals of corrections systems;
5. approval-disapproval of specific prison reforms (e.g., use of solitary confinement, censorship of prisoner mail, etc.); and
6. appropriate treatments for different types of convicted offenders: brief descriptions (vignettes) of convicted offenders allocated by respondents to an appropriate treatment (e.g., parole, probation, incarceration, etc.).

Additional information designed to help interpret each respondent's interview was also obtained, including expectations of public support for corrections reform, and standard demographic and socio-economic data. The interview form used is shown in Appendix B.

The three-state data collected allow the construction of the following measures:

1. salience of prison reform as an issue in each state;
2. receptivity to a variety of change "packages," specific reforms, and changes in the handling of specific types of offenders; and
3. weighting responses according to the "importance" in each states' decision-making accorded to the respondent by other members of the sample or his own assessment of his importance.

A special feature of the study is the application of experimental design techniques to the study of individual attitudes. The offender "vignettes" briefly described in item 6 above were composed of combinations of three characteristics: an offense, varying from vignette to vignette in "seriousness" as measured by scores derived from a separate survey;[15] age of offender; and previous record of the offender, described as ranging from "no previous record" to a record including felonies for crimes against the persons and crimes against property. The three sets of characteristics allowed a very large number of combinations to be constructed (1400 in all). After the basic list of vignettes was reduced about 10 percent by deletion of meaningless combinations (e.g., fifty-year-old truant), each respondent was given a random sample of forty of the approximately 1160 remaining. Since each random sample was statistically equivalent, treatments deemed appropriate by each respondent for various hypothetical convicted offenders could be used to characterize each respondent along a continuum of leniency. In addition, when responses to the samples of vignettes were accumulated across the entire sample of respondents, all of the combinations that went into the full set of 1160 vignettes could be analyzed in order to gauge the relative importance of the three vignette characteristics (offense, age, and previous record) in how respondents allocated hypothetical offenders to different sorts of treatments. The analyses of these results for the three pilot states are contained in later chapters.

It should also be noted that the respondents' receptivity to changes in the corrections system was measured on four levels: a philosophical level involving a hierarchy of fundamental corrections goals; a "global" level in which change was presented as a "package," a "specific practices" level in which changes were broken down into component parts; and an "offender treatment" level in which different types of convicted offenders were considered. These four levels correspond roughly to a continuum from a relatively abstract to a relatively detailed level in which changes in the treatment of specific types of offenders are weighed. We believe that these four levels provide considerable depth to the measurement of receptivity to change.

THE STUDY DESIGN FOR THE FULL
SAMPLE OF TWENTY STATES

Laying out a general approach to a survey is often easier than designing a specific plan, and this study was no exception. The design problems centered around three major sets of decisions: choosing states; choosing positions (and, by implication, respondents) to be interviewed; and constructing a survey instrument.

Designing a Sample of States

Since the basic political units of concern were the fifty states, and resources, even initially, were insufficient to study all fifty, we had to devise a way of selecting some portion of the total set. The original sample size was set at twenty, based partly on the availability of resources and partly on an examination of the distribution of the prisoner population among the states. Since the purpose of the full study was to judge the potential for changes in state corrections systems, the states selected had to represent in some reasonable way the corrections problems of the country as a whole.

The prison systems of some states are so small that they can hardly be said to reflect a significant portion of the general controversy over prison reform. Indeed, some states have so few prisoners that they contract with neighboring states for prison services. Other states (such as New York or California) have such large prison systems serving the needs of their urbanized populations that they house a very large portion of the total prisoner population in the United States. In short, the distribution of the sizes of the adult prison population by states is highly skewed. The largest ten states contain more than half (58 percent) of the total adult state prison population in the United States.[16] The smallest twenty-six states together contain only 15 percent of the state adult prison population. To pick states with equal probability would result in a sample of states in which the state corrections systems housing the largest numbers of prisoners would be in a practical sense underrepresented.

We chose a sampling strategy in which states were selected with probability proportionate to the sizes of their adult prison populations. States were ranked according to their adult prisoner populations, and four strata, as shown below, were devised, each stratum having an associated probability to be used in choosing the specific states for study:

Sample Stratum	Percent of 1970 Adult Prisoners Population	Selection Probability	Number of States Chosen
Stratum I: Ten Largest States	58.2	1.00	10
Stratum II: Next Thirteen Largest States	33.5	.38	5
Stratum III: Next Sixteen Largest States	8.0	.125	2
Stratum IV: Remaining Eleven States	3.0	.09	1

This strategy provided us with a sample of eighteen states, leaving two additional states to be chosen to form strata of states of "special interest."

The states in strata II, III, and IV were chosen using a table of random numbers, with the following results:

Stratum I (All states in this stratum fall into the sample)	Proportion of 1970 U.S. Adult Corrections Population in State
California	14.1
Texas	8.1
New York	6.8
Florida	5.2
Ohio	5.2
Michigan	5.1
Illinois	3.6
Pennsylvania	3.6
North Carolina	3.4
New Jersey	3.2

Stratum II (States picked with probability of .38)

Virginia	2.6
Louisiana	2.4
Missouri	1.9
Tennessee	1.8
Washington	1.6

Stratum III (States picked with probability of .125)

Massachusetts	1.2
West Virginia	.5

Stratum IV (States picked with probability .09)

Wyoming	.09

In consultation with NICJLE staff, two additional strata were formed, stratum V consisting of a state of special interest because of its contemplated reforms, Minnesota, and stratum VI, consisting of one state, Alabama, chosen because none of the states in the Deep South had fallen into the sample picked above. The resulting overall sample of states represents fairly well the corrections systems that handle the state adult prisoner population of the United States, supplemented by states of special interest.

Selection of three states for the first phase of the study was done judgmentally on the basis of trying to assure a geographic spread and to represent neither the most progressive nor the least progressive among the states with relatively large imprisoned offender populations. Florida, Illinois, and Washington seemed to fit those criteria.[17]

Selecting Respondents

The overall plan called for interviewing "decision-makers" and "partisans" in each state. The translation of these terms into specific, identifiable positions was accomplished by relying upon general knowledge about the workings of state governments and upon the advice of experts. The subcategory "decision-makers" was easier to define than "partisans," since the latter were only potentially involved. In defining "partisans" we erred more on the side of inclusiveness, possibly adding persons in positions that ordinarily have little influence on decision-making.[18]

The categories of respondents finally decided upon are shown in the row labels of table 1-1. The numbers in the first column (on the left) refer to the numbers of desired interviews in each state. The three columns on the right contain the numbers of interviews actually obtained in each of the three states.

The "decision-maker" category contains state governors, state legislators, and heads of corrections agencies in each state. In each state thirty-three persons in this category were to be interviewed.

The remainder of table 1-1 describes positions we have labeled "partisans." This general designation covers several subgroups: persons holding positions within the broader criminal justice system (B

Table 1–1.   Overall State Sample Design and Field Experiences in Florida, Illinois, and Washington (as of April 10, 1973)

Position Within State	Number to be Interviewed Per State	Numbers Actually Interviewed (as of April 10, 1973)			Three States Combined
		Florida	Illinois	Washington	
A. *Official Decision-Makers:*					
Present Governor and Previous Governor	2	0	1	2	3
Head of Corrections Agency and Major Deputy	2	2	1	1	4
Chairpersons of Corrections Committees in Both Houses	2	1	2	2	5
Other Members of Corrections Committees in Both Houses[a]	8	9	1	5	15
Party Leaders in Both Houses	4	3	4	1	8
Four Influential Members in Each House[b]	8	6	1	2	9
State Parole Board Chairperson and Two Board Members[a]	3	3	2	3	8
State LEAA Planning Agency Officials	2	2	2	2	6
Juvenile Corrections Agency Head and Major Deputy	2	2	1	1	4
Subtotals	33	28	15	19	62
B. *Partisans: Law Enforcement Officials and Lower Level Corrections Officials:*					
Warden of Largest State Adult Men's Prison and Two Additional Wardens[a]	3	3	3	5	11
Head of Largest Juvenile Detention Facility and Two Other Heads[a]	3	5	2	4	11
Parole Board Functionaries	2	1	2	1	4
Lower Level Corrections Personnel[c]	6	6	9	7	22
Police Chief of Largest City and of all Cities over 50,000	5	5	4	3	12
Head of State Police Force	1	1	0	1	2
Sheriff of Largest County and Three Additional Counties[a]	4	4	4	4	12
Subtotals	24	25	24	25	74

Table 1-1.   Continued

Position Within State	Number to be Interviewed Per State	Numbers Actually Interviewed (as of April 10, 1973)			Three States Combined
		Florida	Illinois	Washington	
C. Partisans: Judiciary, State Attorneys, and Legal Profession:					
Head of State Bar Association and of Largest City or County Bar	2	1	2	2	5
Chairperson of State Bar Association Committee on Criminal Law or Corrections and One Additional Member[a]	2	2	2	1	5
Municipal Court Judges with Criminal Jurisdiction (Sampled as Police Chiefs)	4	5	0	5	10
Judges of State Criminal Courts of First Level[d]	4	4	3	3	10
Judges of State Courts of First Appeal[d]	4	4	3	3	10
Judges of State Courts of Final Appeal[d]	2	2	1	2	5
Probation Officers (Heads of Departments)	5	5	4	5	14
Attorney General	1	0	1	1	2
Prosecuting Attorneys[e]	up to 8	7	3	4	14
Public Defenders[e]	up to 4	4	4	2	10
Subtotals	30-36	34	23	28	85
D. Partisans: Other Public Officials:					
Mayors of Cities Over 50,000	5	6	1	1	8
County Officials (Sampled Similar to Sheriffs)	4	5	4	5	14
Subtotals	9	11	5	6	22
E. Partisans: Other Partisans:					
ACLU Officials and Similar Groups	2	2	1	1	4
Police and Other Law Enforcement Unions and Benevolent Associations	2	1	3	0	4

Continued

Table 1–1.   Continued

Position Within State	Number to be Interviewed Per State	Numbers Actually Interviewed (as of April 10, 1973)			Three States Combined
		Florida	Illinois	Washington	
Citizens' Crime Commissions or Similar Groups	2	2	0	0	2
Other Active Groups[f]	5	4	5	4	13
Subtotal	11	9	9	5	23
GRAND TOTAL	107–113	107	76	83	266

[a]Selected at random from lists of members.
[b]Selected by nominations from respondents in legislature.
[c]Selected by nominations from higher-level corrections officials who are asked names of especially influential rank-and-file employees.
[d]Sampled with probability proportionate to size of jurisdiction.
[e]Sampled as judges but at appropriately lower probability rates.
[f]Chosen from among groups and persons designated by knowledgeable informants and respondents.

and C); "other public officials" (D); and a "residual group" (E) consisting of private associations such as the ACLU and police unions.

The categories were partially fixed and partially variable. For example, in each state the governor and former governor were to be interviewed. Hence, there was no discretion. In contrast, the category "influential members in the state legislature" could be filled with some flexibility. Our intent was to designate specific respondents through information gathered in the field. For example, party heads and committee chairpersons were to be asked to suggest persons who were influential in each house of the legislature.

In order to fulfill the interviewing plan it was necessary to collect names, addresses, and, if possible, telephone numbers of persons who held the specified positions. This was successfully accomplished in advance of field work by consulting state directories, obtaining lists from the relevant agencies, and, in some cases, telephoning the states to obtain information from clerks of the legislature, state librarians, and other informed persons.[19]

Constructing the Interview Schedule

Initially, we planned to interview all decision-makers and mail questionnaires to all partisans. The interview schedule and the questionnaire are therefore virtually identical, with the occasional exception of very minor wording changes.

The questionnaire and interview schedule were written to reflect the general goals of the study outlined earlier in this chapter. Several drafts of the questionnaire-schedule were prepared and modified in consultation with staff members of NILECJ.

A copy of the mailed version of the questionnaire is shown as appendix B.

THE PILOT STUDY: FLORIDA, ILLINOIS, AND WASHINGTON

The larger study departed from "typical" sample surveys in many ways. Respondents were busy members of their state's political "elite." The questionnaire deviated from "typical" formats in being quite complicated and potentially a considerable burden. Furthermore, it was difficult in Baltimore to assemble respondent lists from such distant states of Florida, Illinois, and Washington. Finally, the study was concerned with controversial issues, perhaps, as in Illinois, at the heart of ongoing political disputes. For these reasons, a pilot survey seemed desirable to determine the study's feasibility. At that time, a second phase was also planned (and money appropriated) to be conducted upon demonstrated success of the pilot work.

The pilot study was initiated the week of January 5, 1973 with the instruction of interviewers and the mailing of questionnaires. Each respondent was also sent a letter from Mr. Jerris Leonard, then administrator of the Law Enforcement Assistance Administration, requesting his (or her) cooperation in the study. Audits and Surveys, a commercial survey firm, served as field work subcontractor, mailing questionnaires and using members of their nationwide interviewing staff to conduct personal interviews with decision-makers in the three states.[20]

We had hoped to complete the data collection by March 15, 1973. As table 1–1 indicates, however, we had not completed our interviewing when the study was terminated in April 1973. First of all, we found it extremely difficult to assemble complete lists of names, largely for reasons beyond our control. For example, the three state legislatures were, during January 1973, in the process of organizing themselves—establishing committee memberships, electing party leaders, etc.—and hence names of specific persons holding appropriate positions within each state legislature only gradually became available in the period between January 15 and the end of February. Second, although *no* refusals were obtained by Audits and Surveys interviewers or by the authors, obtaining appointments with these very busy individuals (or obtaining returned questionnaires by mail) was quite difficult. We severely underestimated both the advance preparation necessary in preparing lists of respondents and in carrying out the field work. In addition, the logistics involved in preparing letters in New York for Mr. Jerris Leonard's signature, mailing them to Washington for signature, and having them returned to New York before mailing involved considerable turnaround delays. Indeed, in the middle of February there were still one hundred respondent names to whom letters had not yet been mailed.

We came quite close to fulfilling plans in Florida, with 107 interviews (out of a desired 107–113), faltered in Illinois (with only 76 interviews), but did a bit better in Washington (with 83 interviews). It should be noted that our interviewers went first into Florida and were in the field longest in that state. Interviews in Illinois and Washington were delayed primarily because of the delays in state legislature reorganization.

Examining categories of respondents in table 1–1 shows that we did least well in reaching decision-makers. At least some of our difficulties in this respect stemmed from conditions beyond our control: the Washington and Illinois legislatures did not organize until well into February of 1973. In Illinois, the legislature refused to appoint a commissioner of corrections until long after we had completed our field work. Some of our difficulties were also due to the fact that our respondents were extremely difficult to reach. The governors and former governors of each of the states, for example, never refused outright to be interviewed, and Governor Evans of Washington gave generously of his time. However, Governor Askew made and broke more than a dozen appointments before our field staff gave up, while Governor Walker (according to one of his aides) was simply unable to cooperate "at this time." While recent political events indicate that Governor Walker, despite his rhetoric, is often less than candid, in this instance, fault may well lie with an assistant who was clearly unsympathetic to our efforts. He made numerous promises to the senior author but failed to deliver on a single one. This contrasts markedly with the generous cooperation provided by former Governor Ogilvie.

The other categories of respondents were considerably easier to reach. The judiciary, states attorney's offices, and members of the bar were especially friendly and cooperative, as were corrections officials and other "partisans."

The experiences of the pilot phase provide a firm basis for believing that field work of this sort was feasible. However, we needed more time for field work. We are also confident that personal interviews were considerably more productive than mailing questionnaires. Indeed, by the end of one month's field experience, we decided to shift completely to personal interviews. The mailed returns were so slow in coming back that we despaired that this method could yield more than a fraction of the desired completion rate.

The actual field experiences indicate that respondents found the interviews interesting and relevant. Indeed, more than a score of letters were received by NICJLE from respondents indicating their interest in the study and their pleasure in the interview or questionnaire.

As a personal interview, the schedule typically took about one and a half hours to administer. By any standards, this was a long interview and possibly a burden, especially for these busy respondents. However, a lack of complaints on this score indicated that respondents found the interview interesting and not too burdensome. The personal experiences of the two authors (who participated in the interviewing) bore out this generalization. We found our respondents interested in the study, easily involved in the interviewing situation and, although conscious of the time spent, not unwilling to complete the lengthy session.

All told, our experiences in the pilot study led to several conclusions. First, the major problem in carrying out the field work was logistical. Scheduling interviews and obtaining responses by mail were difficult to carry out over a short period of time. We are confident that given a more leisurely pace of field work, completion rates in each state could easily be expected to attain the level of our Florida experience, or better.

Second, there were *no* reactions from respondents indicating that our questionnaires were biased one way or another. Apparently the questionnaire was sufficiently balanced to allow the expression of a broad spectrum of views on corrections reform. Both "conservatives" and "progressives" could feel that their options were fairly recorded.

Third, we believe that the results from the analyses of the partial data received in the three states are useful. The reader may of course evaluate this directly.

One final methodological note. In the following chapters, three state data are summarized and analyzed with a variety of statistical techniques. Most of the assumptions underlying the use of statistical tests of significance are not fulfilled in these data. In particular, the data are not generated by probability procedures taken from a known universe. Nevertheless, for some of the comparisons, standard errors have been applied, mostly to provide a rough guide in assessing the importance of findings in the context of our sample size and its variance.

We have also employed multiple regression techniques in the analysis of some of the data. Certain aspects of regression analysis are quite robust and survive the worst mishandling. In particular, regression coefficients tend to be more stable under a wide variety of conditions, than correlations coefficients. We therefore warn our readers to pay closer attention to the former than to the latter. In some cases, we also self-consciously used dubious techniques mainly to illustrate how we intended to handle data from the larger twenty state study. The reader should regard these results as especially tentative.

WHO ARE THE RESPONDENTS?

Before proceeding to the substantive chapters, it may be useful to place the respondents within the broader framework of American society. The positions respondents held are not ordinary. Most of the positions require special skills and above average formal education. As a consequence, we can expect respondents to be well educated, predominantly male, white, and middle-aged. Furthermore, we can anticipate that they come from families of relatively high socio-economic standing. These expectations are borne out dramatically in table 1–2.

The average age of respondents is forty-seven, the youngest respondent being twenty-six and the oldest, ninety-one. Nearly two-thirds are between thirty-six and fifty-five, which places one out of three respondents in the stage of maximum social mobility and approaching the peaks of their occupational careers.

For all practical purposes, the respondents are white and male, the respective proportions both being approximately 95 percent. The occupations they hold are predominantly masculine in composition. Apparently few blacks or other nonwhites had broken into the ranks of decision-makers and partisans in the three states.

Three out of four respondents hold the BA degree, and 62 percent have also earned an advanced professional or academic degree. Although we did not ask what degrees respondents held, we can safely assume that law degrees predominate among these advanced degrees, given the positions sampled. Of course, the high educational attainment of our respondents is one of the factors that made it possible to administer so complex an instrument. If formal education does anything for those who suffer through it, it helps provide graduates with the ability to handle complex abstractions.

The last section of table 1–2 contains data on occupations the respondents' fathers held at the time respondents were sixteen. Almost half (48 percent) of the respondents' fathers were white-collar workers, with one in four either holding a professional or managerial position in

Table 1–2.　Age, Sex, Race, Education, and Socio-Economic Backgrounds of Respondents

A. *Age of Respondent:*

	21–35	*36–45*	*46–55*	*56 and Over*	*No Age Recorded*	*100% =*
Percent	14	30	34	20	2	[266]

Average Age = 46.8 years
Range = 26 to 91

B. *Sex of Respondent:*

Percent Male = 94%

C. *Race:*

Percent White = 96%

D. *Educational Attainment:*

	Less Than Nine Years	*9–11 Years*	*High School Graduate*	*Some College*	*College Graduate*	*Advanced Profes- sional or Academic Degree*	*100% =*
Percent	1	3	8	12	14	62	[264]

E. *Father's Occupation When Respondent was 16:*

	Professional and Technical	*Farmers and Farm Managers*	*Managers and Officials Proprietors*	*Clerical*	*Sales*
Percent	20	9	19	3	7

Service Craftsmen	*Operatives*	*Farm Tenants and Laborers*	*Unskilled Laborers*	*Service Workers*
14	6	0.4	2	5

Deceased	*No Answer*	*100% =*
6	8	[266]

the labor force. Conspicuously few fathers were in the lower ranks of the labor force: farm tenants and laborers, unskilled laborers, and service workers.

✳ *Chapter 2*

Elite Assessments of State Corrections Systems

The roots of reform often lie in discontent with significant social institutions. Thus, although change is sometimes desired for its own sake, perhaps to demonstrate modernity or sophistication, more often it is a response to dissatisfaction among one or more influential groups. So it is also with prison systems. The history of prison reform is a chronicle of ongoing discontent.

Who is dissatisfied is obviously critical. One can assume that few prisoners will be content with their surroundings. Yet, if dissatisfaction were limited to prisoners very little change would be projected. Discontent could be easily ignored and unrest summarily crushed. In contrast, were popular opinion, vocal minorities, and/or powerful elites critical of corrections performance, the time for reform might be at hand.[1]

The levels of dissatisfaction expressed by our respondents are of particular interest because of the special powers with which their positions endow them. They are ideally placed to directly influence their state penal codes and to alter the administrative practices of their state prisons. Moreover, many are well-known public officials or criminal justice experts who can mobilize popular opinion through visibility, legitimacy, and perceived expertise.

To begin our interviews, we asked each respondent to tell us what he (there were no women respondents) saw to be the "major strengths" of his state's corrections system and what the major problems were he saw the system facing. The responses to these two questions are ample evidence of the articulateness of our respondents (table 2–1). Nearly nine out of ten were able to cite at least one "major strength," and an

Table 2–1. Perceived Strengths in and Problems Facing State Corrections Systems

A. *Perceived Strengths:*

	Percent Citing At Least One Strong Point In State Corrections System	100% =	Significance[a]
Three States Combined	89%	[244]	
Florida	80%	[97]	
Illinois	91%	[70]	p < .01
Washington	97%	[77]	

B. *Perceived Major Problems:*

	Percent Citing At Least One Major Problem Facing Corrections System	100% =	Significance
Three States Combined	95%	[260]	
Florida	98%	[106]	
Illinois	90%	[72]	p > .05
Washington	95%	[82]	

[a] Since our respondents do not even approximate a probability sample, significance tests are included primarily to meet common practice and for those who feel the probability estimates possess meaning despite sample limitations.

even higher proportion (95 percent) were able to point out at least one "major problem" facing the system. (To facilitate rapid handling of the data to meet severe time constraints in the pilot study, we did not code the content of these responses but simply whether or not a response was given.)

The three states vary more in terms of strengths cited than in terms of problems. Florida respondents were less likely to cite a "major strength" (80 percent) in contrast to Washington's, among whom 97 percent were able to come up with something positive about their corrections systems. Florida respondents cited more major problems (98 percent), closely followed by Washingtonians (95 percent), and trailed only slightly by the Illinois elite (90 percent). It would initially seem, then, that Florida elites might be most critical of their corrections system.

The balance of strengths and problems shown in table 2–1 provides no firm basis on which to assess how much concern respondents express concerning their states' corrections system. A more illuminating set of statistics is contained in table 2–2, where data are shown on how well each corrections system is seen as "doing in meeting its problems." Opinion seems fairly well balanced. Although a few (9 percent) think their system is doing "very well," a similar small proportion (10

Table 2-2. Overall Assessment of State Corrections System

"How well . . . corrections system is doing in meeting (its) problems . . . ?"	*Three States Combined*	*Florida*	*Illinois*	*Washington*	*Decision-Makers*	*Law Enforcement and Corrections Personnel*	*Other Partisans*
Very Well	9%	11%	11%	5%	11%	13%	6%
Adequately	29	18	28	40	31	35	23
So-So	33	35	32	31	36	20	40
Inadequately	20	26	16	16	21	16	22
Very Poorly	10	10	12	8	2	17	10
100% =	[257]	[100]	[74]	[83]	[62]	[71]	[124]
		p > .05				p < .01	
Average Score[a]	2.94	3.06	2.90	2.83	2.71	2.89	3.09

[a] Computed by assigning score values 1, 2, 3, 4, and 5 to the five response categories. The higher the average score, the more critical the assessment.

percent) think the system is doing "very poorly." Indeed, the most popular response is "so-so" (33 percent). If we consider this last response as expressing some criticism, then about two out of three respondents have something critical to say about the way in which their corrections systems are meeting their problems. If we treat this response as expressing at least marginal approval, then two out of three respondents are expressing satisfaction. At minimum, it can be said that one out of four respondents express definite dissatisfaction (the combination of response "inadequately" and "very poorly"). In addition, Florida elites seem the most critical.

The last three columns of table 2–2 contain assessments made by respondents grouped by their positions within the elite. Decision-makers are comprised of those with legal power to make changes (category A in table 1–1), law enforcement and "corrections personel" consist of persons employed in corrections and law enforcement (all titles in category B of table 1–1), and the "partisan" group here consists of all other positions (categories C and D), a rather hetergenious group which will later be disaggregated.

Note that it is the partisans and corrections personnel who are most critical of the corrections system, with decision-makers presenting a more sympathetic view of the systems in their states. Indeed, only 2 percent of the decision-makers think that their corrections system is doing "very poorly," in contrast to 17 percent of the law enforcement and corrections personnel.

ASSESSMENTS OF CORRECTIONS COMPONENT PARTS

A state corrections system ordinarily consists of a number of more or less separate organizational components. In many states, juvenile corrections are administratively distinct from adult corrections. Probation and parole are often separated from each other and from the administration of prisons and reformatories. The assessments we have obtained so far have been concerned with the performance of the total corrections system, and distinctions among component parts have been buried. It is these components to which we turn now.

In table 2–3, respondents' assessments of six separate components of their states correctional systems are shown. The greatest contrasts in assessment can be obtained by comparing assessments of juvenile institutions and adult men's prisons. Forty-four percent of the respondents think that adult men's prisons are doing "inadequately" or "very poorly," while only 28 percent think similarly about juvenile institutions. An alternative expression of this contrast is the averages computed for these two components, 2.8 and 3.3, computed by giving arbitrary values of 1, 2, 3, 4, and 5 respectively to the most favorable to the least favorable responses; a high average represents a more critical assessment.

Another way of assessing the perceived performance of the six corrections institutions on table 2–3 is to compare mean ratings. While most of the differences between means are too small to take seriously, one can order the six as follows: adult men's prisons (3.3), community facilities (3.3), probation department (3.1), parole department (3.0), parole department (3.0), parole board (2.9), and juvenile institutions (2.8). In short, while there is not a great deal of variation, adult men's prisons and juvenile institutions hold down the negative and positive ends of the scale respectively. Perhaps more to the point, since a mean of 3.0 is "so-so," the balance of opinion seems to fall in this somewhat critical category.

The overall ratings conceal some interesting differences among the states in the evaluation of specific components. For example, major interstate differences center around the parole board and parole and probation departments, where Florida residents are more critical. In contrast, Washington elites think more highly of their probation and parole systems. However, without more specific knowledge about the departments in question, it is difficult to interpret these findings further.

At the bottom of each panel of table 2–3, assessments are tabulated separately for decision-makers, corrections personnel, and partisans (as in table 2–2). Note that with one exception, partisans tend to be a bit harsher in their assessments of each of the components than either of the other two groups. We will return to this issue later.

One might wonder about the degree to which respondents who judge one component of their corrections system unfavorably tend to have similar feelings about other components. One can answer this question by looking at correlations among the assessment items considered in the previous pages (table 2–4). It is apparent from the positive signs that criticisms tend to be made across the board. In addition, all the specific components correlate positively with the "overall" assessment. Nevertheless, some correlations are clearly higher than others, which suggests that there is a tendency for judgments to cluster. In particular, larger correlations appear among the three parole and probation components, while assessments of community corrections facilities are a bit more independent of the other evaluations.[2]

One can summarize the clusters of the correlations in table 2–4 by factor analyzing the seven items. Table 2–5 shows factor loadings for the two factors that appear. While the two are not nearly as distinct as

Table 2-3. Assessment of Specific Components of State Corrections Systems

	Average Score[a]	Rating of Performance					100% =	Significance
		Very Well	Adequately	So-So	Inadequately	Very Poorly		
A. Juvenile Institutions and Reformatories								
Three States Combined	2.8	17%	32	23	15	13	[235]	
Florida	2.8	19%	27	25	15	14	[93]	
Illinois	3.2	6%	32	22	20	20	[65]	$p < .05$
Washington	2.4	23%	38	22	10	6	[77]	
Decision-Makers	2.4	17%	50	17	11	6	[54]	
Law Enforcement and Corrections Personnel	2.6	23%	32	18	12	14	[65]	$p < .051$
Partisans	3.0	14%	23	28	18	16	[116]	
B. Adult Men's Prisons								
Three States Combined	3.3	4%	26	26	24	20	[257]	
Florida	3.5	4%	18	24	30	24	[102]	
Illinois	3.2	5%	32	22	20	20	[74]	$p > .05$
Washington	3.1	2%	31	35	18	14	[81]	
Decision-Makers	2.7	11%	31	36	21	2	[68]	
Law Enforcement and Corrections Personnel	2.9	13%	35	20	16	17	[65]	$p > .05$
Partisans	3.1	6%	23	40	22	10	[124]	

Rating of Performance (continued)

C. Parole Board

	Average Score[a]	Very Well	Adequately	So-So	Inadequately	Very Poorly	100% =	Significance
Three States Combined	2.9	11%	33	25	16	16	[245]	
Florida	3.3	10%	21	23	21	24	[99]	p > .01
Illinois	2.8	10%	40	24	15	12	[68]	
Washington	2.6	14%	41	28	9	8	[78]	
Decision-Makers	2.8	10%	43	12	24	10	[58]	
Law Enforcement and Corrections Personnel	3.2	9%	22	31	18	19	[67]	p < .05
Partisans	2.8	13%	33	28	10	16	[120]	

Rating of Performance

D. Parole Department

	Average Score[a]	Very Well	Adequately	So-So	Inadequately	Very Poorly	No Institution In State	100% =	Significance
Three States Combined	3.0	9%	29	31	19	10	1	[242]	
Florida	3.1	11%	24	22	24	17	1	[98]	p < .05
Illinois	2.9	8%	34	31	20	8	0	[65]	
Washington	2.8	56%	32	44	13	4	1	[79]	
Decision-Makers	2.9	7%	40	21	24	9	0	[58]	
Law Enforcement and Corrections Personnel	3.0	6%	28	36	22	7	1	[69]	p > .05
Partisans	3.0	11%	25	35	15	13	1	[115]	

Table 2-3. Continued

	Average Score[a]	Rating of Performance						No Institution In State	100% =	Significance
		Very Well	Ade-quately	So-So	Inade-quately	Very Poorly				
E. Probation Department										
Three States Combined	3.1	10%	27	27	20	14		3	[244]	
Florida	3.1	15%	22	23	26	12		2	[96]	
Illinois	3.6	7%	22	18	21	25		7	[68]	p < .01
Washington	2.8	6%	36	39	14	5		0	[80]	
Decision-Makers	3.3	5%	29	20	25	16		5	[56]	
Law Enforcement and Corrections Personnel	3.1	9%	26	27	27	8		3	[66]	p > .05
Partisans	3.0	12%	26	30	15	16		2	[122]	
F. Community Treatment Facilities										
Three States Combined	3.3	10%	24	20	27	14		5	[231]	
Florida	3.2	10%	30	17	24	16		3	[93]	
Illinois	3.2	29%	20	22	29	14		6	[65]	p > .05
Washington	3.4	10%	20	20	30	12		7	[73]	
Decision-Makers	2.8	14%	38	14	21	9		4	[56]	
Law Enforcement and Corrections Personnel	3.2	13%	28	19	20	13		71	[69]	p < .05
Partisans	3.6	5%	15	23	35	18		5	[106]	

[a]Computed by assigning values, 1, 2, 3, 4, and 5 to the responses. The high average represents a more critical assessment.

Table 2–4. Intercorrelations Among Assessments of Corrections Performance

		1	2	3	4	5	6	7
Juvenile Institutions	1		.34	.29	.30	.25	.25	.38
Adult Men's Institutions	2			.44	.35	.29	.23	.56
Parole Board	3				.64	.50	.02	.35
Parole Dept.	4					.60	.08	.32
Probation Dept.	5						.12	.28
Community Facilities	6							.31
Overall Assessment of State Corrections	7							

one might like, the first might be called "released felons supervisory component" and the second might be called "incarceration component." The former is clearly dominated by the three parole and probation items (as the correlation matrix suggested), while the latter most directly reflects the performance of adult men's prisons and the "overall" assessment. Still, perhaps the most important message is that all of the items tend to correlate in positive and nontrivial ways, suggesting that while respondents make distinctions among corrections components, they are likely to be critical of all components if they are critical of some.

The analysis presented in the previous pages has been mainly aimed at providing a description of the larger contours of opinion on state corrections, an analysis of marginals. In focusing now on variation between respondents, we note that despite considerable homogeneity in background, there are some potentially important biographical variables such as age and educational attainment. We also know that Florida respondents differ from Illinois respondents for example, in the state corrections system they face. Similarly one can expect that police,

Table 2–5. Factor Loadings For Assessments of Corrections Performance (Varimax Rotation)

Variable	Released Felons Supervisory Component	Incarceration Component
Parole Dept.	.83	.16
Parole Board	.75	.22
Probation Dept.	.64	.17
Adult Men's Institutions	.38	.61
Juvenile Institutions	.26	.46
Community Facilities	−.01	.45
Overall	.25	.73
Eigenvalues	3.07	1.25

prosecutors, corrections officials, etc., all have different viewpoints, however slight, that arise from the varying perspectives their positions afford.

To explore the importance of such biographic and positional differences among the respondents, we resorted to multiple regression analysis, and as table 2–6 suggests, biographic and positional variables account for only a modest proportion of the variance in overall assessments of state corrections systems. Only 9 percent of the total variation is explained, although if one wants to take the F-Test seriously, the model does make the .05 level. Certainly, none of the independent effects of any variable seem large either by significance tests criteria or the amount of variance each uniquely accounts for (the square of the part, not partial correlation).

Since none of the biographic and positional variables reach conventional significance levels, one might reasonably conclude that biographic and positional variables mean very little. If we relax conventional standards and use the rule that a variable must account for at least one-half of one percent of the variance uniquely, one finds that older respondents and statewide elected officials tend to assess their corrections system more favorably. In contrast, police and Florida residents tend to be more critical.

Table 2–6. Low Overall Assessment of Corrections Performance Regressed on Biographical and Positional Variables[a]
($N=253$, $R^2=.09$, $F=1.90$, $P<.05$)

Variable	Units	Regression Coefficient	t-Value	Unique Variance
Age	Years	−0.01	−1.09	.005
Education	Six Levels	−0.03	−0.37	.001
State Politicians	Dummy (1=Yes)[b]	−0.41	−1.43	.008
Correction Officials	Dummy (1=Yes)	−0.25	−0.93	.003
Police	Dummy (1=Yes)	0.42	1.48	.008
Judges	Dummy (1=Yes)	−0.04	−0.13	.000
Prosecutors	Dummy (1=Yes)	−0.08	−0.21	.000
Bar Association and Public Defenders	Dummy (1=Yes)	0.34	0.96	.003
Local Politicians	Dummy (1=Yes)	0.11	0.36	.000
Partisans	Dummy (1=Yes)	0.48	1.39	.007
Florida	Dummy (1=Yes)[c]	0.20	1.21	.006
Illinois	Dummy (1=Yes)[c]	0.01	0.01	.000

[a] High value means corrections system doing poorly (1=very well, 2=adequately, 3=so-so, 4=inadequately, 5=very poorly.)

[b] Low level corrections personnel dummy dropped.

[c] Washington dummy deleted.

Four methodological points about table 2–6 should be mentioned, in part, in preparation for future regression runs. First, we have used a far more detailed occupational group breakdown than previously. While we are able to probe for more subtle effects in this manner, the relatively small number of cases in each occupation causes each dummy variable to have very little variance and hence makes statistical significance more difficult to attain.

Second, we have included no attitudinal material as independent variables. While we could easily increase variance explained and produce larger regression coefficients, it seems hard to argue that attitudes "cause" assessments or vice versa. For example, we might have used the assessment of adult men's prisons as a predictor of the overall assessment, but the more general evaluation may actually be a cause of the more specific. In general, we will be reluctant to use attitudes as causal explanations for other attitudes. (We also considered at great length the possibility of moving to structural equation models with unmeasured variables where simultaneous effects could be addressed empirically. However, since we had little theory to guide our specifications, we would have put ourselves at the mercy of statistical artifacts and, hence, at the mercy of Type I errors. This seemed both unnecessary and unwise.)

Third, as in our earlier material, significance tests are included largely in honor of convention, since our "sample" does not approximate selection through probability procedures. Typically, we will rely on the size of some measure of effect rather than the alpha level to indicate "important" variables.

Finally, we will often discuss the "raw" regression coefficients (i.e., unstandardized), since our data comes in a form amenable to their use. For example, in addition to noting that "state pols" (elected state officials) explains .008 of the variance uniquely, one might consider that if a respondent is a "state pol" compared to a rank and file corrections officer (the deleted occupational dummy variable), he is .41 of a unit less critical of corrections performance on our five-point scale (holding other variables in the equation constant).

While regression analysis did not do especially well for the overall assessment of state corrections, quite different results obtain for each separate corrections component. We regressed each of the six specific evaluations on the same set of biographical variables and, somewhat to our surprise, explained between 10 and 19 percent of the variance. We will not burden the text with tables for each equation; the following are the highlights.

For juvenile institutions we account for 17 percent of the variance. Two variables have especially large effects, accounting for well over half of the R^2 by themselves. Illinois residents are far more critical of their juvenile facilities (unique variance equals .041) while state bar association officials and public defenders are by far the most critical occupational group (unique variance equals .035). (In our data, unique contributions in excess of .020 usually have t-values larger than 1.96, the .05 level.) Looked at in another way, on our five-point scale the former has a regression coefficient of 0.68, while the latter has a regression coefficient of 1.21.[3]

For adult men's prisons one finds a pattern much like that found for the overall assessment, which is not surprising, since they are correlated .56. Ten percent of the variance is explained, with the effects of each variable very similar to the earlier model. The major difference is that the impact of living in Florida stands out far more saliently, with a unique contribution to variance explained of .025 and a regression coefficient 0.45.

Our regression model does better on the assessment of the parole board than any other corrections evaluation. Nearly 20 percent of the variance is explained with several variables having large effects. Older residents are typically far less critical, while corrections officials, police, local politicians, and partisans are far more critical. And again, Florida residents are the most displeased. All of these independent effects reflect unique contributions to explained variance in excess of .020, with the Florida contribution the largest at .046.

We are able to account for 14 percent of the variance in assessments of the parole department, and again police are very critical relative to other occupations. They alone account for .057 of the variance, which is twice the impact of the other two critical occupations: local politicians and partisans. Interestingly, state of residence has very small effects.

Biography and position explain 16 percent of the variance in assessments of community corrections. Here a somewhat different configuration of effects appears, with older and more highly educated respondents somewhat more critical, followed closely by police (again!). However, for the first time prosecutors surface as salient critics, and they alone account for .022 of the variance. In contrast, corrections officials are more favorable. No state effects appear.

What can one conclude from these regression equations? To begin, there does appear to be some important variation between states, holding other respondent variables constant. In particular, Florida elites are more critical, especially of their men's prisons and their parole board; Illinois residents are more critical of their juvenile facilities and their probation department. Since juveniles are more likely to obtain probation, this may reflect a more general unrest with the way young offenders are handled. Note that these state effects are not only of substantive interest, but bode well for studies including a larger sample of states. States may really differ in how well their corrections system is doing and therefore may vary in their readiness for reform. The occupational effects are also intriguing, because they imply that, holding age and education constant, support for change will often differ. In particular, police are very unhappy with the corrections system, and especially those components that may shorten sentences in traditional prisons. We will examine this proposition in the next chapter.

CERTAINTY OF CORRECTIONS ASSESSMENT

It has been the experience of sample survey researchers over the past three decades that it is possible to obtain evaluations from respondents on almost any conceivable topic. Often, however, such opinions are held with little conviction or intensity. Although it appeared to us unlikely that members of this elite would have casual assessments of corrections, we explored the matter by asking respondents to indicate how certain they were of their judgments of the juvenile institutions and the adult men's prisons. The cross-tabulation of opinions and certainty for these two institutions is shown in table 2–7.

The top panel of table 2–7 shows the relationship between certainty of judgment and the assessments given of adult men's prisons. Note that the more negative the assessment, the more certain the opinion. Indeed, 33 percent of those who rate the adult men's prisons as doing "very poorly" hold those opinions with "absolute certainty," in contrast to only 9 percent of those who think these institutions are doing "adequately." Conversely, almost two out of three of the latter claim they are "unsure" or only "fairly sure" about their opinions, in contrast to 26 percent of those who think the prisons are doing "very poorly." In short, those who think well of the adult men's prisons hold those opinions with some reservations and doubt, while those who think the prisons are not doing well are more convinced that they are correct in their assessments. One may interpret this finding as indicating that opinions will be more readily shifted still further in an unfavorable direction.

The bottom half of table 2–7 presents a somewhat contrasting situation with respect to juvenile institutions. In this case those who are especially favorable tend to hold those opinions with a bit more certainty, while it is those with lukewarm and negative assessments who

Table 2–7. Assessment of Adult and Juvenile Institutions and Certainty of Assessments

A. *Concerning Adult Men's Prisons*

Certainty of Assessment	Respondents' Assessment of Adult Men's Prisons					
	Very Well	Ade- quately	So- So	Inade- quately	Very Poorly	Total Sample
Absolutely Certain	40%[a]	9%	7%	18%	33%	17%
Very Sure	20[a]	26	35	37	41	34
Fairly Sure	30[a]	54	44	37	20	40
Unsure	10[a]	8	12	7	6	8
Not Sure at All	—	3	2	2	—	2
100% =	[10]	[66]	[68]	[60]	[51]	[255]

B. *Concerning Juvenile Institutions and Reformatories*

Certainty of Assessment	Respondents' Assessment of Juvenile Institutions					
	Very Well	Ade- quately	So- So	Inade- quately	Very Poorly	Total Sample
Absolutely Certain	35%	11%	7%	12%	26%	16%
Very Sure	42	30	32	35	26	33
Fairly Sure	22	40	48	47	45	41
Somewhat Unsure	—	16	9	6	3	9
Not Sure at All	—	3	4	—	—	2
100% =	[40]	[74]	[54]	[34]	[31]	[233]

[a] Percentages based on ten cases and hence especially unreliable.

are generally less sure. The patterning with respect to juvenile institutions also suggests greater potential conflict, since there are more equal groups of elite respondents holding widely divergent opinions, each fairly convinced of their position. (We only asked about "certainty" for adult men's prisons and juvenile institutions.)

Although the data are not shown here, inspection of degrees of certainty for decision-makers, corrections personnel, and partisans shows no difference among the three groups. Apparently, no one of these segments of the elite seem to be more "opinionated" than any other.

We also regressed each assessment on the relevant "certainty" variables and pretty much replicated the tabular findings. For men's prisons we are able to account for about 5 percent of the variance, largely attributed to certainty about men's prison assessment. Only one-half of one percent of the variance is accounted for in the certainty about juvenile institutional assessments.

SERIOUSNESS OF PRISON PROBLEMS

Considering only men's prisons, as in table 2–8, we now focus on seventeen specific corrections problems. Descriptions of these problems were presented to our respondents, who were asked to state whether each problem was "very serious," "moderately serious," "a minor problem," or "no problem at all."

Two of the problems—overcrowding and inadequate psychiatric counseling—are considered very serious by more than a majority of the elite respondents. Of the remaining problems, three receive ratings as "very serious" by more than a third: "inadequate financial support," "inadequate vocational training," and "public apathy about prisons."

Conditions viewed by many as not being a problem at all include "court interference in prison administration," "harsh treatment by prison guards," "lack of adequate security," and "inadequately trained prison administrators." The remaining problems are viewed as very serious by minorities of up to a third of the respondents.

The general portrait that emerges is of prison systems that have exceeded capacity, are faced with public apathy, lack appropriate rehabilitative programs, and are beset with financial problems. Prison administrators are adequately trained, guards are not brutal, and the prisons have the means to restrain inmates. Issues that loom large in some states—prison uprisings, drug use among prisoners, and rampant homosexuality—appear not to be very salient in the three states studied here.

One might feel little need for additional comment on this overall pattern were there not some important implications. One may infer from the data that respondents are less uneasy about the current philosophies and goals of their corrections systems (particularly rehabilitation) than with an inability to implement programs at the proper level of intensity in the proper kind of environment. In some sense this seems an argument for "more of the same" and clearly does not suggest anything like the massive reform that some critics have proposed.[4] At most, the respondents may be endorsing a different *kind* of correctional program but certainly not an elimination of the state's role in processing convicted offenders toward a goal of rehabilitation.

When we consider the variation in these items among the three states, considerable heterogenity is immediately apparent (table 2–9). "Statistically significant" differences among the three states occur for fourteen of the seventeen rated problems. Perhaps the most dramatic difference is shown with respect to overcrowding: 93 percent of the Florida respondents claim this to be a very serious problem, in

Table 2–8.   Assessments of Seriousness of Specific Problems in State Prisons

Prison Problem	Very Serious	Moderately Serious	Minor Problem	Not a Problem	100% =	Percent Don't Know	Average Score[a]
Overcrowding	51%	23	13	13	[259]	3	1.87
Inadequate Financial Support	38%	44	11	6	[250]	6	1.85
Poorly Trained Guards	27%	44	16	13	[234]	12	2.15
Antiquated Buildings	30%	43	19	8	[256]	4	2.05
Violence Among Prisoners	19%	38	37	6	[236]	11	2.31
Racial Antagonism Among Prisoners	24%	47	24	6	[233]	12	2.11
Inadequate Vocational Training	35%	38	16	11	[253]	5	2.02
Inadequate Psychiatric Counseling	55%	29	10	6	[242]	9	1.67
Prisoner Uprising Against Prison Conditions	10%	32	42	15	[252]	5	2.62
Public Apathy About Prisons	46%	31	13	11	[261]	2	1.87
Court Interference in Prison Administration	8%	10	24	57	[242]	9	3.31
Harsh Treatment by Prison Guards	3%	20	39	38	[215]	19	3.11
Lack of Adequate Security	10%	16	34	41	[239]	10	3.07
Homosexuality Among Prisoners	29%	40	26	4	[209]	21	2.06
Drug Use Among Prisoners	22%	40	29	9	[213]	20	2.25
High Proportion of Hardened Offenders	26%	41	23	10	[215]	19	2.17
Inadequately Trained Prison Administrators	11%	29	31	29	[232]	13	2.78

a Computed by assuming score values of 1, 2, 3, and 4 for response categories. A low average means a condition was considered relatively serious.

contrast to only 17 percent in Washington. Shortly before interviewing began, the head of Florida's Corrections Department refused to accept any more prisoners from the courts on the grounds that the adult prisons were overloaded to a point that additional inmates would create hazardous conditions. This was the second time he had refused to accept prisoners from the courts over the past several years. His refusal received national coverage in the media and a great deal of attention within Florida.

Financial support is another problem that clearly differentiates the three states: more than half (51 percent) of the Florida respondents claim this to be a very serious problem, in contrast to 34 and 25 percent for Illinois and Washington respectively. Florida also exceeds the other states with respect to the problems of homosexuality among prisoners, psychiatric counselling, high proportions of hardened offenders, inadequate vocational training, and court interference in prison administration. Indeed, the average percentage of claims of "very serious" for Florida's respondents is 34 percent, in contrast to 26 percent and 16 percent for Illinois and Washington. In short, the Florida prison system is seen to be in deeper trouble than its counterparts in the other two states.

The responses from Florida respondents foreshadow a major theme that runs through this book. In many respects, Florida stands out as having especially difficult problems with its corrections system and respondents who are more divided in their evaluations. Indeed, as we will see in the next chapter, there is also less consensus in that state on what should be done about corrections.

Illinois comes in for its share of problems too: antiquated buildings, violence among prisoners, racial antagonism among prisoners, public apathy about prisons, and inadequately trained administrators are highest in seriousness in Illinois.

All would be relatively idyllic in Washington were it not that state's elites claim that drug use is a very serious problem among prisoners. In all other respects, Washington comes off as the least troubled state, as elites see it.

Another way of looking at the seriousness of specific problems ratings is provided in table 2–10, where the correlations among *pairs of ratings* are presented. A high correlation means that respondents who rate one particular problem as serious are more likely to rate the other problem as serious. Almost all of the correlations in table 2–10 are positive, indicating that generally respondents who think any particular problem is serious are also likely to think that any other problem is also a serious one. As with the broader evaluations discussed earlier, this indicates that respondents probably have a general

Table 2-9.   State Assessment of Seriousness of Specific Problems in State Prisons

Prison Problem	Percent Rating Problem "Very Serious"						Significance
	Florida	100% =	Illinois	100% =	Washington	100% =	
Overcrowding	93	[106]	28	[45]	17	[66]	p = < .01
Inadequate Financial Support	52	[102]	34	[68]	25	[65]	p = < .01
Poorly Trained Guards	28	[95]	35	[69]	17	[59]	p = > .05
Antiquated Buildings	33	[100]	35	[74]	23	[82]	p = > .05
Violence Among Prisoners	22	[94]	25	[68]	8	[74]	p = < .01
Racial Antagonism Among Prisoners	29	[91]	39	[67]	5	[75]	p = < .01
Inadequate Vocational Training	45	[102]	31	[72]	27	[79]	p = < .05
Inadequate Psychiatric Counseling	67	[99]	42	[69]	51	[74]	p = < .01
Prisoner Uprising Against Prison Conditions	11	[98]	21	[71]	0	[83]	p = < .01
Public Apathy About Prisoners	59	[106]	51	[72]	25	[83]	p = < .01
Court Interference In Prison Administration	13	[95]	10	[69]	1	[78]	p = < .01
Harsh Treatment by Prison Guards	5	[85]	5	[63]	0	[67]	p = < .01
Lack of Adequate Security	11	[98]	10	[68]	7	[73]	p = > .05
Homosexuality Among Prisoners	44	[91]	25	[59]	10	[59]	p = < .01

Drug Use Among Prisoners	24	[83]	12	[56]	27	[74]	p = < .01
High Proportion of Hardened Offenders	37	[91]	22	[60]	12	[64]	p = < .05
Inadequately Trained Prison Administrators	8	[87]	18	[68]	9	[77]	p = < .05
Average % =	34		26		16	

Table 2–10. Intercorrelations Among Respondent Ratings of the Seriousness of Specific Problems

	1	2	3	4	5	6	7	8	9	10	11	12	13	14	15	16	17
1 Overcrowding (Resources)		34	15	25	21	27	25	14	06	07	10	26	09	11	21	06	-05
2 Finances			29	28	23	38	28	11	-03	11	14	07	15	-18	15	01	03
3 Guards				37	39	32	35	53	20	33	29	12	16	18	06	04	47
4 Buildings					25	32	21	28	15	26	21	11	10	16	15	-02	15
5 Vocational Training						56	41	38	13	20	14	11	04	12	04	-15	22
6 Psychiatric Counsel							30	19	11	18	17	17	-07	25	21	-06	06
7 Public Apathy								41	15	21	24	19	11	11	20	00	09
8 Harsh Treat.									28	28	30	22	15	01	04	-01	36
9 Violence (Prisoner Control)										62	46	39	33	23	20	15	26
10 Race											40	44	32	27	13	16	24
11 Uprisings												20	29	18	18	23	27
12 Homosexuality (Prisoner Behavior)													25	18	41	23	00
13 Security														32	18	23	15
14 Drugs															33	11	20
15 Hardened Criminals																14	-03
16 Courts																	01
17 Prison Admin.																	

assessment of the overall seriousness of prison problems, as well as assessments of very specific problems.

Table 2–10 also contains hints that some prison problems tend to be more closely associated with each other, either because some respondents pay more attention to such features of prisons or because certain conditions tend to occur together. These groups of problems can be identified through the patterning of correlations in table 2–10, problems cohering together tending to have higher coefficients among themselves than with other problems.

As a first approximation to specifying such clusters of ratings, the correlations in table 2–10 have been arranged so that adjacent problems are more highly correlated with each other. Groups of correlations with consistently higher inter-relationships are identified by being enclosed in triangles. The first triangle designates a set of problems which might be called "resources," consisting of concern over finances, overcrowding, antiquated buildings, inadequate vocational and psychiatric counseling, and concern over public apathy. Note that the correlations enclosed within this triangle tend to be rather high in comparison with correlations involving those variables and others outside the triangle.

The second cluster may be called "prisoner control problems" and consists of harsh treatment by guards, violence among prisoners, racial conflict, prisoner uprisings, and homosexuality. Statistically, public apathy also fits in with this cluster.

The third cluster, which overlaps heavily with the second, may be called "prisoner behavior problems" and is composed of violence, racial conflict, uprisings, homosexuality, security and drug use, and hardened criminals.

The correlation matrix of table 2–10 can also be subjected to factor analysis (table 2–11). Not surprisingly, the factors that appear reflect what we observed directly in table 2–10. In particular, a factor representing problems with prisoners emerges as especially salient. It is clearly dominated by such items as prisoner violence, racial antagonisms, and homosexuality. In addition, what we labeled as "problems with resources" above now appears better viewed as consisting of two factors: problems with corrections personnel and problems with other resources. The former is most directly defined by poorly trained guards, harsh treatment by prison guards, and inadequately trained prison administrators. The latter most strongly reflects overcrowding, inadequate financial support, and public apathy. Still, these factors are not nearly as distinct as one might like, suggesting our earlier generalization: respondents who tend to feel there are problems in one area feel similarly about other areas.

Table 2–11. Factor Loadings for Specific Prisoner Problems (Varimax Rotation)

Variable	Problems With Prisons	Prison Personnel	Resources and Rehabilitation
Violence	.76	.22	−.10
Race	.65	.28	.03
Homosexuality	.64	−.11	.26
Uprisings	.46	.34	.14
Security	.39	.19	.10
Hardened Criminals	.36	−.13	.34
Drugs	.35	.09	.17
Courts	.28	−.10	.08
Harsh Treatment	.26	.53	.23
Prison Administration	.12	.66	−.12
Guards	.11	.70	.31
Finances	−.03	.16	.56
Overcrowding	.11	−.04	.55
Public Apathy	.18	.21	.44
Pyschiatric Counseling	.06	.09	.39
Buildings	.12	.28	.35
Vocational Training	.03	.27	.26
Eigenvalues	3.8	1.5	1.1

If these clusters were to persist in a better sample of states, they would provide important clues to the ways in which corrections problems are seen by elites. In short, some elite members may be more concerned with the resources available to the prisons, others with problems of control of prisoners within prisons, and others more concerned with the quality of corrections personnel. Corresponding to these different emphases may be different degrees of receptivity to change. For example, those concerned with prisoner behavior problems may well be less receptive to proposed changes in their state's corrections system that would involve placing prisoners in community treatment facilities.

CONTACT WITH AND KNOWLEDGE OF CORRECTIONS SYSTEM

Assessments and opinions may be rooted in intimate knowledge of a problem, based mainly on mass media reports, or, at an extreme, mainly on-the-spot conjectures. Another way of evaluating a set of assessments is to probe into the experiential bases for these judgments.

Table 2–12 presents data on whether elite members have ever visited state prisons, talked with correction officials, or met with prisoners (or ex-prisoners) to discuss prison conditions. A surprisingly

Table 2–12. Firsthand Contact with Prisons, Corrections Officials, and Prisoners

A. *Visits to State Prison Facilities*

	Never Visited	Once	A Few Times	Many Times	Job Requires Visits	100% =	Significance
Three States Combined	12%	4	41	25	18	[266]	
Florida	17%	3	42	19	20	[107]	
Illinois	9%	3	42	25	21	[76]	p > .05
Washington	8%	6	37	34	14	[83]	
Decision-Makers	13%	0	40	27	19	[62]	
Law Enforcement and Corrections Personnel	5%	4	39	26	26	[74]	p > .05
Partisans	15%	5	42	24	14	[130]	

B. *Talked to Corrections Officials*

	Never Talked	Once	A Few Times	Many Times	100% =	Significance
Three States Combined	13%	.4	38	49	[261]	
Florida	22%	1	30	47	[105]	
Illinois	12%	0	41	47	[73]	p < .01
Washington	4%	0	43	53	[83]	
Decision-Makers	7%	0	30	63	[60]	
Law Enforcement and Corrections Personnel	7%	1	33	58	[72]	p < .01
Partisans	12%	0	43	36	[129]	

C. *Met With Prisoners or Ex-Prisoners About Prison Problems*

	Percent Who Have Met	100% =	Significance
Three States Combined	61%	[264]	
Florida	54%	[105]	
Illinois	58%	[76]	p < .05
Washington	72%	[83]	
Decision-Makers	73%	[62]	
Law Enforcement and Corrections Personnel	74%	[73]	p < .01
Partisans	48%	[129]	

large amount of contact is claimed by the respondents. Eighty-eight percent claim to have visited a state prison at least once, and one in four have visited the prison facilities "many times." Almost the same percentage (87 percent) have talked at least once about corrections problems with corrections officials, and one in two have talked with such officials "many times." Three out of five claim to have talked with prisoners and ex-prisoners about prison conditions. In short, this group has had more than ordinary amounts of contact with prisons, corrections officials, and prisoners. Even if such contacts were fleeting and superficial, it is clear that these members of the state elite have had considerably more firsthand contact than the general public or persons coming from the similar social classes of American society.

In the top panel of table 2–12, where data on the frequency of visits to state prisons are shown, we can observe that there are differences between the three states' elites: 92 percent of Washington's elites have visited their prisons, as contrasted with 83 percent of Florida's elite members. (This difference is not statistically significant.) Obviously, most law enforcement and corrections personnel have visited prisons, although we may note that the visits of a few of the law enforcement and corrections personnel have not been very frequent: 39 percent have only visited a few times, mostly police and staff personnel in parole and probation.

The three states vary in the extent to which their elite members have talked to corrections officials, as shown in the middle panel of table 2–12. Ninety-six percent of Washington's elite have done so, in contrast to only 78 percent of Florida's elite, with Illinois' elite members occupying an in-between position. This finding may represent differences in the public relations aggressiveness of the three state corrections system. Indeed, Washington elites consistently have had more contact with their corrections systems than the elites of either of the two other states.

Obviously, corrections officials have talked to corrections officials, but only slightly more than decision-makers. A little less than one in seven partisans have never talked to corrections officials.

The bottom panel of table 2–12 presents proportions of the elites who have met with prisoners (or ex-prisoners) about prison conditions. Large differences appear among the states and among subgroups of the elites. Nearly three out of four (72 percent) Washington elite members have attended such meetings, but only 54 percent of the elite members from Florida. Decision-makers and law enforcement–corrections personnel are about equally likely to have been at such meetings, in contrast to the only 48 percent of partisans who have met with prisoners.

If knowledge about the problems and conditions within a corrections system is fostered by such contacts, then the elites whom we interviewed should be relatively knowledgeable. Indeed, when presented with a list of questions about features of their corrections system, almost all were aware of such matters as the existence in their states of separate facilities for juveniles and adults, whether the system had counseling programs for prisoners, and so on. There was so much unanimity among respondents that we did not think it useful to present the results in this chapter.[5]

Several measures of knowledge did turn out to be of some descriptive utility (table 2–13). Each respondent was asked to estimate the recidivism rates experienced by his state, and to estimate the annual costs of maintaining both adult and juvenile offenders in state institutions.

One in four of the respondents could not give recidivism estimates, and the average of those who could was 46 percent. (It could be argued that those who refused to make estimates were more knowledgeable than those who gave such estimates. The measurement of recidivism is by no means easy either conceptually or operationally, and most estimates are severely flawed.) Recidivism rates were estimated highest in Florida and lowest in Washington, 51 and 40 percent respectively, with Illinois elites, as usual, maintaining an in-between position, with an average estimate of 47 percent. Corrections officials gave the lowest estimate (43 percent) and partisans, the highest (50 percent).

Fewer elites were willing to estimate the annual per capita costs of maintaining an adult prisoner in state institutions: 36 percent refused to give an estimate, but those that did gave estimates that averaged $6800. Illinois elites estimated the highest per capita annual cost, $7700, but only half of them contributed to this estimate. Decision-makers were the least reluctant to make estimates, and partisans the most hesitant, although estimates across the three groups did not vary by very much.

An even larger proportion (44 percent) were reluctant to guess at the costs of maintaining a juvenile in state institutions. Those who did gave estimates that averaged $8200, a cost $1400 higher than for adult prisoners. Washington respondents yielded the highest cost estimates, $9100, although the differences among states did not reach statistical significance. Again partisans were most reluctant to make guesses (48 percent), with corrections–law enforcement officials (42 percent) and decision-makers (37 percent) more willing to do so. Decision-makers gave the highest estimates, $8500.

It is difficult to judge the accuracy of such knowledge without extensive additional data estimating per capita costs within each of the

Table 2–13. Knowledge of Corrections Systems

A. *Estimates of Recidivism Rates*

	Average Estimated Recidivism	N =	Percent Not Estimating
Three States Combined	46%	[199]	25%
Florida	51%	[82]	23%
Illinois	47%	[52]	32%
Washington	40%	[65]	22%
Decision-Makers	46%	[51]	18%
Law Enforcement-Corrections	43%	[57]	23%
Partisans	50%	[91]	30%

B. *Estimates of Costs of Maintaining Adult Prisoners*

	Average Estimated Cost Per Prisoner	N =	Percent Not Estimating
Three States Combined	$6800	[171]	36%
Florida	$6600	[70]	35%
Illinois	$7700	[38]	50%
Washington	$6500	[63]	24%
Decision-Makers	$6700	[52]	16%
Law Enforcement-Corrections	$8000	[44]	40%
Partisans	$6200	[75]	42%

C. *Estimates of Costs for Maintaining Juvenile Prisoners*

	Average Estimated Cost Per Prisoner	N =	Percent Not Estimating
Three States Combined	*$8200*	[150]	44%
Florida	$7500	[57]	47%
Illinois	$7800	[36]	53%
Washington	$9100	[57]	31%
Decision-Makers	$8500	[39]	37%
Law Enforcement-Corrections	$8300	[43]	42%
Partisans	$8000	[68]	48%

states.[6] The best we can say about these data is that they represent, at least partially, the willingness of respondents to *claim* knowledge. In this respect, we can see that Washington elites claim more knowledge and, compared to partisans, decision-makers, and corrections–law enforcement officials, are more likely to claim knowledge. Yet, overall it is interesting to note that about a third of our respondents, picked because of their potential influence on corrections, claimed an inability to estimates recidivism rates and per capita costs.

One might argue, of course, that these experiential and knowledge variables are only important to the degree that they affect opinions about problems with correction and the readiness for reform. While we would not fully endorse this view, we did regress both the assessments of corrections components and scales developed from the questions about specific problems in men's prisons on the experiential and knowledge variables. By and large the effects were not dramatic, with typically far less than 5 percent of the variance explained. In addition, since both sets of independent variables are correlated with biography and position, one needs to hold age, education, and occupation constant to get a more accurate reading. Hence, a more complicated analysis is needed, and we will postpone further discussion of experiential and knowledge variables until it has been introduced.

SUMMARY AND CONCLUSIONS

There are a number of ways one might summarize and highlight critical aspects of this chapter. One useful summary can be obtained by using biography, position, corrections knowledge, corrections experience, and certainty of one's assessments as predictors of corrections assessments. Thus, we regressed the evaluations of corrections components and the overall rating on certainty, biography, position, experience, and knowledge. None of the independent effects were especially large, and in no case was the increment to explained variance obtained by adding the certainty, experience, and knowledge variables to biography and position substantial. Where there was some hint of possible effects, the tendency was for more knowledgeable and experienced respondents to be more critical.

Applying the same general analytical strategy on the views of specific problems with men's prisons first required some form of data reduction. Here we capitalized on our earlier factor analysis (table 2–11) and simply added items that loaded highly on a given factor. (We experimented with fancier aggregation techniques, but they had little impact on the results and thus seemed unnecessarily complicated.) We then regressed the resulting three indices on biography, experience, and knowledge (tables 2–14, 2–15, and 2–16).

For "Problems with Corrections Resources" (table 2–14) we are able to account for 21 percent of the variance. None of the experiential or knowledge variables appear significant, however, and the general result is that people who are more educated, work as police or prosecutors, and live in Florida and Illinois see resource problems as more severe.[7] Of these, it is clear that "Florida" is by far the dominant variable, explaining over 14 percent of the variance by itself. In addi-

Table 2–14. Problems with Corrections Resources Index Regressed on Biographical and Positional Variables and Corrections Familiarity
(N=174, R²=21, F=9.09, P<.05)

Variable	Units	Regression Coefficient	t-Value	Unique Variance
Education	Six Levels	0.67	3.08	.045
Police	Dummy (1=Yes)	1.50	2.04	.019
Prosecutors	Dummy (1=Yes)	2.15	2.28	.025
Florida	Dummy (1=Yes)	3.03	5.49	.141
Illinois	Dummy (1=Yes)	1.09	1.76	.015

Note: High index value means a serious problem (sum of overcrowding, finances, buildings, psychiatric counsel, public apathy with Table 2.8 codes in reverse order).

Table 2–15. Problems with Prisoner Index Regressed on Biographic and Positional Variables and Corrections Familiarity
(N=149, R²=.10, F=3.07, P<.05)

Variables	Units	Regression Coefficient	t-Value	Unique Variance
Certainty in Assessment of Adult Prisons	Five Levels	0.81	2.34	.035
Certainty in Assessment of Juvenile Prisons	Five Levels	−0.55	−1.68	.018
Not Interested in Corrections Literature	Four Levels	1.15	1.59	.016
Estimated Recidivism	Proportion	0.02	1.74	.019
Florida	Dummy (1=Yes)	1.00	1.71	.019

Note: High index value means a serious problem (sum of violence, race, uprisings, homosexuality, security, drugs, hardened criminals with Table 2.8 codes in reverse order).

Table 2–16. Problems with Corrections Personnel Index Regressed on Biographical and Positional Variables and Corrections Familiarity
(N=179, R²=.10, F=3.26, P<.05)

Variable	Units	Regression Coefficient	t-Value	Unique Variance
Certainty of Juvenile Prisons	Five Levels	−0.27	−1.58	.013
Met With Prisoners	Dummy (1=Yes)	0.59	1.73	.016
Cost/Year Adults	Hundreds	0.006	1.53	.012
Education	Six Levels	0.27	1.94	.020
Partisans	Dummy (1=Yes)	1.28	1.99	.021
Illinois	Dummy (1=Yes)	0.73	1.98	.020

Note: High index value means a serious problem (sum of guards, harsh treatment, prison administrators with Table 2.8 codes in reverse order).

tion, it is interesting to speculate that since police and prosecutors are the most concerned occupations, it may well be law and order types rather than liberals who see the corrections system as needing help. However, since more highly educated types are also concerned, it may be the liberals and conservatives are equally worried, but with different issues in mind.

For table 2–15, "Problems with Prisoners," we account for only 10 percent of the variance. In addition, none of the unique contributions are overwhelming, with the only statistically significant t-value being for certainty about one's assessments of adult institutions. Nevertheless there is a hint that Florida residents and people who estimate higher recidivism rates, are less interested in reading about corrections, and are less certain about their assessments of juvenile institutions are more concerned. People who are more certain about their assessments of adult institutions are more worried. With the exception of the certainty effects, the findings are consistent with expectations. Why the two certainty measures should have opposite effects is unclear.

"Problems with Corrections Personnel" (table 2–16) is also not well explained by our data. Only 10 percent of the variance is explained, and again, none of the independent variable effects are especially striking. Illinois residents and respondents who are partisans, more highly educated, and who estimate higher prisoner costs, have met with prisoners, and who are less certain about their assessments of juvenile institutions are more concerned. All but the last effect are fully consistent with expectations and earlier findings. While the certainty measure is also consistent with earlier material (table 2–15), we are still left with no obvious explanation for its impact.

Where does all this leave us? To begin, it is clear that in 1973 among elites in the three states we sampled there exists widespread dissatisfaction with many aspects of corrections. In particular, a large proportion cite a lack of resources for rehabilitative programs as a serious problem. This implies a philosophical support for many current meliorative practices and a belief that "more of the same" could be effective.

Equally important, our data indicate that such concerns involve far more than the psychological predispositions of our respondents. Holding a variety of background variables constant, there seems to be important variation between states in assessments of corrections performance. In particular, Florida and Washington hold down opposite ends of the spectrum, although Illinois residents are more likely to be broadly critical of their juvenile programs and Floridians are especially worried about the lack of resources for adult facilities.

There is also some limited evidence that respondents who are more interested in corrections matters, have more firsthand contact with the corrections system, and who by various "objective" indicators find the system less cost effective are more critical. Again, this suggests that there is some reality out there to which elites may react.

Finally, our data indicate that both liberal and law-and-order types (especially police) may be unhappy, though probably for somewhat different reasons. One might further speculate that there is considerable readiness for corrections reform, but that the specific nature of that reform will depend on a complicated interaction of proposed alternatives, specific criticisms held by different kinds of actors, and the relative influence of these parties in the state's structure of power.

✳️ *Chapter 3*

Goals, Futures, and Reforms: Support for and Opposition to Corrections Changes

It is usually easier to perceive a problem than to propose feasible solutions, and social problems are no exception.

Formulating viable policies for large-scale institutions is no easy matter; we may easily sympathize with respondents asked to give their views on a range of corrections reforms.

Obviously, many obstacles lie in the way of making assessments of alternative corrections policies. First of all, such judgments may tap antagonistic social values. A regard for civil liberties for example, may conflict with prisoner rehabilitation. Are convicted offenders to be understood as victims of behavioral disorders or as persons who have made rational choices? Does a proposed "treatment" violate important procedural ideals such as "due process?"[1]

Second, there are judgments about the effectiveness of proposed changes. As social scientists, we know that most rehabilitation practices turn out on close inspection to be ineffective. But what about well-conceived programs that have been poorly implemented? And what about programs that have yet to be tried? Moreover, even when corrections outcomes are well documented, (e.g., incarceration does put the potential repeat felon out of circulation), there still remains the question whether they are cost effective in the sense of producing sufficient benefits to justify the tax dollars spent. Finally, even when one can justify a reform both in terms of its moral worth and effectiveness, there remains the issue of pragmatic policies: Is there enough support for a given policy to justify efforts on its behalf and the resulting expenditure of scarce political capital?

Third, proposed reforms float in the intellectual atmosphere at several levels of specificity. On the most general level, reforms usually possess labels that connote a more or less general cast of intent. Thus, the label "community corrections reform" may mean a wide variety of specific practices that have in common the idea of placing convicted offenders within local communities under some sort of modified restraint. Similarly, current slogans emphasizing the deterrent effects of imprisonment are consonant with a wide variety of prisons and a range sentences. At the opposite extreme, there are some very specific reforms aimed at replacing one particular practice with another, as for example, in a reform providing legal counsel for offenders during parole hearings. In short, corrections reform can in principle occur at many different levels.

While we clearly could not simplify the underlying intellectual task, we did attempt to provide a variety of ways in which respondent views could be expressed. At the most general level we asked respondents about the overall goals of their corrections system; in contrast, at the other extreme we asked whether they supported each of a long list of very specific changes. Thus, our analyses in this chapter move from the general to the specific. We begin with responses to broad philosophical issues and end with responses to particular types of correctional practices. In general, as the questions address more narrow and concrete issues, the answers show more variability and complexity.

DEGREES OF SUPPORT FOR CORRECTIONAL GOALS

To probe with any degree of sensitivity the subtleties of anyone's social philosophy is difficult within the confines of a questionnaire. Thoughtful and informed respondents present particularly difficult problems, because we can expect that their views will be especially rich and well developed. Hence, our questionnaires were necessarily rather blunt instruments for the task. Compromises were required between the desire to do justice to our respondents and the limitations of technique, time, and our expertise.

Given these constraints, we decided to have respondents evaluate several overall corrections goals abstracted from their justifications, qualifications, and elaborations. Although this strategy obscures subtleties in correctional philosophies, we hope it did not produce serious distortions. Fortunately, in a sense our instrument mirrors life: when people have to make decisions leading to actions, subtle caveats must usually be left behind. Working over fine.points is a luxury for those with time to ponder them. Decisions to act are typically dichotomous: one is for something or against it. Hence, as aggregate measures of general patterns, assessments of abstracted correctional goals may actually be better predictors of action than more subtle approaches.

Table 3–1 shows the degrees of support that certain correctional goals received from our respondents. (The actual questions can be found in appendix B.) Consistent with our earlier analysis of specific corrections problems, rehabilitation is by far the most popular, with 84 percent of the sample giving it "highest priority" and 11 percent "high priority." Also endorsed are the goals of deterring crime and protecting the public, though the proportions rating these goals as of "high" or "highest" priority drop to about half the sample. (Given the recent visibility of numerous studies showing the impotence of rehabilitative

Table 3–1. Elite Ratings of Goals of Corrections Systems

| Goal | Priority of Goal to Respondents | | | | | | 100% = | Sig- nifi- cance |
	Highest	High	Impor- tant	Use- ful	Not Use- ful	Counter Produc- tive		
A. *Deterring Crime*								
Three States Combined	21%	26	26	15	9	3	[266]	
Florida	25%	25	23	14	10	2	[107]	
Illinois	18%	29	24	20	9	0	[76]	p > .05
Washington	19%	24	32	11	7	6	[83]	
B. *Protecting the Public*								
Three States Combined	22%	28	28	8	4	10	[265]	
Florida	23%	29	29	6	4	9	[107]	
Illinois	22%	24	29	14	5	5	[76]	p > .05
Washington	20%	29	26	6	5	15	[82]	
C. *Administering Punishment*								
Three States Combined	6%	10	16	13	18	37	[264]	
Florida	9%	13	19	12	19	28	[107]	
Illinois	4%	8	12	19	21	36	[75]	p > .05
Washington	2%	8	16	10	15	49	[82]	
D. *Rehabilitating Prisoners*								
Three States Combined	84%	11	4	.4	.4	0	[264]	
Florida	90%	8	3	0	0	0	[105]	
Illinois	79%	14	4	1	1	0	[76]	p > .05
Washington	82%	13	5	0	0	0	[83]	

CARNEGIE LIBRARY
LIVINGSTONE COLLEGE
SALISBURY, N. C. 28144

programs, a similar survey in 1976 might reveal a somewhat different ordering of priorities.) In contrast, the goal of administering punishment is rejected by 37 percent as "counterproductive," with only 16 percent believing it to be of "high" or "highest priority."

The bottom portion of each panel in table 3–1 contains the responses given by each state's elites. By and large, state differences were not very large, although, curiously, Florida respondents persistently show slightly higher proportions of "highest priority" ratings to each of the goals. Perhaps Florida's elite are more divided over the priorities, with different groups strongly endorsing different corrections goals. Or perhaps some Floridians expect their system to achieve all of these four goals and see no contradiction in giving high priority ratings to all of them.

As in the previous chapter, one may undertake a more elaborate analysis than that readily available through contingency tables such as 3–1. Consistent with our earlier models we regressed the priority given to each of the four broad corrections goals on independent variables reflecting biography, position, knowledge of the corrections system, and experience within various aspects of corrections. Tables 3–2 through 3–5 present the results.

Table 3–2 shows that we are able to explain nearly 20 percent of the variance in support of the goal of deterring crime. (These are "final" models in the sense described earlier. However, an examination of the "full" models showed identical substantive effects.) By far the largest effect is shown for education, with more educated respondents being far less likely to give deterrence a high priority. Note that this variable alone accounts for 7.5 percent of the variance. Respondents who have met with prisoners are also less likely to support the goal of deterrence. However, police, prosecutors, judges, and local politicians are more in favor of a high priority for deterrence. Lest we automatically assume

Table 3–2. Low Priority for the Goal of Deterring Crime Regressed on Biography, Position, Knowledge, and Experience ($N=262$, $\bar{R}^2=.19$, $F=9.97$, $P<.05$)

Variable	Units	Regression Coefficient	t-Value	Unique Variance
Met Prisoners	Dummy (1=Yes)	0.38	2.26	.016
Education	Six Levels	0.33	4.86	.075
Police	Dummy (1=Yes)	−0.59	−2.38	.018
Judges	Dummy (1=Yes)	−0.71	−2.82	.025
Prosecutors	Dummy (1=Yes)	−1.00	−3.03	.029
Local Politicians	Dummy (1=Yes)	−0.65	−2.30	.017

Note: A high index score means low priority (1=highest priority, 2=high, 3=important, 4=useful but not important, 5=neither useful nor important, 6=counterproductive).

Table 3-3. Low Priority for the Goal of Protecting the Public Regressed on Biography, Position, Knowledge, and Experience ($N=260$, $R^2=.11$, $F=6.20$, $P<.05$)

Variable	Units	Regression Coefficient	t-Value	Unique Variance
Talked with Corrections Personnel	Four Levels	0.23	2.45	.021
State Politicans	Dummy (1=Yes)	0.50	1.89	.013
Corrections Officials	Dummy (1=Yes)	0.58	2.27	.018
Bar	Dummy (1=Yes)	.062	1.79	.011
Partisans	Dummy (1=Yes)	1.27	3.50	.043

Note: High index score means low priority (1=highest priority, 2=high, 3=important, 4=useful but not important, 5=neither useful nor important, 6=counterproductive).

Table 3-4. Low Priority for the Goal of Administering Punishment Regressed on Biography, Knowledge, and Experience ($N=233$, $R^2=.30$, $F=10.67$, $P<.05$)

Variable	Units	Regression Coefficient	t-Value	Unique Variance
Uncertain about Juvenile Institutions	Five Levels	0.18	1.81	.010
Have Met Corrections Personnel	Four Levels	0.35	3.54	.039
Estimated Recidivism	Proportion	0.007	2.14	.014
Education	Six Levels	0.27	3.43	.037
State Politicians	Dummy (1=Yes)	0.63	2.35	.017
Corrections Officials	Dummy (1=Yes)	0.99	3.72	.043
Local Politicians	Dummy (1=Yes)	−0.76	−2.19	.015
Partisans	Dummy (1=Yes)	0.70	1.86	.011
Florida	Dummy (1=Yes)	−0.50	−2.65	.022

Note: High index score means low priority (1=highest priority, 2=high, 3=important, 4=useful but not important, 5=neither useful nor important, 6=counterproductive).

Table 3-5. Low Priority for Goal of Rehabilitation Regressed on Biography, Position, Knowledge, and Experience ($N=262$, $R^2=.10$, $F=5.56$, $P<.05$)

Variables	Units	Regression Coefficient	t-Value	Unique Variance
Estimated Cost of Adult Prisons	Hundreds	0.002	2.07	.015
Police	Dummy (1=Yes)	0.31	2.95	.031
Local Politicians	Dummy (1=Yes)	0.29	2.39	.020
Florida	Dummy (1=Yes)	−0.15	−2.11	.016

Note: High index score means low priority (1=highest priority, 2=high, 3=important, 4=useful but not important, 5=neither useful nor important, 6=counterproductive).

that these occupations tend to be filled by mindless law-and-order types, it should be recalled that recent sophisticated thinking has clearly shifted in support of their views. Norval Morris, for example, has recently argued that "penal purposes are properly retributive, deterrent and incapacitative."[2]

As table 3–3 shows, we are able to account for only 11 percent of the variance in the priority of protecting the public, and few of the independent effects are especially large. Respondents who have met with corrections personnel, or are corrections officials, state level politicians, members of the bar, or partisans, are somewhat more likely to give "protecting the public" a low priority. This does not mean, of course, that protection is totally unimportant for these respondents, just that it is less important than some other goals. It may also reflect the feeling that since many dangerous convicted offenders already serve long prison terms, the corrections system is presently doing all it can in the way of protecting the public and should shift its priorities elsewhere.

Table 3–4 indicates that we are able to account for more variance in the priority of "administering punishment" than for any of the other goals. Thirty percent of the variance is explained, and with two exceptions, all of the independent effects reflect less support for punishment. Once again, education, contact with corrections personnel, and being a corrections official appear to especially reflect "liberal" persuasions. Also, state-level politicians and respondents who estimate higher recidivism rates are less in favor of punishment. In contrast, local politicians (but not police and prosecutors) and respondents from Florida seem more bent on punishment. Apparently Floridians not only see their corrections system in more trouble, but are also more likely to feel punishment may be a response to these difficulties.

While we are only able to account for 10 percent of the variance in support for the goal of rehabilitation (table 3–5), the independent effects both confirm and extend findings from the first three regression tables. Floridians not only gave punishment a higher priority, but now are also more likely to support rehabilitation. While the same respondents may not be endorsing both goals simultaneously (of course they may be, although this would necessarily involve well-known contradictions),[3] this at least suggests considerable pluralism in corrections philosophy among Floridians. The other three variables all indicate lower priorities for rehabilitation: police, local politicians, and respondents who estimate higher current costs per adult offender. Once again, before one automatically brands these actors as draconic, one must recognize that in some sense these respondents may have been in the vanguard of current corrections thinking.

To summarize, it is clear that rehabilitation is the corrections goal that dominates the thinking of our respondents. Conversely, punishment per se is widely rejected. Deterrence and protection of the public fall in between. In addition, support for these various goals varies somewhat, with police, local politicians, and prosecutors more in what some might call a "law-and-order" camp, and corrections officials, respondents with higher education, more contact with corrections personnel and prisoners in the "liberal" camp. Florida respondents may be more confused, polarized, or simply desperate.

Elites are of course only one major factor in policy-making. Elected officials have some obligation to represent their constituencies, and appointed officials have some obligation to the "general public." Hence, while elite views are of obvious interest, of equal interest are the elite views of how the "general public" views the same concerns. Table 3–6

Table 3–6. Elite Perceptions of Public's Goals

| Goal | Perceived Priority of Goal for General Public | | | | | | | |
	Highest	High	Impor-tant	Use-ful	Not Use-ful	Counter Produc-tive	100% =	Sig-nifi-cance
A. *Deterring Crime*								
Three States Combined	38%	38	16	5	3	0	[262]	
Florida	44%	31	16	5	4	0	[106]	
Illinois	36%	39	14	8	3	0	[74]	p > .05
Washington	30%	46	20	2	1	0	[82]	
B. *Protecting the Public*								
Three States Combined	63%	29	6	1	1	0	[263]	
Florida	67%	26	7	0	1	0	[106]	
Illinois	59%	32	5	3	1	0	[76]	p >.05
Washington	60%	31	7	0	0	1	[81]	
C. *Administering Punishment*								
Three States Combined	32%	38	20	5	4	0	[260]	
Florida	40%	38	15	3	4	0	[105]	
Illinois	31%	34	23	5	7	0	[74]	p < .01
Washington	24%	42	24	7	2	1	[81]	
D. *Rehabilitating Prisoners*								
Three States Combined	22%	27	33	14	2	2	[268]	
Florida	29%	27	29	11	2	3	[105]	
Illinois	16%	25	37	17	4	1	[76]	p > .05
Washington	20%	30	35	13	1	0	[87]	

presents data on this topic: elite perceptions of how the "general public" would rate the same set of corrections goals. The questionnaire items are identical to those of table 3–1, except that the respondent was asked for the public's priorities.

Strong majorities of our respondents believe the public places deterring crime, protecting the public, and administering punishment as "high" or "highest priority." In contrast, only 49 percent felt the public views rehabilitation as highest or high priority. Table 3–6 dramatically shows that our respondents see themselves as quite different from the public in the priorities given to correctional goals. Table 3–1 indicated a rather "progressive stance"; table 3–6 indicates that our respondents view the public as somewhat more "conservative."

An examination of the correlations between items from tables 3–1 and 3–6 extends this conclusion. While there is a slight tendency for perceptions of public opinion to mirror the respondent's own views (positive correlations), the largest correlation is .30 (for the "punishment" goal) and most hover around zero. In contrast, correlations among the respondent's own priorities have absolute values between .12 and .45. The first three goals are positively related to each other and negatively related to the rehabilitative goal. In short, the views of elites seem at this point (with the possible exception of punishment) *unrelated* to perceptions of public opinion.

In addition, as the elites see it, popular concerns emphasize protecting the "general public" by removing offenders to prison, thereby preventing them from committing additional offenses. This goal does not have an overriding priority, but is just somewhat more important than the other goals in table 3–6. Thus, the data also suggest that the general public is perhaps viewed by the elite as not having as well focussed a view of the goals of the corrections system as they themselves hold.

In the bottom half of each panel in table 3–6, state-by-state tabulations are shown. Only one set of the state differences is large enough to reach statistical significance, apparently because the Florida elite members think that state's general public gives especially strong emphasis to the goal of administering punishment, a tendency similar to that shown by Florida elites. In addition, there is a tendency for Florida respondents to attribute to the general public slightly more endorsement of each of the goals of corrections, a pattern that also mirrors their own priorities, as shown in table 3–1.

The general portrait emerging from these data on overall corrections system priorities is that of an elite that personally believes strongly in rehabilitation, but who perceive themselves as having to deal with a public that heavily endorses a custodial and punitive view of the corrections. Of course, it is not at all obvious that the elites are correct in their views of their general publics, nor whether the public, if in possession of the information placed at the command of the elite, would not alter their priorities to be more in line with elite opinion. We can do no more than raise this issue in the absence of relevant data.

SUPPORT FOR ALTERNATIVE FUTURES

Overall goals may describe a philosophy of corrections, but any given corrections system runs according to a set of laws and administrative practices which may more or less faithfully correspond to a given philosophical stance. To get closer to the level at which decisions are made, we need to further operationalize abstract goals. Thus, our next level of increasing concreteness consists of a series of questions concerning alternative directions (futures) which corrections systems might take. These were described as "packages of reforms," with the respondent being asked to express his endorsement or rejection of each package. We also tried to vary some of the consequences of each of the "futures" so that we could observe how decisions might be affected by a set hypothetical outcomes.

Each alternative future was described to the respondent, who was then asked whether he favored or opposed the proposal under the specific conditions of no resulting changes in costs of handling offenders and no resulting changes in recidivism rates. If a respondent *opposed* a given future, he was then presented with four additional specifications which were calculated to reveal the conditions under which he would change his mind and support the program. These four were:

A. 25 percent decrease in costs of handling offenders
B. 50 percent decrease in costs of handling offenders
C. 10 percent decrease in rates of recidivism
D. 30 percent decrease in rates of recidivism

All conditions were posed independently, though an obvious dependence exists between the first two and the last two: clearly, if a person changed his mind to support a proposed "future" in reaction to a hypothetical 25 percent decrease in costs, he would continue to support the proposal under a 50 percent decrease in costs. A similar logical dependence obtains with respect to the specified changes in rates of recidivism.

If the respondent *favored* a particular alternative future he was presented with four conditions parallel to those described above calculated to reveal the conditions under which he would change from support to opposition. These four conditions were:

A.   25 percent increase in costs of handling offenders
B.   50 percent increase in costs of handling offenders
C.   10 percent increase in rates of recidivism
D.   30 percent increase in rates of recidivism

Again, all conditions were posed independently so that the respondent was never asked to evaluate more than one change at a time. It would have been interesting to alter both the cost and recidivism conditions simultaneously (along with some other dimensions). However, since the task, as posed, proved quite difficult for many respondents (with "don't knows" to items of up to 10 percent) complicating it would have had the likely outcome of decreasing usable responses significantly.

The first alternative future was described as follows:

> Some people are advocating a general tightening up of our corrections system in which convicted offenders would be given fixed sentences based on the type of offense. Paroles and pardons would be given to just a small percentage of the offenders. Under this proposed alternative most offenders would serve out their full sentence in traditional prisons.
> Assuming that it could be shown that these changes would lead to *no increase* in the cost of handling offenders and *no increase* in the rate of repeat offenders among those released, would you favor or oppose changes in this direction for this state?

Twenty-two percent of the respondents favored this "punitive," proposal while 78 percent opposed it. (In our earlier analyses of these data, we labeled this future "traditional." Now, given the apparent demise of rehabilitation, it is increasingly in vogue for its alleged ability to deter, protect the public, and satisfy social and individual retributive needs. For want of a better summary label, we are now calling this future "punitive.") Apparently our sample interviewed in 1973 found this model for future corrections systems largely unacceptable. Table 3–7 shows how initial stances of support or opposition were affected by changes in projected costs and rates of recidivism. Looking first at the upper two lines, one can see how opposition dwindles as costs (on the left-hand side) and recidivism (on the right-hand side) decrease. Both start at 78 percent. A 50 percent decrease in costs lowers opposition to 62 percent. Decreasing the rate of recidivism by 30 percent drops the proportion of those opposed to 20 percent. Even though contrasts between the effects of changing costs and recidivism rates must be han-

Table 3-7. Elite Acceptance of Punitive Alternative Future[a]

	Change in Costs[b]			*Change in Recidivism[b]*		
	No Δ Costs	25% Δ Costs	50% Δ Costs	No Δ Recidivism	10% Δ Recidivism	30% Δ Recidivism

[a] See text for description of Punitive Alternative Future.
[b] For those opposed "Δ" means *decrease* in costs or recidivism. For those in favor "Δ" means *increase* in costs or recidivism.

dled very cautiously because of noncomparable metrics, it is clear that for the conditions posed here, people seem far more likely to change their minds from opposition to support as a result of changes in recidivism than changes in costs.

The interviewing experiences of the authors suggest why this occurs. Many respondents who opposed this future considered themselves progressive on corrections matters and opposed the "punitive" alternative primarily on principle, bolstered by a belief that it had failed in the past. Almost regardless of costs, the proposal was unacceptable. Their primary goal was rehabilitation, and they did not see this future as useful toward that end. However, if rates of recidivism dropped drastically, the "punitive" alternative became, almost by definition, "rehabilitative." Hence, they could then support it. This, of course, dramatizes a point many reformers have recognized. The line between "punishment" and "rehabilitation" is very hard to draw in practice and, as both are operationalized in prisons, blend so that the potential for "real" rehabilitation is usually lost.

Looking now at the bottom two lines in table 3–7, one can gauge the effects of varying conditions on the 22 percent who initially favored the "traditional" proposal. Again changes in rates of recidivism have a larger effect, but the difference in impact is not nearly as great as for those initially opposed. Support drops to 11 percent under the conditions of a 50 percent decrease in costs and to 4 percent for a 30 percent decrease in recidivism rates. The recidivism rates cannot have as striking an effect in this case because the proportion in favor cannot go below zero percent. Had the proportion in favor been larger initially, the effects of reductions in recidivism might have been greater.

The second alternative future involved programs emphasizing rehabilitation through indeterminate sentences:

> Another set of proposals advocates a corrections system in which all convicted offenders would be given sentences of unspecified length. The major emphasis would be on rehabilitation through job training, group and individual psychiatric counseling and other rehabilitation measures. Under this proposed alternative, most prisoners would be released on parole when they have improved enough to take a normal place in the community.
>
> Assuming that it could be shown that these changes would lead to *no increase* in the costs of handling offenders and *no increase* in the rate of repeat offenders among those released, would you favor or oppose changes in this direction for this state?

Under conditions of no resulting change in the costs of handling offenders and no change in rates of recidivism, 84 percent favored the proposal and 16 percent opposed. Table 3–8 shows how these initial proportions were affected by changing the projected outcomes of the proposal. Looking at the upper two lines representing those who initially favor the rehabilitative package, once again changes in rates of recidivism appear to have a far larger impact than changing costs. As the increase in recidivism reaches 30 percent, support for the program drops to 12 percent. Increasing the costs of handling offenders by 50 percent drops support only to a still solid majority of 64 percent. The explanation may be similar to the one presented earlier. If the goal of a program is rehabilitation and recidivism increases markedly, the program is clearly a failure and undeserving of support.

For the lower two lines representing the proportions who opposed the proposal, neither decreases in cost or decreases in recidivism have much impact, although recidivism changes appear to reduce opposition more than cost changes. But again, starting with such a small percentage there is little room for an effect to appear and opposition to drop.

Table 3–8. Elite Acceptance of Rehabilitative Alternative Future[a]

	Change in Costs[b]			Change in Recidivism[b]		
	No Δ Costs	25% Δ Costs	50% Δ Costs	No Δ Recidivism	10% Δ Recidivism	30% Δ Recidivism

100%

90% 84%   84%

80%   77%

70%   Favor

60%   Favor   64%

50%

40%   38%

30%

20% 16%   16%   Oppose

10%   13%   10%   7%   12%

0%   Oppose   4%

[a] See text for description of "Rehabilitative Future."
[b] For those opposed "Δ" means *decrease* in costs or recidivism. For those in favor "Δ" means *increase* in costs or recidivism.

The third alternative future emphasized supervision of offenders rather than incarceration. The description reads:

> Still another set of proposals would design a corrections system in which incarceration would be a treatment given only to a very small minority of offenders, such as habitual felons, and persons who had committed particularly serious crimes. Under this system, most offenders would be released under supervision to their local communities or committed to part-time confinement in community based corrections centers. Offenders would be released from supervision or part-time confinement as soon as they showed successful readjustment to the community.
>
> Assuming that it could be shown that these changes would lead to no increase in the costs of handling offenders and no increase in the rate of repeat offenders among the released, would you favor or oppose changes in this direction for this state?

Seventy-nine percent favored this proposal, while 21 percent opposed. Table 3–9 shows how these percentages were affected by changes in projected outcomes. Those favoring are represented again in the upper lines of the two graphs. As we found above, changes in recidivism appear to have far greater effects than changes in costs. As recidivism increases, the support drops to 12 percent. As cost increases, the support drops to 61 percent.

At the bottom of the table we are faced with such a low level of initial opposition that neither decreases in cost or recidivism have much scope for change. Nevertheless, decreasing recidivism rates does seem to have a larger impact on reducing opposition.

In summary, the "punitive" proposal stressing incarceration in traditional prisons received very limited support. In contrast, the two packages involving rehabilitation and community supervision were widely endorsed. Changing the projected costs of a program typically altered initial percentages of support and opposition between 10 and

Table 3–9.   Elite Acceptance of Community Based Corrections Alternative Future[a]

	Change in Costs[b]			*Change in Recidivism*[b]		
	No Δ Costs	25% Δ Costs	50% Δ Costs	No Δ Recidivism	10% Δ Recidivism	30% Δ Recidivism

[a]See text for description of "Community Based Corrections Future."
[b]For those opposed "Δ" means *decrease* in costs or recidivism. For those in favor "Δ" means *increase* in costs or recidivism.

20 percent. Changing the projected recidivism rates altered initial support and opposition as much as 70 percent. Despite the somewhat arbitrary levels of costs and recidivism used as projected outcomes, the differential effects are most striking. Our respondents are saying that a change in costs of handling offenders as large as 50 percent would be far less likely to affect their support or opposition than a change in rates of recidivism of up to 30 percent. In times (1973) of popular complaints about inflation, high taxes, and fiscal responsibility these findings were quite unexpected.

The above findings also raise important questions about the political feasibility of the alternative futures. Our respondents seem to be saying that they heartily endorse the more "progressive" programs and that costs are (to them) less relevant. This is most striking, since earlier we noted that they saw the public as supporting *least strongly* the corrections priority of rehabilitation. Thus, our respondents would perhaps be placed in a difficult position were they to act publicly on their preferences, especially if their constituents or the general public were visibly cost-conscious. Moreover, as we noted earlier, they would find it hard to marshal evidence that their favored programs would actually reduce recidivism.

The plight of our respondents is further emphasized in the support for each future which they perceive among several potential constituencies. Table 3–10 shows the support or opposition our respondents expected for the "punitive" corrections model. The vast majority thought the police and the general public would endorse that future. Seventy-nine percent claimed the public would support the "punitive" future, and 86 percent said the police would provide support. Indeed, 56 percent felt the police would support it strongly. In contrast, civil liberties groups, corrections officials, and state courts were viewed as likely to be in opposition. Eighty-one percent felt that civil liberties groups would oppose strongly. In the middle was the state legislature, with 58 percent of the sample feeling they would favor this "punitive" package, although only 11 percent thought legislators would provide strong support. These findings indicate that our respondents, who typically opposed this alternative, might initiate alliances with the courts, corrections officials, and civil liberties groups against the public and the police.

It appears here that our respondents see more support for the "punitive" future than in fact exists among some groups. For example, the state legislatures are seen as leaning towards at least some support, although since a good proportion of the respondents themselves fall into this group, it seems hardly likely that there is that much support among state legislators. It may well be that in this case, the respon-

Table 3–10.   Elite Perception of Support from Among Selected Groups for Punitive Future

Group	Support		Neutral	Opposition		100% =	Signifi-cance
	Strong	Some		Some	Strong		
A. *General Public*							
Three States Combined	36%	43	8	9	4	[260]	
Florida	42%	42	7	7	3	[106]	
Illinois	36%	39	7	7	8	[72]	p > .05
Washington	28%	49	13	13	2	[82]	
B. *State Legislature*							
Three States Combined	11%	47	8	21	13	[256]	
Florida	15%	44	5	24	13	[102]	
Illinois	12%	45	8	18	16	[73]	p >.05
Washington	6%	53	11	20	10	[81]	
C. *States Courts*							
Three States Combined	9%	28	13	27	23	[253]	
Florida	12%	31	11	26	20	[100]	
Illinois	7%	29	15	25	24	[72]	p > .05
Washington	7%	25	12	30	26	[81]	
D. *The Police*							
Three States Combined	56%	30	4	6	4	[261]	
Florida	58%	31	3	7	2	[106]	
Illinois	57%	27	7	3	7	[75]	p > .05
Washington	54%	31	4	8	4	[80]	
E. *Corrections Officials*							
Three States Combined	11%	18	5	22	43	[254]	
Florida	12%	15	3	19	52	[103]	
Illinois	16%	20	4	21	39	[71]	p > .05
Washington	8%	21	8	28	36	[80]	
F. *Citizens' Rights or Civil Liberties Organizations*							
Three States Combined	6%	4	2	8	81	[251]	
Florida	3%	4	1	10	82	[98]	
Illinois	8%	4	3	8	76	[72]	p > .05
Washington	6%	3	1	6	84	[81]	

dents are not making estimates of sentiments as much as they are making estimates of action. That is to say, regardless of how state legislators might feel in the privacy of their questionnaires, if such legislation were introduced, their support might have to reflect their constituencies rather than their own personal opinions.

The bottom parts of each panel in table 3–10 contain data from each of the three states involved. Although again, state differences are not large enough to reach conventional standards of statistical significance, our elite respondents in Florida see themselves as surrounded by a particularly "punitive" future-oriented general public, and have legislators, police, and states courts that are also more enamored with this future. Thus, in Florida there may well be constituencies who are more likely to support the "punitive" future than there are in either of the other two states.

Table 3–11 shows a somewhat different picture. The rehabilitation future draws substantial anticipated endorsements from all parties except the police. Eighty-nine percent of our respondents thought that civil liberties groups would favor this future, an expectation that may have been correct at the time, but in contradiction to the present ACLU opposition to indeterminate sentences. Eighty-four percent felt that there would be support from corrections officials. Majorities also thought the public, state legislature, and courts would be in favor. Hence, despite lukewarm public enthusiasm, the rehabilitation model seems to be a proposal that is not only consistent with the preferences of our respondents but, from their 1973 point of view, perhaps the most politically feasible.

The state-to-state differences in perceived support for the "rehabilitation" future are apparently a bit stronger than in the case of the "punitive" future. Particularly strong are the differences in the perceived support of the general public, with Florida and Illinois seeing both more extreme support for rehabilitation and more extreme opposition. A similar pattern is shown for perceived support of the police: Illinois elites see the police as providing more support than in other states as well as strong opposition. It appears that the respondents from Florida and Illinois see the population of their state as more divided on this issue than is the case for the other two states, while respondents from Illinois see the police as more divided. Without knowing more about these groups and about each of the states, it is difficult to interpret these patterns. We may suggest, as have many observers, that because of heavy in-migration over the past two decades, Florida is really "two states." An explanation for the pattern in Illinois might hinge on the perceived difference between the Chicago

Table 3–11.   Elite Perception of Support from Among Selected Groups for Rehabilitation Future

Group	Support		Neutral	Opposition		100% =	Significance
	Strong	*Some*		*Some*	*Strong*		
A. *General Public*							
Three States Combined	6%	46	8	28	13	[262]	
Florida	9%	39	10	24	18	[105]	
Illinois	8%	43	3	29	17	[75]	p < .01
Washington	1%	57	8	32	1	[82]	
B. *State Legislators*							
Three States Combined	12%	56	8	18	7	[256]	
Florida	16%	52	7	16	9	[101]	
Illinois	12%	51	7	19	10	[72]	p > .05
Washington	7%	64	8	19	1	[83]	
C. *States Courts*							
Three States Combined	23%	45	12	15	5	[258]	
Florida	23%	44	10	18	6	[103]	
Illinois	12%	53	14	12	8	[72]	p > .05
Washington	32%	39	13	13	2	[83]	
D. *The Police*							
Three States Combined	7%	23	8	33	30	[262]	
Florida	7%	25	7	34	28	[104]	
Illinois	13%	17	9	20	40	[75]	p < .01
Washington	1%	25	7	43	23	[83]	
E. *Corrections Officials*							
Three States Combined	46%	38	4	9	2	[258]	
Florida	52%	35	2	9	2	[102]	
Illinois	46%	35	4	10	4	[76]	p > .05
Washington	39%	45	8	8	1	[80]	
F. *Citizens' Rights or Civil Liberties Organizations*							
Three States Combined	77%	12	2	4	4	[255]	
Florida	75%	16	3	2	4	[101]	
Illinois	75%	11	3	7	4	[71]	p > .05
Washington	82%	2	1	4	5	[83]	

police department and all other police forces. But these ad hoc explanations are clearly speculation.

Table 3–12 shows the degree of anticipated support for the "community supervision" future, suggesting a pattern somewhere between the earlier two. A majority see support coming from civil liberties groups, corrections officials, courts, and the legislature. In strong opposition are likely to be the police, the general public, and especially people living in communities where community treatment centers would be located. Ninety-two percent of the sample felt that neighbors of community corrections facilities would oppose them. Hence, though our respondents strongly favor community treatment programs, their expectation of considerable opposition may prevent them from publically endorsing such programs.

The only reasonably persistent state differences with respect to the "community supervision" treatment is the smaller amount of perceived strong opposition in Washington. In each of the two other states, approximately the same patterns of support and opposition appear. This pattern may well reflect the fact that Washington was the only state among the three having any significant experience with community-based corrections. It may also be that this alternative future was not yet visible enough in the media and in other public forums for clear patterns of opposition and support to appear in Florida and Illinois. Thus, the configurations for these two states shown in table 3–12 may rest on guesses by our respondents extrapolating from general trends in opinions among these groups.

Given the complex political realities just discussed, which futures are seen by our respondents as most likely to be implemented? In the questionnaire were items after each alternative future asking: "How likely do you think it is that the corrections system in this state will move in a direction like the one described above?" The results can be seen in table 3–13. The "punitive" model is seen as unlikely by 74 percent. The other two futures are seen as about equally probable, though 41 percent feel the rehabilitation future is very likely, while 32 percent feel the community treatment future is very likely. These findings suggest that our respondents believe the coalition around rehabilitative programs, which essentially includes everyone but the police, is the one most likely to implement its program. The coalition around the community treatment programs, which excludes the public as well as police, is also likely, but less so, to implement its program.

Perhaps the most important conclusion coming from the past few pages is that the corrections trends anticipated by our elite respon-

Table 3–12.   Elite Perception of Support from Among Selected Groups for Community Supervision Future

Group	Support Strong	Support Some	Neutral	Opposition Some	Opposition Strong	100% =	Significance
A. *General Public*							
Three States Combined	4%	33	5	32	26	[263]	
Florida	6%	27	2	31	34	[105]	
Illinois	4%	33	5	27	31	[75]	p < .05
Washington	2%	41	8	37	12	[83]	
B. *State Legislators*							
Three States Combined	6%	47	10	26	12	[260]	
Florida	10%	43	7	26	15	[105]	
Illinois	4%	42	12	22	19	[73]	p < .05
Washington	2%	55	11	29	32	[82]	
C. *States Courts*							
Three States Combined	12%	50	15	17	7	[256]	
Florida	11%	44	14	20	12	[102]	
Illinois	8%	45	25	16	6	[73]	p < .01
Washington	16%	60	9	14	1	[81]	
D. *The Police*							
Three States Combined	3%	16	6	31	44	[260]	
Florida	2%	18	7	31	43	[103]	
Illinois	4%	16	5	23	52	[75]	p > .05
Washington	2%	15	7	38	38	[82]	
E. *Corrections Officials*							
Three States Combined	31%	38	7	16	7	[255]	
Florida	37%	33	3	19	8	[102]	
Illinois	33%	38	6	12	11	[72]	p < .05
Washington	22%	46	14	16	2	[81]	
F. *Citizens' Rights or Civil Liberties Organizations*							
Three States Combined	81%	6	2	0	1	[256]	
Florida	78%	19	1	1	1	[101]	
Illinois	82%	14	3	0	1	[73]	p > .05
Washington	83%	13	4	0	0	[82]	

Table 3–12. continued

| | Support | | | Opposition | | | |
Group	Strong	Some	Neutral	Some	Strong	100% =	Signifi-cance
G. *Community Members in Neighborhoods Where Treatment Centers Might Locate*							
Three States Combined	2%	4	3	26	66	[262]	
Florida	3%	6	1	17	73	[105]	
Illinois	0%	5	4	27	64	[74]	p > .05
Washington	1%	1	4	36	58	[83]	

dents are predicted *despite* projected public opinion. While the public is viewed as less enthusiastic about rehabilitation and community corrections, this is precisely where the states are thought to be going. In contrast, the "punitive" future is seen as widely popular, but not a likely direction of change. Besides the substantive importance of this conclusion, it suggests that one could use our data more effectively to analyze the sources of support and opposition for our alternative futures: we have a sample of elites, and these are the groups that may really matter.

Therefore, our next step is to regress support for each of the three futures on the same sorts of independent variables considered earlier. First, for each alternative future, a dependent variable must be defined, and unlike our earlier models, this is not straightforward. In particular, we need a way to take into account each respondent's reluctance or readiness to change his mind in the face of changing costs and recidivism rates, while at the same time adjusting for the fact that all three futures showed rather limited variance in initial support and opposition. Second, we need a way to assess parsimoniously each respondent's judgments about the impact of the alternative futures on his own job and aspirations. In other words, we have to begin to grapple more seriously with the *realpolitik* of corrections reform.

We attempted to solve the former problem by constructing indices for each of our three futures for each of the two types of changes in outcomes: costs and recidivism. A respondent got a "one" for falling in the dominant category initially: "oppose" for the "punitive" future, and "support" for both the rehabilitative and community-based approaches. Then the respondent got one additional point for sticking to that view in the face of a 25 percent change in costs, and yet another point for holding his views in the face of a 50 percent change in costs. Thus, for all three futures, three indices were constructed to reflect

Table 3-13. Estimates of Likelihood of Alternative Futures for Corrections

| | Perceived Likelihood of Implementation | | | | |
	Very Likely	A Possibility	Unlikely	100% =	Significance
A. *Puntive Future*					
Three States Combined	7%	19	74	[259]	
Florida	12%	21	68	[102]	
Illinois	5%	16	78	[74]	p > .05
Washington	4%	19	77	[83]	
B. *Rehabilitation Future*					
Three States Combined	41%	39	20	[251]	
Florida	36%	39	24	[102]	
Illinois	34%	40	26	[70]	p < .05
Washington	53%	37	10	[79]	
C. *Community Supervision Future*					
Three States Combined	32%	46	22	[252]	
Florida	30%	40	29	[102]	
Illinois	24%	50	26	[68]	p < .01
Washington	42%	50	8	[82]	

"inflexibility" in the face of changing costs, and each index ranged from zero to three. We considered several other weighting schemes, but in the absence of some common metric on which to array these changes, it was very unclear how to proceed. Hence, we opted for the simpliest scaling system and the few other systems we tried produced virtually the same substantive results.

Similar procedures were employed for changes in recidivism. One could get a score from zero to three depending on the tenacity with which one's initial views were held in the face of alteration in the recidivism rates. Thus, we constructed six indices in all, and these will be the dependent variables in the pages to follow. In essence, higher scores reflect the tenacity of support or opposition for the three futures.

For the second problem we relied on four questionnaire items asked after each of the three alternative futures:

If you were to actively support changes like this, would your support make any difference for your work in the future. Would it improve your *prospects*, worsen your *prospects*, or not matter much one way or the other?

If you were to actively oppose changes like these, would your opposition make any difference for your work in the future. Would it improve your *prospects*, worsen your *prospects*, or not matter one way or the other?

Suppose such changes actually came about. Would it make your current work *harder*, *easier*, or not matter much one way or the other?

Suppose such changes came about. Would it make any difference for your work in the future? Would it improve your *prospects*, worsen your *prospects*, or not matter much one way or the other?

Even a casual reading of these questions suggests what we were trying to gauge. The first two items were attempts to measure the anticipated political costs and benefits from participation in corrections change. The second two items were attempts to measure the anticipated costs and benefits from the actual corrections future for the daily work the respondent did. While none of these questions necessarily assume our respondents were maximizing utilities, they do assume that respondents would be influenced by rational self-interest.

With these four "interest" variables added to the set of biography, position, knowledge, and experimential variables used earlier, we attempted to predict each of the six dependent variables described above. The results can be found on tables 3–14 through 3–19.

Table 3–14 attempts to predict continued opposition to the "punitive" future in the face of lower costs. We are able to account for 36 percent of the variance, and five of the six independent variables have

Table 3–14. Opposition to Punitive Future Despite Low Costs Regressed on Biography, Position, Knowledge, Experience, and Interests
(N=208, R² =.36, F=18.73, P<.05)

Variable	Units	Regression Coefficient	t-Value	Unique Variance
Talked to Corrections Personnel	Four Levels	0.22	2.93	.027
Not interested in Corrections Literature	Five Levels	−0.67	−3.59	.041
Education	Six Levels	0.34	5.52	.097
Opposition Hurts Prospects	Three Levels	−0.25	−1.78	.010
Reform Would Hurt Prospects	Three Levels	0.47	3.92	.049
State Politicians	Dummy (1=Yes)	0.42	2.00	.013

Note: High index score means continued opposition to punitive future in the face of lower costs (sum of oppose, oppose despite 25 percent decrease in cost, 50 percent decrease in costs).

Table 3–15.   Opposition to Punitive Future Despite Lower Recidivism Regressed on Biography, Position, Knowledge, Experience, and Interests (N=201, R²=.19, F=9.21, P<.05)

Variable	Units	Regression Coefficient	t-Value	Unique Variance
Not Interested in Corrections				
Literature	Five Levels	−0.36	−1.98	.016
Age	Years	−0.01	−1.61	.011
Education	Six Levels	0.19	3.09	.040
Reform Hurts Prospects	Three Levels	0.47	4.20	.073
State Politicians	Dummy (1=Yes)	0.49	2.40	.024

Note: High index score means continued opposition to punitive future in the face of decreased recidivism (sum of oppose, oppose despite 10 percent drop in recidivism, 30 percent drop in recidivism).

rather large effects. (These are "final" models in the sense described earlier.) State elected officials, more highly educated respondents, respondents who have talked with corrections personnel, and respondents who claim that the "punitive" future would worsen their prospects are far more likely to continue their opposition despite lower costs. In contrast, respondents who are not interested in reading about corrections matters are more likely to alter their views from opposition to support in the face of lower costs. Note that once these variables have had their impact, the only occupational dummy variable of any importance is state elected officials.

One cannot help but be struck by the continued opposition to the "punitive" future by state-level elected officials. One would think that

Table 3–16.   Support for Rehabilitative Future Despite Increased Costs Regressed on Biography, Position, Knowledge, Experience, and Interests (N=211, R²=.30, F=17.30, P<.05)

Variable	Units	Regression Coefficient	t-Value	Unique Variance
Not Interested in Corrections				
Literature	Five Levels	−0.38	−2.21	.017
Support for Reform Hurts				
Prospects	Three Levels	−0.45	−3.37	.039
Reform Makes Job Easier	Three Levels	0.38	3.85	.051
Reform Hurts Prospects	Three Levels	−0.46	−2.89	.029
Local Politicians	Dummy (1=Yes)	−0.61	−2.50	.021

Note: High index score means continued support for rehabilitative future despite increased costs (sum of support, support despite 25 percent increase in cost, support despite 50 percent increase in costs).

Table 3–17. Support for Rehabilitative Future Despite Increased Recidivism Regressed on Biography, Position, Knowledge, Experience, and Interests (N=207, R²=.21, F=10.52, P<.05)

Variable	Units	Regression Coefficient	t-Value	Unique Variance
Not Interested in Corrections Literature	Five Levels	−0.35	−2.38	.022
Age	Years	−0.009	−1.64	.011
Support Reform Hurts Prospects	Three Levels	−0.39	−4.17	.069
Reform Makes Job Easier	Three Levels	0.36	4.33	.074
Partisans	Dummy (1=Yes)	−0.54	−2.35	.022

Note: High index score means continued support for rehabilitative future despite increased recidivism (sum of support, support despite 10 percent increase in recidivism, support despite 30 percent increase in recidivism).

unresponsiveness to costs flies in the face of their constituency's interests. The picture is further complicated by table 3–15, which shows that state politicians also are more likely to continue to oppose the "punitive" future despite lower recidivism rates. Again this effect appears with several other variables held constant: education and the reform's negative consequences, which both foster stubbornness, in contrast to age and lack of interest in reading about corrections, which both discourage stubbornness.

In short, tables 3–14 and 3–15 suggest that holding self-interests constant, more highly educated respondents, respondents who may have more interest in and contact with corrections matters, and state

Table 3–18. Support for Community Corrections Despite Increased Costs Regressed on Biography, Position, Knowledge, Experience, and Interests (N=217, R²=.27, F=13.22, P<.05)

Variable	Units	Regression Coefficient	t-Value	Unique Variance
Talked to Correction Personnel	Four Levels	0.23	2.90	.029
Education	Six Levels	0.16	2.48	.021
Support Reform Hurts Prospects	Three Levels	−0.64	−5.32	.098
Reform Makes Job Easier	Three Levels	0.27	2.68	.025
Corrections Officials	Dummy (1=Yes)	0.33	1.66	.010
Prosecutors	Dummy (1=Yes)	−0.69	−2.14	.016

Note: High index score means continued support despite increased costs (sum of support, support despite 25 percent increase in costs, support despite 50 percent increase in costs).

Table 3–19.   Support for Community Corrections Despite Increased Recidivism Regressed on Biography, Position, Knowledge, Experience, and Interests (N=207, R^2=.21, F=8.61, P<.05)

Variable	Units	Regression Coefficient	t-Value	Unique Variance
Talked to Corrections Personnel	Four Levels	0.17	2.70	.029
Not Interested in Corrections Literature	Five Levels	−0.30	−1.90	.014
Support Reform Hurts Prospects	Three Levels	−0.36	−3.56	.050
Reform Makes Job Easier	Three Levels	0.26	3.08	.038
Judges	Dummy (1=Yes)	−0.63	−2.38	.023

Note: High index score means continued support despite increased recidivism (sum of support, support despite 10 percent increase in recidivism, support despite 30 percent increase in recidivism).

politicians are more likely to ignore reduced costs and reduced recidivism and continue to oppose the "punitive" future. This implies some sort of intellectual or ideological stance beyond the *realpolitik* of corrections change.

Where reactions to the "punitive" future in the face of changing costs and recidivism rates may reflect considerable intellectual and ideological content, support for the "rehabilitative" future despite higher costs and higher recidivism rates seems almost exclusively determined by rational self-interest. Table 3–16 shows that we are able to account for 30 percent of the variance in continued support for rehabilitation in the face of higher costs with the lion's share of that variance attributed to three interest variables. However, consistent with our earlier two tables, respondents who are less interested in reading about corrections matters are less likely to hold to rehabilitation despite higher costs. Finally, local politicians are also less inflexible.

The prediction of continued support for the rehabilitation future despite higher recidivism is more difficult to achieve. Table 3–17 shows that we can account for only 21 percent of the variance. Nevertheless, once again our interest variables really tell most of the story, with older respondents, respondents who are less interested in reading about corrections matters, and partisans being more responsive to changes in recidivism rates.

Table 3–18 and 3–19 shows the continued support for community corrections despite higher costs and recidivism rates has a pattern closer to the interest model than the intellectual-ideological model. Familiar variables again appear, with our measures of rational self-interest taken together by far the most important. However, in addition it seems that prosecutors and judges will be more likely to change from support to opposition, while corrections officials seem a bit more committed to community corrections.

What can one conclude about the alternative futures? Perhaps most important, it is clear that the "punitive" future is far less popular than the rehabilitative and community corrections approaches.

Second, support for these packages of reforms is strongly influenced by the levels of cost and particularly the levels of recidivism analyzed in this study. While some respondents stick to their original assessments, most alter their views.

Third, we are typically able to account for more of the variance in support or opposition in instances where costs are altered, as opposed to recidivism rates. This suggests that assessments in the face of increased or decreased costs are more a function of the independent variables we have considered (biography, position, knowledge, experience and interests) than assessments in the face of changes in recidivism. Changes in projected recidivism are thus more likely to affect elites in similar ways.

Fourth, there is some evidence that more highly educated, knowledgeable, and experienced respondents are less influenced by the levels of cost and recidivism with which we presented them. It is hard to say precisely what this means except to suggest that perhaps moral or ideological positions on these futures are more salient. Alternatively, they may be so heavily swayed by other existing evidence about these futures that our varying consequences had less impact. For example, they might feel that the "punitive" future leads to prison unrest and therefore feel that much lower costs and recidivism rates are necessary to justify it.

Finally, it is fairly clear where opposition and support for these programs will come from. Higher-level corrections officials and state-level politicians are more likely to oppose the "punitive" future while supporting the others. Police, judges, prosecutors, corrections personnel, and local politicians will be more likely to support the "punitive" future and oppose the other two. However, with the possible exception of the "punitive" future, rational self-interest clearly dominates the picture, so that it would seem that all parties are likely to change if they perceive a changing political climate. In other words, few respondents will stubbornly hold their views in the face of high political and practical costs, a circumstance that suggests legislative and administrative reforms are possible. There seems plenty of room for negotiation and compromise, and plenty of room to respond to new political realities.

SUPPORT FOR SPECIFIC CHANGES

To tap the most concrete level of corrections changes, a group of items in the questionnaire asked respondents whether they favored, opposed, or were neutral about a series of specific corrections practices. The resulting data are tabulated in table 3–20. Looking first at the results for the three states combined, it is clear that there is considerable variability in support for these practices. Virtually everyone favors

Table 3–20.   Elite Support for Specific Changes in Corrections Systems

	Oppose	Neutral	Favor	100% =	Significance
A. *Reinstatement of Death Penalty for Habitual Offenders*					
Three States Combined	42%	10	48	[252]	
Florida	31%	9	60	[98]	
Illinois	44%	11	45	[75]	p < .05
Washington	53%	10	37	[79]	
B. *Abolition of Censorship of Prisoners' Mail*					
Three States Combined	42%	11	47	[262]	
Florida	52%	8	40	[105]	
Illinois	32%	19	49	[75]	p < .05
Washington	39%	7	54	[82]	
C. *Methadone Maintenance Programs in Prisons*					
Three States Combined	23%	15	63	[246]	
Florida	25%	13	62	[99]	
Illinois	20%	16	65	[71]	p > .05
Washington	22%	17	62	[76]	
D. *Greater Use of Solitary Confinement for Offenses Committed in Prison*					
Three States Combined	61%	19	20	[252]	
Florida	52%	21	27	[101]	
Illinois	65%	24	11	[71]	p < .05
Washington	69%	12	19	[80]	

Table 3–20. continued

	Oppose	Neutral	Favor	100% =	Significance
E. *Increased Emphasis on Vocational Training Closely Related to Jobs*					
Three States Combined	1%	4	95	[265]	
Florida	2%	1	97	[107]	
Illinois	0%	0	100	[75]	p > .05
Washington	1%	0	99	[83]	
F. *Greater Use of Corporal Punishment for Offenses Committed in Prison*					
Three States Combined	70%	10	20	[259]	
Florida	68%	8	25	[105]	
Illinois	73%	14	14	[73]	p > .05
Washington	69%	11	20	[81]	
G. *Permitting Visits by Prisoners' Spouses for Sexual Purposes*					
Three States Combined	23%	17	59	[253]	
Florida	18%	14	68	[103]	
Illinois	28%	18	54	[74]	p > .05
Washington	25%	22	53	[76]	
H. *Prisoners to be Represented by Counsel at Prison Offense Hearings*					
Three States Combined	26%	13	62	[258]	
Florida	32%	15	53	[102]	
Illinois	22%	14	65	[74]	p > .05
Washington	21%	10	70	[82]	
I. *Prisoners Represented by Counsel at Parole Hearings*					
Three States Combined	18%	7	75	[261]	
Florida	18%	7	75	[105]	
Illinois	13%	5	81	[75]	p > .05
Washington	24%	8	68	[81]	
J. *Parolees Represented by Counsel at Parole Revocation Hearings*					
Three States Combined	6%	5	88	[264]	
Florida	5%	7	89	[106]	
Illinois	8%	5	86	[76]	p > .05
Washington	7%	4	89	[82]	

Continued

Table 3–20.   continued

	Oppose	Neutral	Favor	100% =	Significance
K. *More Group Therapy for Prisoners*					
Three States Combined	4%	13	83	[262]	
Florida	4%	4	92	[106]	
Illinois	4%	24	72	[74]	p < .05
Washington	5%	13	82	[82]	
L. *Greater Use of Halfway Houses for Prisoners Awaiting Full Release*					
Three States Combined	5%	4	92	[261]	
Florida	5%	2	94	[105]	
Illinois	4%	5	91	[75]	p > .05
Washington	5%	5	90	[81]	
M. *Greater Use of Community Corrections Centers for Part-Time Confinement of Some Offenders*					
Three States Combined	6%	5	89	[261]	
Florida	6%	2	92	[105]	
Illinois	8%	5	86	[74]	p > .05
Washington	5%	8	87	[82]	
N. *Routine Weekend Furloughs to Allow Prisoners to Visit Their Communities*					
Three States Combined	31%	13	56	[257]	
Florida	25%	14	61	[103]	
Illinois	23%	14	63	[73]	p < .05
Washington	44%	12	43	[81]	
O. *Prisoner Participation in Self-Government*					
Three States Combined	31%	13	56	[263]	
Florida	32%	16	52	[106]	
Illinois	37%	16	47	[75]	p < .05
Washington	23%	7	70	[82]	
P. *Strengthening the Powers of Prison Guards in Disciplining Prisoners*					
Three States Combined	61%	18	21	[248]	
Florida	66%	16	19	[97]	
Illinois	51%	23	26	[73]	p > .05
Washington	64%	15	20	[78]	

more vocational training, availability of counsel at prison offense hearings, at parole hearings, and parole revocation hearings, and group therapy, halfway houses, and community treatment facilities. Only three practices receive a majority in opposition: the use of solitary confinement, strengthening the power of prison guards in disciplining prisoners, and corporal punishment. With respect to other practices, we find respondents about evenly divided between those favoring and those opposing.

Table 3–20 also reveals some state differences, although they are often small and inconsistent and therefore difficult to summarize easily. Florida elites seem more in favor of some punitive measures such as the death penalty, solitary confinement, and corporal punishment. On the other hand, they are more lenient on other issues, being more likely to favor group therapy, furloughs, and conjugal visits. Similarly, Washington residents appear to more strongly favor the abolition of censorship and representation at prison offense hearing, and prison self-government, but oppose furloughs. The volatility of such opinions is reflected by an incident that occurred shortly before our interviewing began. In 1972 several prisoners on furlough in Washington had committed some particularly heinous crime and the practice of furloughs came under serious attack whose efforts were still apparent in our finding. Illinois residents are less in favor of some of the punitive measures and are at the same time less in favor of increased use of group therapy and prisoner self-government.

To reduce analytical complexity, we examined clusters of reforms that tended to be supported by the same respondents in the hope that we could move from a discussion of each individual prison reform to broader, empirically derived aggregates of practices. Building on a correlation matrix involving the items from table 3–20, table 3–21 shows the necessary factor analysis. Apparently, the reforms are best expressed by three types of factors: "coercive reforms," "legal reforms," and "rehabilitative reforms." We then added the items from table 3–20 which loaded most heavily on each of the factors to construct three new indices of prison reforms.

Using these three indices as dependent variables, regression analyses were performed in which each index was regressed on the same biographical, positional, knowledge, and experiential variables used in previous analyses. Table 3–22 shows that we are able to account for 33 percent of the variance in support for coercive reforms. Virtually the whole story is told by two variables: education and having met with prisoners. In both cases their effect is greatly to reduce support for coercive reforms. In addition, partisans are less in

Table 3–21. Factor Loadings for Specific Corrections Reforms (Varimax Rotation)

Specific Reform	Coercive Reforms	Legal Reforms	Rehabilitative Reforms
Guards Discipline	.74	−.13	−.29
Corporal Punishment	.66	−.01	−.18
Solitary Confinement	.59	−.07	−.10
Death Penalty	.56	−.08	−.17
Counsel Parole Revocation	−.09	.73	.10
Counsel Parole Hearings	−.08	.72	.06
Counsel Prison Offenses	−.15	.52	.09
Community Corrections	−.11	.05	.68
Halfway Houses	−.19	.07	.50
Self-Government	−.37	.18	.42
Furloughs	−.18	.14	.41
Therapy	−.14	−.001	.36
No Mail Censorship	−.43	.16	.26
Conjugal Visits	−.25	.06	.23
Vocational Training	.06	−.04	−.01
Methadone	.05	.17	.02
Eigenvalue	3.52	1.24	1.04

favor of coercive reforms, while Floridians and respondents with little interest in reading about corrections matters are more in favor. Note that these prison practices involve far more than simply locking up convicted offenders, but include capital punishment, solitary confinement, corporal punishment, and increasing the disciplinary power of prison guards. Where in earlier analyses in this chapter we have hesitated to label "punitive" practices as draconic, in the case of this index the label seems warranted. The reader may recall that we earlier argued that some of our more punitive-oriented respondents may actually have been in the sophisticated corrections vanguard. These

Table 3–22. Support for Coercive Reforms Regressed on Biography, Knowledge, and Experience (N=222, R^2=.33, F=21.39, P<.05)

Variable	Units	Regression Coefficient	t-Value	Unique Variance
No Interest in Corrections Literature	Five Levels	0.88	2.40	.018
Met Prisoners	Dummy (1=Yes)	−1.22	−4.06	.051
Education	Six Levels	−0.90	−7.46	.172
Partisans	Dummy (1=Yes)	−1.64	−2.87	.026
Florida	Dummy (1=Yes)	0.55	1.86	.011

Note: High score means reforms favored (sum of death penalty, solitary, corporal punishment, guard's power).

Table 3-23. Support for Legal Reforms Regressed on Biography, Experience, and Knowledge (N=254, R²=.10, F=4.66, P<.05)

Variable	Units	Regression Coefficient	t-Value	Unique Variance
Estimated Cost of Adult Prisoners	Hundreds	0.005	2.22	.018
Education	Six Levels	0.16	1.81	.012
Corrections Officials	Dummy (1=Yes)	−0.54	−1.87	.013
Police	Dummy (1=Yes)	−1.05	−3.00	.033
Prosecutors	Dummy (1=Yes)	−0.93	−2.00	.015
Partisans	Dummy (1=Yes)	0.81	1.94	.013

Note: High score means reforms favored (sum of counsel at prison offense hearings, counsel at parole hearings, counsel at parole revocation hearings).

findings require that we now qualify that assessment. To some degree, our earlier analyses have lumped together persons who see incarceration as a necessary *and sufficient* function of prisons with persons who would add more painful coercive measures. The former may be in some sort of vanguard, the latter hearken back to more brutal times.

Table 3–23 shows that we can explain only 10 percent of the variance in support for legal reforms. The largest effect is for police, who are less likely to support legal reforms. Prosecutors and corrections officials seem to hold somewhat similar views. Partisans appear more in support of legal reforms along with persons having more education and persons who estimate higher costs of keeping prisoners in jail. In short, law enforcement interests oppose legal reforms.

Finally, table 3–24 shows that we are able to explain 25 percent

Table 3-24. Support for Rehabilitative Reforms Regressed on Biography, Knowledge, and Experience (N=219, R²=.25, F=10.16, P<.05)

Variable	Units	Regression Coefficient	t-Value	Unique Variance
Uncertainty about Juvenile Institutions	Five Levels	0.21	1.60	.009
Met with Prisoners	Dummy (1=Yes)	0.72	2.65	.025
Estimated Cost of Juvenile Prisoners	Hundreds	−0.004	−1.57	.009
Education	Six Levels	0.63	5.60	.111
Police	Dummy (1=Yes)	−0.75	−1.83	.012
Judges	Dummy (1=Yes)	−1.24	−3.05	.033
Prosecutors	Dummy (1=Yes)	−1.59	−2.95	.031

Note: High score means reforms favored (sum of therapy, halfway houses, community corrections, furloughs, self-government).

of the variance in rehabilitative reforms. A very familiar pattern emerges once again. Police, judges, and prosecutors are less likely to support rehabilitative programs. More highly educated respondents and respondents who have met with prisoners are more in favor.

In summary, these data seem to sharpen earlier distinctions, and perhaps the most important insight is that for many of our respondents, "punitive" reforms mean draconic reforms. Moreover, such elites have less education, less interest in the literature on corrections, and less contact with prisoners. One is tempted to call them the yahoos of corrections. Fortunately, it appears that such respondents are the minority, at least in 1973.

Also of some interest is the finding that law enforcement types are most in opposition to the legal reforms covered in this study. It remains to be seen, however, if these groups possess sufficient power to thwart such changes.

Finally, support for rehabilitative practices shows the now familiar pattern. The picture is dominated by respondents with higher education, who are as positive about rehabilitation as they are negative about coercion.

CORRECTIONS REFORMS AND STATE ELITES

The political elites of the three states studied as a group subscribed to the then current reform position on adult men's prisons. A strong majority endorsed a view of the corrections system as centered around the rehabilitation of prisoners and on moving the prison system away from imprisonment in institutions as a single mode of treatment toward a series of graduated forms of incarceration including such measures as community-based corrections, part-time prisons, and extensive use of parole.

This overall stance manifested itself on several levels. First, the elites endorsed rehabilitation as a major goal of corrections in general. Second, reform "packages" that emphasized rehabilitation and community corrections institutions received majority endorsements. Finally, specific reform measures that were punitive in character were rejected, while those that emphasized rehabilitation were endorsed.

The majority view of corrections was held with particular strength by elites who were better educated, more interested in corrections, and who served as elected officials. A minority viewpoint that emphasized corrections as serving a deterrent or retributive function was held by those who were not interested in corrections as an issue, by the less well educated, and by the police. Sometimes the police were joined by prosecutors and judges, especially on issues that involved extending additional civil liberties to prisoners.

Although elites did not regard it as likely that corrections would move in the direction of emphasizing punitive and deterrent functions, they saw the general public as endorsing that view. Indeed, it was clear that the general public was seen in each of the three states as holding views about corrections that were at variance with the elites' viewpoints. Without independent measures of actual public opinion in the three states, it is difficult to assess whether the elites were more or less accurately reporting on this matter or simply expressing a stereotyped view of the public as generally unenlightened. Yet, there is some evidence that the elites were misestimating some opinions: They saw their colleagues as less liberal than themselves, a finding that suggests that there is not much communication on prison reform within elite circles, much less, public debate on the issues.

In short, corrections reforms promising rehabilitation would have found a receptive audience among our state elites. The obstacles to these reforms lay mainly in uncertainty about public opinion and its reactions to such measures. It should be noted that many of the elites were also rather sensitive to the possibility of political losses resulting from support of reform. Were strong antireform sentiment to arise in any of the states—perhaps led by law enforcement interest groups— many of our elites would probably back off from a public liberal stand.

✻   *Chapter 4*

The Politics of Corrections:
Patterns of Influence

In the voting booths where elections are decided, it is one vote per person. For revisions of corrections legislation or administrative procedures, there is hardly a comparably simple formula. Persons vary in their ability to influence outcomes not only because of their formal positions, but because of their informal contacts. Hence, to properly assess the potential for change within each state requires that one take into account existing patterns of authority and influence, particularly as related to corrections issues. We need to know precisely who is the "more equal" than others in order to accurately project the direction and likelihood of reform. We also require quantitative estimates of differential influence in order to adjust our earlier findings to the *realpolitik* of each state. While governors, for example, are formally and in broad terms more powerful than the administrators they appoint, the necessary delegation of responsibilities may alter day-to-day balances of influence in both qualitative and quantitative terms. To ignore such complications is to ignore the realities of corrections reform.

Obviously the first step is to describe the patterning of influence. However, we will be concerned here not with general patterns of influence, but those patterns that have been established with respect to formulating, initiating, and validating changes in corrections systems. A later chapter will be concerned with applying the knowledge gained here in an attempt to devise a rational system for weighting elite interviews according to the opinion-holders' importance in decision-making.

85

Our respondents were selected because their opinions on corrections were likely to have some significant impact. Moreover, we deliberately included as many persons and groups as could be reasonably expected to be [vitally] concerned with the issues involved. The success of this dragnet operation can be seen in the fact that, as shown in chapter 2, we have a more than usually knowledgeable and interested group of respondents. Within this elite group, however, we can anticipate that some are more active than others in the decision-making process.

Over the past decade, a considerable controversy has agitated the fields of political sociology and behavioral political science over appropriate methods for studying patterns of influence in political decisions. On the one hand, there are those who insist that the only appropriate way to proceed is to study a number of concrete decisions, inducing from such instances what are customary patterns of influence. There is much to say for this position, especially its close attention to actual practice. On the other hand, the opposing point of view claims that the study of specific decisions obscures the important overall patterning which can be best uncovered by studying the reputations that individuals and organizations enjoy as influential and powerful social units. As is often the case with such controversies, there is some merit on both sides. Even more important, however, is the fact that studies employing one or the other method are often not as far apart in their findings as antagonists claim. Reputations are not manufactured out of whole cloth: they have some basis in practice. Specific decisions are often influenced not only by those with reputations but also by others whose interest in a particular decision may be very high. Thus, one may find that the governor's office is usually regarded as extremely influential with respect to state legislation. Yet, one may also find that in the case of a particular piece of legislative action, the governor's office may have had no influence on the outcome.

This particular research relies on the reputational approach, not so much out of the conviction that this approach is the best possible, but because it is more feasible to obtain reputations in sample surveys than it is to study specific decisions.

Properly to interpret our findings is to regard them as outlining the *potentials* for influence in each of the three states. The reputations we collected are based upon the collective experiences of our elite respondents with decision-making in the past, a sort of informal average over the years previous to 1973. It is problematic how much decision-making in the future may depart from the practices of the past. We can safely wager, however, that, while some states may show marked deviation from the patterns, reputations predicting the overall patterning of the past will tend to persist at least into the proximate future. We advance this prediction mainly out of regard for the remarkable persistence of customary behavior.

WHO IS ACTIVE ON CORRECTIONS ISSUES?

The first question to raise is who usually participates in corrections policy-making and legislating? Respondents were asked to rate the activity levels of a number of groups and persons with respect to corrections issues in their state. The resulting data are shown in table 4–1, for respondents for all three states combined.

The percentages indicate wide variability in the degree of participation across groups and persons. For example, governors are assessed as

Table 4–1. Active Groups on Corrections Issues—Three States Combined

	Activity Level				
Person/Group	*Plays No Role*	*Rarely Active*	*Sometimes Active*	*Always Active*	*100% =*
Governor	0%	3	32	65	[257]
Citizens' Crime Commission	13%	12	42	33	[227]
Democratic Leader in State Senate (Upper House)	7%	20	51	22	[237]
Republican Leader in State Senate (Upper House)	8%	21	51	20	[238]
Democratic Leader in State Senate (Lower House)	6%	21	52	21	[235]
Republican Leader in State Senate (Lower House)	6%	21	52	21	[232]
State Senate Corrections Committee	2%	3	27	69	[233]
State House Corrections Committee	2%	5	27	66	[234]
LEAA State Planning Agency	8%	10	38	43	[224]
Head of State Corrections Dept.	0.4%	2	14	84	[248]
State Attorney-General	2%	7	44	47	[248]
State Bar Association	4%	24	51	20	[249]
Police Chiefs of Large Police Depts.	6%	19	51	24	[249]
American Civil Liberties Union (ACLU)	4%	8	40	48	[246]
State Parole Dept. and Staff	2%	14	28	56	[246]
Ex-Offenders Organization	28%	25	30	17	[210]
Associations of Corrections Personnel	16%	23	39	21	[218]
Prominent Criminal Lawyers in State	13%	29	46	13	[238]
Associations of Police Personnel	12%	26	48	14	[241]
Prison Reform Groups	4%	0	35	62	[26]
Public Defenders	0%	10	47	43	[30]
Other Public Officials and Agencies	3%	10	49	38	[39]
Other Private Persons and Groups	0%	12	62	26	[34]

quite active, while associations of lower-level corrections personnel are relatively inactive. Sixty-five percent of the respondents say the governors of their state are "always active." In contrast, only 21 percent say that associations of corrections personnel as "always active." The most active "groups" are the governor, the corrections committees of both houses, the head of the State Department of Corrections, and the State Parole Board.

Some of the groups listed in the bottom four rows of the table also show high levels of activity. However, these were groups or persons who respondents volunteered as additions to a standard list of nineteen groups. Consequently, each addition was assessed by small numbers of respondents. The percentages involving these groups are based on a very small number of ratings, consequently we will not refer to these groups any further in this chapter.

Table 4–2 contains average activity levels for each group in each state. The averages were calculated by forcing the categories of activity into a four-point scale ("no role" = 1, "rarely active" = 2, "sometimes

Table 4–2. Average Group Activity Levels by State

| | Average Activity Levels for Each State | | | | | |
| | Florida | | Illinois | | Washington | |
Person/Group	$\bar{X}$	N =	$\bar{X}$	N =	$\bar{X}$	N =
Governor	3.6	[101]	3.5	[74]	3.8	[82]
Citizens' Crime Commission	2.7	[85]	3.1	[64]	3.2	[78]
Democratic Leader in State Senate (Upper House)	2.9	[71]	3.1	[42]	2.7	[81]
Republican Leader in State Senate (Upper House)	2.8	[91]	3.1	[66]	2.7	[81]
Democratic Leader in State Senate (Lower House)	2.9	[92]	3.0	[64]	2.8	[79]
Republican Leader in State Senate (Lower House)	2.9	[92]	3.0	[63]	2.7	[77]
State Senate Corrections Committee	3.7	[94]	3.7	[65]	3.5	[74]
State House Corrections Committee	3.7	[97]	3.5	[62]	3.5	[75]
LEAA State Planning Agency	3.2	[87]	3.0	[62]	3.3	[75]
Head of State Corrections Dept.	3.8	[99]	3.9	[67]	3.6	[82]
State Attorney General	3.5	[100]	3.1	[67]	3.4	[82]
State Bar Association	2.9	[97]	2.8	[70]	2.9	[82]
Police Chiefs of Large Police Dept.	2.8	[98]	2.9	[69]	3.2	[82]
American Civil Liberties Union (ACLU)	3.2	[96]	3.3	[67]	3.4	[83]
State Parole Department and Staff	3.6	[99]	3.2	[66]	3.4	[81]
Ex-Offenders Organizations	2.0	[81]	2.5	[58]	2.7	[71]
Associations of Corrections Personnel	2.4	[68]	2.8	[62]	2.9	[70]
Prominent Criminal Lawyers in State	2.5	[91]	2.7	[68]	2.5	[79]
Associations of Corrections Personnel	2.5	[94]	2.7	[68]	2.8	[79]

active" = 3, "always active" = 4). A mean of 3, for example, would indicate that a group was given an average rating of "sometimes active." A mean of 3.5 would indicate an average amount of activity about midway between "sometimes" and "always active." (We assume, with some uneasiness, that the levels of activity form an interval scale.)

Averages over 3.5 have been circled in table 4–2. In general, the groups with high mean ratings are the same groups that were active as shown in the percentage distributions of table 4–1. (It would be surprising were they not.) However, there are some state differences. Were one to take some very small differences seriously, the state patterns suggest that groups judged as active in the total sample have somewhat different degrees of activity in each individual state. In particular, Illinois has the lowest relative average for its governor. It also has the highest mean for its corrections head. In contrast, Washington has the highest mean for its governor and the lowest for its corrections head. This suggests that amounts of activity may be in part a function of the activity of other actors within a given state.

It should be noted that Illinois Governor Walker, a Democrat, was in the fall of 1972 newly elected against the opposition of the "regular" Democrats and was then confronted by a house and senate in which Republicans predominated. Shortly thereafter, the legislature refused to confirm Governor Walker's candidate for head of corrections and overrode his veto of some extraordinary financial aid for the Chicago Transit Authority. In short, Governor Walker was a governor at odds with strong groups in his own party and faced by a legislature dominated by the opposing party. His was not a position that could be called one of great power.

Three states are too small a sample to do cross-state comparisons in any compelling way, especially with such small differences between mean values. Even though a difference of .5 in the four-point scale might have substantial substantive meaning, a difference of that size could easily be a function of measurement and sampling error. Further, it is a bit fatuous to talk about a pattern with three data points. Nevertheless, it may be reasonable for heuristic purposes to proceed with a systematic cross-state analysis, relying mainly on the consistency of patterns that may appear in different sets of data.

Table 4–3 presents a correlation matrix relating the mean activity levels of the five most active parties computed across the three states. The correlations fluctuate widely, as one might expect from such a small sample. Nevertheless, the pattern is far from random and suggests that the more active the governor, the less active the other parties. Further, the other four groups and individuals tend to cluster so that if one is active the others are active.

Table 4–3. Correlations for Mean Activity Across the Three States

		Governor	Senate Corrections Committee	House Corrections Committee	Head of Corrections	Parole Department
		1	2	3	4	5
Governor	1		−.79	−.41	−.99	−.32
Senate Corrections Committee	2			.88	.86	.36
House Corrections Committee	3				.51	.73
Head of Corrections	4					.21
Parole Department	5					

Since table 4–3 indicates that when a governor is more active in corrections matters, other groups are less active, one may perhaps infer that some balance of power is involved. The differential activity may stem from a deliberate partitioning of the political pie in which certain issues become the "turf" of certain actors, or may reflect an unintended consequence of political activity. In either case, the correlations contradict the idea that if either the governor or key legislators become active on corrections matters, others automatically jump on the bandwagon. Were these findings to hold in a larger sample of states, it would indicate that legislative activity on corrections would not necessarily involve all, or even a large number, of potential actors. Each state would have a few key people who typically showed interest in these issues and, barring unusually controversial proposals introduced with wide publicity, success or failure of corrections bills would result from the actions of these few.

Another way to evaluate these data is to examine the extent to which respondents differ in attributing to groups more or less activity in corrections legislative matters. Since the elite members are supposedly reacting to these questions as informants, the major differences among respondents should arise out of their positions and the states in which they reside, with correspondingly little difference among respondents according to their educational level, age, and other purely biographical characteristics. To test these expectations, we ran regressions of state, positional, and biographic characteristics on the attribution of activity levels to each of the groups shown in table 4–3.

The results of the regressions are too tedious to report here. In none of the five regressions were significant results obtained. In only one case, involving the activity level of the governor, did any one of the variables attain close to conventional levels of statistical and substantive significance. As we could anticipate from the results of table 4–2, Illinois elite members were a bit more likely to attribute a lower level of activity to the governor of that state. In other respects and in the cases of activity levels for the other major actors shown in table 4–3, respondents hardly differed in any systematic way that could be captured by biographical, experiential, or positional characteristics. In short, respondents across states and with different backgrounds were apparently reporting much the same perceptions of the major active groups in legislative activities involving corrections.

WHO IS REPUTED TO WIELD THE POWER?

In order to understand which bills are likely to pass, one must know far more than who is typically active in corrections matters. Crucial is which parties have the "clout" to impose their goals on legislation. Our questionnaire examines this issue in several ways.

One way to discover who wields power on corrections matters is to simply ask. Though this reputational approach has known weaknesses, it is a useful first approximation, especially when checked against other kinds of data. One measure of reputation was to ask: "If you wanted to get a piece of corrections legislation through the state legislature, which of these groups or persons [on the list shown in table 4–1] would be very important to get on your side?" A second item asked: "Whose opposition could make it impossible or very difficult to get corrections legislation passed?" The resulting responses are summarized in table 4–4. The left-hand column shows the proportions of respondents who said a given group was very important for passage, and the right-hand column shows the proportions of respondents who said a given group could probably stop passage.

On several individuals and groups there is high consensus. The governor, Democratic and Republican leaders of both houses, and corrections committees of both houses were seen by at least 40 percent of the respondents as very important for passage and also having the ability to stop legislation. In addition, the head of corrections was seen by over 50 percent as being very important for passage.

It is interesting to compare these results with table 4–1 showing groups' levels of activity. Governors and corrections committees are both seen as always active and very powerful, but the political chamber leaders are seen as, at best, somewhat active and very power-

Table 4–4. Reputations for Power on Corrections Issues (N = 266)

Person/Group	Percent Claiming Group Very Important for Bill Passage	Percent Claiming Group Can Stop A Bill
Governor	74%	79%
Citizens' Crime Commission	25%	17%
Democratic Leader in State Senate (Upper House)	62%	61%
Republican Leader in State Senate (Upper House)	51%	47%
Democratic Leader in State Senate (Lower House)	62%	59%
Republican Leader in State Senate (Lower House)	49%	45%
State Senate Corrections Committee	59%	53%
State House Corrections Committee	56%	52%
LEAA State Planning Agency	16%	7%
Head of State Corrections Dept.	55%	36%
State Attorney-General	35%	34%
State Bar Association	20%	18%
Police Chiefs of Large Police Depts.	17%	18%
American Civil Liberties Union (ACLU)	12%	10%
State Parole Dept. and Staff	22%	13%
Ex-Offenders Organizations	6%	1%
Associations of Corrections Personnel	10%	7%
Prominent Criminal Lawyers in State	10%	9%
Associations of Police Personnel	9%	11%

ful. This suggests, that even though these partisan leaders are not typically involved and active in corrections matters, they must be won over for a bill to pass.

In general, parties seen as essential for passage are also seen as able to stop passage. The correlation between the two columns of proportions on table 4–4 is .95. However, there are several interesting exceptions to this pattern. The LEAA State Planning Agency is seen by a few respondents (16 percent) as important for passage, but by virtually no one (7 percent) as able to block corrections legislation. A similar pattern appears for the state parole department and staff: more people feel they are important for passage (22 percent) than feel it can block legislation (13 percent). The most striking example of this perceived ability to aid passage of legislation but not to prevent it is the head of corrections; 55 percent felt the corrections head very important for support of a bill, but only 36 percent felt he could stop a bill. One may think of these three groups as performing "staff functions"; they are probably very important in the development and writing of corrections legislation, but exercise little direct power in the legislature. If they are not prepared to work on a bill's development, it may never get into the legislative process. However, once the bill is submitted, they apparently can do little to affect its passage.

Table 4–5 presents data on the perceived power of groups within states. Rather than complicate matters unnecessarily in this analysis by showing the proportions in each state that say a given individual or group can aid passage and stop it, we have taken advantage of the .95 correlation between perceived ability to aid and perceived ability to block, a relationship so high we can use either measure as an index of power. We have chosen to use perceived ability to aid passage as our index. Hence, the columns in table 4–5 show the percentage of respon-

Table 4–5. Reputations for Power in Corrections Issues in Each State

Person/Group	Florida (N = 107)	Illinois (N = 76)	Washington (N = 83)
Governor[a]	78%	69%	81%
Citizens' Crime Commission[a]	13%	20%	45%
Democratic Leader in State Senate (Upper House)[a]	62%	67%	59%
Republican Leader in State Senate (Upper House)[a]	39%	70%	48%
Democratic Leader in State Senate (Lower House)[a]	59%	67%	60%
Republican Leader in State Senate (Lower House)[a]	38%	68%	46%
State Senate Corrections Committee[a]	64%	51%	57%
State House Corrections Committee[a]	62%	50%	54%
LEAA State Planning Agency	18%	12%	18%
Head of State Corrections Dept.[a]	52%	57%	57%
State Attorney-General[a]	37%	20%	46%
State Bar Association	18%	22%	22%
Police Chiefs of Large Police Depts.[a]	52%	57%	25%
American Civil Liberties Union (ACLU)	37%	20%	17%
State Parole Dept. and Staff[a]	26%	7%	30%
Ex-Offenders Organization	2%	4%	13%
Association of Corrections Personnel	3%	11%	19%
Prominent Criminal Lawyers in State	10%	11%	8%
Associations of Police Personnel	4%	9%	16%

[a]Person/Group for which at least 25 percent of a state's sample said they were very important for passage of corrections legislation.

dents in each state who said the individual or group is very important for passage.

Table 4–5 still presents a large amount of data, making comparisons between states somewhat difficult. To aid in making comparisons, we have indicated those individuals or groups in a given state designated by at least 25 percent of state respondents as very important for passage. Focusing on these twelve groups, there are some provocative differences between states. The governor, corrections committee, attorney-general, and parole department are seen as considerably less likely to be essential in Illinois than in the other states. In contrast, the party leaders of both houses (especially Republicans) are likely to be seen as more essential for Illinois than in the other states.

Following this lead, a correlation matrix was constructed using the state as the unit of analysis and the proportion saying a given party was essential for passage as each observation (table 4–6). The correlations cluster strongly. The correlations among ratings of groups can be arranged so that two very distinct blocks of ratings are formed, each block primarily containing variables that correlate positively with each other, but negatively with ratings that involve the groups contained in the other block. These two blocks are outlined with triangles in table 4–6. States that have a governor perceived as powerful also regard as powerful the crime commission, corrections committee, attorney-generals, parole departments, and police chiefs of large cities. Further, when the governor is seen as more powerful, party leaders in both houses are seen as far less powerful, along with the head of corrections.

Although the substantive meaning of the correlations must necessarily be regarded quite tentatively, the consistency of the signs in table 4–6 apparently indicates that the configuration of reputational power around corrections issues falls into two broad categories. First, some states may possess an "administrative coalition," in which there exist close connections between the governor, the corrections committees, and most criminal justice agencies. Though not part of state government, police chiefs of large city departments and citizen crime commissions are linked to this network, possibly through the governor and the attorney-general's office. Crime commissions may be drawn into the executive fold because they are typically appointed by the governor and work closely with the state's attorney's office. Because prosecutors and police are usually in close contact with one another on the job, the former may also participate in the "executive coalition."

The second type of state may be more dominated by legislators than executives. Here the power resides in the leaders of the political parties and especially those who are active in the legislature. For our

Table 4–6. Interstate Correlations in Ratings of Groups as Essential for Aid in Passage of Corrections Legislation

	1	2	3	4	5	6	7	8	9	10	11	12
Democratic Senate Leader	1	78	87	80	14	−99	−03	−58	−45	−99	−30	−90
Republican Senate Leader	2		98	99	72	−86	−03	−96	−90	−80	−46	−96
Democratic House Leader	3			98	59	−93	−19	−89	−82	−89	−33	−91
Republican House Leader	4				70	−87	−05	−95	−89	−82	−35	−90
Head of Corrections	5					−27	66	−88	−95	−17	−43	−35
Governor	6						57	68	57	99	74	99
Citizens Crime Commission	7							−25	−38	61	87	57
Senate Corrections Committee	8								98	60	32	60
House Corrections Committee	9									48	11	63
Attorney-General	10										81	98
Police Chiefs	11											69
Parole Department	12											

three states, however, the pattern is not as neat as one might like. Although party leaders all tend to be powerful together in a given state, when they are more powerful, the corrections committees are less powerful. Hence, in legislative-dominated states, not all relevant actors in the legislature share dominance. Moreover, a nonlegislative figure, the head of corrections, may be a relatively important figure in such states.

In summary, one can think of two "ideal types" of configurations of power around corrections issues. Illinois is apparently closest in our example to legislative dominance, and Florida and Washington are examples of executive coalition domination. Were these categories to hold up in a larger sample of states, it would suggest different change strategies for each type. In the executive type, the views of the administrative coalition will be far more important than those of party leaders in the legislature. In the legislative type, the party leaders are the actors whose opinions on corrections matter most. However, in the latter states, efforts at persuasion may be more difficult than for executive coalition states: party leaders are not especially active in corrections matters and may prefer to focus their legislative efforts in other directions.

The last few paragraphs of this section illustrate how a much larger sample of states may provide data that are useful for the planning of strategies in approaching states according to how power is divided between the governor and his allies and the party chiefs in the state legislatures. It should be emphasized that with only three states, the patterns shown here are quite heavily dependent on the particulars of one state, Illinois. In addition, our Illinois data was gathered just after Governor Walker took office and his administration was still being put together. The pattern might be somewhat different today. In any case, a larger sample of states may or may not include others with this pattern, and hence, the triangles of table 4–6 may be somewhat idiosyncratic.

The same issue of consensus arises in connection with attributions of power to influence legislation as earlier with respect to reputed legislative activity. If these reports of influence are to be regarded as having some validity, we should find that there are few differences among elite respondents except those that may be generated by interpositional and interstate differences. Biographical differences resting on such characteristics as educational attainment should in contrast be relatively slight. To test these expectations, regressions were run on major biographical, positional, and state variables, using the attribution of influence to the major actors as dependent variables.[1] None of the regressions turned out to be statistically or substantively significant, and only residence in Illinois came close to attaining a large regression coefficient. While consensus, so defined, is hardly proof that we have captured the essence of the configurations in influence surrounding corrections legislation, such reliability does bolster this assertion.

WHO KNOWS WHOM?

The exercise of political influence requires communication. Some interaction is necessary not only to transmit information, but also for the negotiation processes that go on in all parliamentary bodies. Hence, the next step in our examination of the configuration of influence around corrections is to trace out the interpersonal networks within which each state capitol functions.

Two items on the questionnaire were aimed at assessing the amount of contact between various groups. One asked: "Are there any groups in which you know some key members well enough to call them about something concerning corrections issues?" A second item asked: "Have you ever contacted any of these individuals or group members about corrections issues?" In both cases, respondents had before them the list of groups and individuals mentioned earlier and simply indicated for which persons and/or groups the answer to either question was "yes."

Table 4–7 shows the percentages of respondents in each state who claimed contact with each group on the list. Thirty-two percent of the respondents claim to know the "average" group included on the list well enough to call them on corrections matters, and 21 percent claim to have actually made such contacts. Focusing on the left-hand columns ("know well enough to call"), there is a tendency for Illinois respondents to know groups less well. Possibly more interesting is that the standard deviation for Illinois is also lower, suggesting that not only do respondents feel they know fewer people, but the variability from group to group is not as large. Comparing the pattern of percentages in Illinois' column with the other two suggests why the standard deviation and mean are lower. The head of corrections plus several we have identified earlier as part of the executive coalition tend to have fewer respondents who know them well enough to call. This makes sense, since many new appointments are involved. However, these lower percentages relative to other states do not substantially change the *ordering* of groups and individuals in Illinois relative to the other states. Correlations between the three columns of percentages show high positive correlations of the order of .75.

The state of Washington presents a different, almost cozy, pattern. Not only do more respondents claim to know each group, but the low

Table 4–7.   Extent of Personal Contact on Corrections Matters by State

Person/Group	Percent Knowing Group Well Enough to Call			Percent Who Have Contacted Person/Group		
	Florida	Illinois	Wash-ington	Florida	Illinois	Wash-ington
Governor	50%	32%	46%	30%	29%	30%
Citizens' Crime Commission	15%	22%	35%	13%	21%	26%
Democratic Leader in State (Upper House)	40%	30%	40%	24%	25%	17%
Republican Leader in State Senate (Upper House)	31%	30%	41%	23%	26%	16%
Democratic Leader in State Senate (Lower House)	40%	29%	39%	23%	24%	17%
Republican Leader in State Senate (Lower House)	31%	30%	36%	24%	24%	14%
State Senate Corrections Committee	42%	32%	32%	31%	26%	28%
State House Corrections Committee	44%	28%	31%	36%	22%	24%
LEAA State Planning Agency	28%	28%	43%	22%	26%	32%
Head of State Corrections Dept.	47%	40%	46%	38%	37%	40%
State Attorney-General	54%	32%	59%	23%	22%	43%
State Bar Association	36%	28%	39%	17%	16%	6%
Police Chiefs of Large Police Depts.	28%	29%	40%	12%	16%	23%
American Civil Liberties Union (ACLU)	19%	18%	29%	8%	14%	19%
State Parole Dept. and Staff	38%	30%	45%	26%	21%	35%
Ex-Offenders Organizations	8%	14%	28%	3%	10%	17%
Associations of Corrections Personnel	12%	18%	31%	8%	9%	20%
Prominent Criminal Lawyers in State	29%	18%	25%	8%	10%	12%
Associations of Police Personnel	16%	18%	26%	8%	10%	13%
$\overline{X}\%$ =	32.0	26.7	37.4	19.9	20.6	23.9
SD =	13.1	6.3	8.1	10.1	7.2	8.8
N =	[107]	[76]	[83]	[107]	[76]	[83]
	Grand Mean = 32.0			Grand Mean = 20.2		

standard deviation suggests a rather even distribution of interpersonal networks. Perhaps after the dust settled in Illinois, a Washington pattern appeared.

Somewhat in contrast to Illinois and Washington, corrections politics in Florida seems more atomized. The mean percent is considerably lower than Washington, while the standard deviation is by far the largest of the three. In short, there are fewer interpersonal networks more unevenly distributed among political actors.

The means for the three right-hand columns ("have contacted") are virtually identical. Hence, in spite of a lower proportion of respondents in Illinois claiming to know important persons and groups, in practice it does not seem to matter too much at the aggregate level. All three states show an overall amount of actual contact that is approximately equal. (In part this may result from Illinois respondents referring to officeholders of the prior administration since some posts, such as head of corrections, had not been filled by the time the data was gathered.) Correlations between the three columns of percentages show consistently high positive values of approximately .70, suggesting that the states show roughly the same *percentage orders* of magnitude of contacts with groups within each state.

In summary, on the average, the persons and groups are well enough known to be contacted on corrections matters by 32 percent of our respondents. The level of contact for groups is smaller, 20 percent. Apparently some persons and groups are more heavily tied into communication networks than others. In general, the governor and his executive departments who work in the criminal justice field are likely to be most familiar to the respondents than the other groups listed. In Illinois, this tendency is greatly reduced and the patterns of actual contact show somewhat less selectivity. Although the parties that are known are also the ones more likely to be contacted, the differences between groups that are contacted and those that are not are not nearly as strking. These findings essentially support the material presented earlier. Generally, those groups who are active and influential in corrections are also those most tied into the interpersonal corrections network.

RESPONDENT VARIATION IN KNOWLEDGE AND CONTACT

Up to this point, our attention has been focussed mainly on which groups on our list of potentially important political actors are known to the elite respondents and on the frequency with which they are contacted. In that analysis, the collective judgments of the respondents are taken as reflecting objective differences among the three states and among the groups being studied.

Looked at in a different way, the same data can be used to illuminate differences among elite respondents. Some respondents can be expected to be quite familiar with a wide range of groups and to have had some contact with many groups. Other respondents may have a much more restricted range in either knowledge or contact. The data bear out these expectations: a few of the elite respondents (5 percent) claim to know "some of the key members" in *every* one of the nineteen groups on the list; a larger proportion (21 percent) know *no* key members in any of the groups. On the average, however, our elite members know some of the key members in about one third of the groups (6.1), with the median number being 4.5.

Since contact presupposes some knowledge, the correlation between the number of groups known and the number contacted is quite high (+.73) even though on the average a smaller number of groups have actually been contacted (4.1). Indeed it appears that the distribution of range of contact is quite skewed. More than a third (37 percent) of the respondents have had no contacts with members of any of the groups; but those who have contacted any groups have contacted 6.5, on the average.

To capture the individual extent of knowledge and contact we have formed two scores for each elite respondent. The number of groups known was calculated for each respondent and called the "knowledge score." A similarly calculated measure was formed for contacts with members of each of the nineteen groups and entitled the "contact score." Using these scores as dependent variables, regressions were run with a variety of respondent characteristics as independent variables (table 4–8).

The two regressions each explain useful amounts of the variation in knowledge and contact scores, 40 and 33 percent respectively. Note, however, that only a few of the variables in table 4–8 have regression coefficients that are significantly different from zero. In the case of knowledge scores, being a state elected official means that you know 5.8 more "key members" of the nineteen groups. Being a local elected official means more knowledge, although on a smaller scale, 4.26 more groups in which key members are known. Obviously, being an elected official either on the state or local level means that you more easily acquire knowledge of the key actors in the state political system and also some reason to contact such persons in the past.

Having had some reason to visit state prisons and to contact corrections officials also increases knowledge of the key actors. Persons who have visited the prisons know .89 more of group key members and talking to corrections officials means that one knows 1.19 additional key members for each of the variable's four levels of interaction. (Of course, since corrections officials are one of the nineteen groups, this last finding indicates that our respondents are consistent in their responses to the questionnaire!)

Among biographical characteristics, only educational attainment makes a difference, each level of educational attainment meaning an additional 1.06 groups whose key members are known to the respondent. Since most of our respondents have earned a bachelor's degree,

Table 4–8. Regression of Knowledge and Contact Scores on Elite Respondent Characteristics (N = 266[a])

Respondent Characteristics	Knowledge Scores[b]		Contact Scores[b]	
A. *Position*[c]				
Corrections Officials	1.42	(.68)[b]	1.60	(.96)
State Elected Officials	5.80[f]	(10.2)	3.69[f]	(4.53)
Local Elected Officials	4.26[f]	(4.15)	1.01	(.26)
Criminal Court Judges	−.55	(−.64)	−1.25	(−.37)
Prosecutors	1.17	(.24)	1.27	(.30)
Police	.41	(.05)	.00	(.00)
Bar Association and Public Defenders	−.88	(−.00)	−.79	(−.14)
Other Partisans	2.82	(1.71)	3.27	(2.52)
B. *State*[d]				
Illinois	−.98	(−.74)	.06	(.35)
Florida	−.23	(−.46)	.11	(.01)
C. *Knowledge and Experience*[e]				
Visited Prisons	.89[f]	(3.23)	.73	(2.42)
Met with Prisoners	1.02	(.92)	.40	(.16)
Talked with Corrections Officials	1.19[f]	(4.56)	1.23[f]	(5.40)
Estimated Recidivism	−.01	(−.13)	−.01	(−.28)
Estimated Juvenile Costs	−.04	(−.70)	−.05	(−1.04)
Estimated Adults Costs	−.05	(−.52)	−.02	(−.79)
Reads about Corrections	−.94	(−.71)	−1.20	(−1.20)
D. *Biographic Characteristics*				
Age (Years)	−.18	(−.143)	.12	(.76)
Education	1.06[f]	(4.95)	.72	(2.5)
E. *Regression Constant*	−6.7	(−2.08)	−6.3	(−2.04)

$R^2 =$	.40[f]		.33[f]
F =	3.54		2.67

[a]Scores computed by summing, respectively, for each respondent the number of groups known and contacted.
[b]Numbers in parentheses are t-values for regression coefficients.
[c]Omitted category is corrections rank-and-file personnel.
[d]Omitted state is Washington.
[e]See previous tables for definitions of these variables.
[f]Significance level of .01.

this coefficient mainly means that those who have had advanced training—mainly attendance at a law school—are more likely to have higher knowledge scores.

In short, a wide range of acquaintance with key members of the nineteen groups is characteristic of elected officials. Their concern with the range of issues that come to their attention may mean that over time they have built a network of personal acquaintance that ranges widely over the groups that become involved in corrections legislation and other issues. Elite members who have shown a special involvement in corrections to the extent of visiting prisons and talking to corrections officials are also more knowledgeable than the average elite member, possibly expressing that special interest.

Fewer respondent characteristics seem important when we examine in table 4–8 the regression analysis of contact scores. State elected officials have contacted 3.69 more groups than the average, but local officials cannot be meaningfully distinguished from the average elite member. Having talked to corrections officials means that you have contacted 1.23 more groups than the average elite member for each of the variable's four levels.

The findings concerning contact resemble those concerning knowledge, albeit in a weaker form. Those concerned with state-level decision-making are more likely to have a wide range of contacts, especially if they are also lawyers.

PATTERNS OF GROUP INFLUENCES ON ELITES

In an earlier section of the chapter, our attention was focussed on the reputations of each of the nineteen groups and their abilities to facilitate or impede the passage of legislation affecting corrections. The "power" reputations uncovered in that section referred to power wielded in a particularly important arena: legislative changes in corrections.

But there is another face to influence, possibly a step or more removed from legislative change, involving affecting the views of key actors. Thus an official in the corrections sytem might have little leverage to *directly* affect corrections legislation, yet through his ability to persuade and convince, he may be able indirectly to affect changes. To tap this different form of influence, we asked our elite respondents which of the nineteen groups have influenced them on corrections matters, and which among them the respondents were able to influence. We were especially concerned with this "influence" aspect to power since our respondents are considerably more than ordinary citizens, and hence the groups that excercised some influence over their views are especially important in the understanding of how change comes about. Since influence is usually a two-way street in which persons who are influenced by someone are often in turn influential with that person, our measures of this form of influence took that reciprocity into account.

Two items were used in the questionnaire. The first item read: "For which groups or individuals, (on this list) if any, do you feel you have significant influence on the positions they take?" The second read:

"Which of the groups or individuals, if any, do you feel have a significant influence on the positions you take?"

The results of these influence questions can be seen in table 4–9. It is difficult to digest the large amount of data on table 4–9 because one would like to make both vertical and horizontal comparisons. The means and standard deviations at the bottom of the table are of some help as summary statistics, but it is hard to make a compelling case for the substance that the numbers reflect.

Table 4–10 attempts to simplify the analysis. We selected the twelve groups noted earlier as those for which at least 25 percent of the sample in one state said they were either very important for passage or could block it. The means and standard deviations show essentially the same pattern as seen in table 4–9 for the total number of groups and persons, a finding that suggests that by limiting our analysis to the groups who are reputationally important we do not change the overall

Table 4–9. Patterns of Influence by State

Person/Group	Florida (N = 107) Have Influenced	Florida (N = 107) Influenced by	Illinois (N = 76) Have Influenced	Illinois (N = 76) Influenced by	Washington (N = 83) Have Influenced	Washington (N = 83) Influenced by
Governor	22%	37%	18%	16%	19%	41%
Citizens' Crime Commission	11%	8%	13%	16%	19%	24%
Democratic Leader in State Senate (Upper House)	16%	17%	17%	10%	14%	7%
Republican Leader in State Senate (Upper House)	12%	11%	16%	8%	12%	7%
Democratic Leader in State Senate (Lower House)	15%	18%	17%	12%	14%	8%
Republican Leader in State Senate (Lower House)	12%	10%	13%	10%	10%	5%
State Senate Corrections Committee	20%	21%	14%	13%	20%	19%
State House Corrections Committee	22%	24%	13%	12%	17%	14%
LEAA State Planning Agency	16%	16%	13%	14%	23%	23%
Head of State Corrections Dept.	17%	28%	25%	33%	28%	37%
State Attorney-General	11%	23%	8%	16%	24%	34%
State Bar Association	12%	11%	14%	13%	17%	17%
Police Chiefs of Large Police Depts.	5%	10%	8%	12%	18%	12%
American Civil Liberties Union (ACLU)	6%	8%	8%	9%	11%	14%
State Parole Dept. and Staff	16%	16%	17%	16%	19%	24%
Ex-Offender Organization	3%	5%	8%	7%	11%	12%
Associations of Corrections Personnel	8%	8%	10%	12%	16%	16%
Prominent Criminal Lawyers in State	8%	10%	7%	7%	11%	6%
Associations of Police Personnel	4%	5%	3%	7%	10%	6%
X% =	12.3	15.2	12.8	12.7	16.5	17.2
SD =	5.6	8.3	5.1	5.7	5.1	10.6

Table 4–10.   Patterns of Influence by State for Most Powerful Persons Only[a]

Person/Group	Florida (N = 107) Have Influenced	Florida Influenced by	Illinois (N = 76) Have Influenced	Illinois Influenced by	Washington (N = 83) Have Influenced	Washington Influenced by
Governor	22%	37%	18%	16%	19%	41%
Citizens' Crime Commission	11%	8%	13%	16%	19%	24%
Democratic Leader in State Senate (Upper House)	16%	17%	17%	10%	14%	7%
Republican Leader in State Senate (Upper House)	12%	11%	16%	8%	12%	7%
Democratic Leader in State Senate (Lower House)	15%	18%	17%	12%	14%	8%
Republican Leader in State Senate (Lower House)	12%	10%	13%	10%	10%	5%
State Senate Corrections Committee	20%	21%	14%	13%	20%	19%
State House Corrections Committee	22%	24%	13%	12%	17%	14%
Head of State Corrections Dept.	17%	28%	25%	33%	28%	37%
State Attorney-General	11%	23%	8%	16%	24%	34%
Police Chiefs of Large Police Depts.	5%	10%	8%	12%	18%	12%
State Parole Dept.	16%	16%	17%	16%	19%	24%
$\bar{X}\%$ =	14.9	18.5	14.9	14.5	17.8	19.3
SD =	5.0	8.5	4.6	6.4	5.0	12.7

[a]Person/Group for which at least 25 percent of a state's sample said they were very important for passage of corrections legislation.

patterns of summary statistics. We appear to have retained the same pattern of central tendencies and variabilities.

Focusing now on table 4–10, a number of patterns appear. First, overall, people are a bit more likely to say that they were influenced than to say they exercised influence. We would have been surprised had it come out the other way, since the person and groups selected here represent the most powerful actors we considered and our sample of respondents includes many relatively unimportant persons.

Second, the columns of percentages show some interesting differences. Governors, for example, stand out in two of three cases (Illinois is the exception) as the most powerful influencers, while not especially different from other persons and groups in the amount they are influenced by others. In all three states, the head of corrections stands out as an influencer but not especially as someone who is influenced. Obviously there are a very large number of such comparisons. One way to reduce some of the complexity is to examine the correlations between the patterns of influence from state to state, in this case correlations between the columns of percentages on table 4–11.

Table 4–11. Correlations Between Influence Patterns by State

A. *For All Person/Groups*[a]

			Florida		Illinois		Washington	
			1	2	3	4	5	6
Florida	Have Influenced	1	X	(83)	75	47	52	46
	Influenced By	2		X	64	61	65	73
Illinois	Have Influenced	3			X	(71)	53	46
	Influenced By	4				X	85	77
Washing-ton	Have Influenced	5					X	(83)
	Influenced By	6						X

B. *For Twelve Most Powerful Person/Groups*[b]

			Florida		Illinois		Washington	
			1	2	3	4	5	6
Florida	Have Influenced	1	X	(72)	56	18	15	32
	Influenced By	2		X	43	47	53	72
Illinois	Have Influenced	3			X	(59)	20	28
	Influenced By	4				X	82	75
Washington	Have Influenced	5					X	(84)
	Influenced By	6						X

[a]Computed by intercorrelating the columns of tables 4-9 and 4-10.
[b]Person/Group for which at least 25 percent of a state's sample said they were very important for passage of corrections legislation.

Table 4–11 contains two correlation matrices. The upper matrix shows the correlations between the patterns of influence based on the total list of nineteen groups and persons.[a] All of the correlations are rather high and positive, though the highest correlations tend to occur for the two types of influence within a state (circled correlations). The lower matrix involves the same kinds of comparison but based on the limited set of the twelve most powerful groups. We will focus on this matrix. In passing, however, it is useful to note that although the sizes of some of the correlations differ in the two matrices, the patterns within each are essentially the same.

Probably the most obvious pattern involves the high correlations that reflect the associations within a given state. Groups who influence are also those that are influenced. Note that one could have expected quite the opposite: people who influence others are less likely to be influenced. The latter pattern does hold true for a few actors in some

[a] Correlations computed across the columns of tables 4-9 and 4-10. Thus, a high correlation between "have influenced" and "been influenced" means that groups with high percentages of respondents claiming to have influenced such groups are also groups for which high percentages claim to have *been* influenced by.

states, usually the governor and his corrections-related department, but these are rather exceptional. While the influence patterns within Florida and Washington correlate .72 and .84 respectively, the correlation for Illinois is only .59. This may be yet another indicator of the Illinois government being in transition.

The bottom matrix of table 4–11 contains quite low correlations involving cross-state comparisons. Looking first at the correlations involving "have influenced" across the three states (variables 1, 3, 5), Florida and Washington have the most different (though still positively associated) pattern. The correlation between variables 1 and 3 is .56, between 3 and 5 is .20, and between 1 and 5, the correlation is .15. If we want to assume that one should be able to "predict" 1 from 5 based on a linear correlation (clearly, by assuming linearity we have already greatly decreased the ways the two patterns could differ from one another), then we can be more specific about the differences in patterns. A two-variable regression will indicate in its residuals which parties are most deviant.

Table 4–12 shows the residuals arising from predicting "have influenced" in Florida from "have influenced" in Washington. Clearly, the governor in Florida is far more likely to have been influenced than expected. In contrast, the chiefs of police from large cities are far less likely to have been influenced than expected. The two corrections committees in Florida are moderately more likely to have been influenced, and the Citizens Crime Commission and state attorney-general are less likely to have been influenced. These patterns are difficult to

Table 4–12.   Residuals for "Have Influenced" for Florida Predicted from "Have Influenced" for Washington

Person/Group	Florida Observed	Florida Estimated	Residual
Governor	22	15	7
Citizens' Crime Commission	11	15	−4
Democatic Leader in State Senate (Upper House)	16	14	2
Republican Leader in State Senate (Upper House)	12	14	−2
Democratic Leader in State Senate (Lower House)	15	14	1
Republican Leader in State Senate (Lower House)	12	14	−2
State Senate Corrections Committee	20	15	5
State House Corrections Committee	22	15	7
Head of State Corrections Dept.	17	16	1
State Attorney-General	11	16	−5
Police Chiefs of Large Police Depts.	5	15	−10
State Parole Dept. and Staff	16	15	1

interpret without further analysis involving more information about Florida and Washington and, more important, additional states. The differences do not fit into our executive versus legislative states in part because both states have been labeled executive. However, the findings are provocative, since they suggest that within our category of executive centered states, there may be important subtypes.

Returning again to table 4–11 and the bottom matrix, we can examine the pattern of correlations between the percentages of people in each state who claim to have influenced the groups, the correlations between variables 2, 4, and 6. It is not especially clear which of the pairs of states is more alike. The correlations are all fairly high. However, Florida and Washington appear to be slightly more alike.

These findings suggest that it may be useful to return to a mode of analysis we used earlier when comparing states on the perceptions of respondents about who was very important for bill passage and who could block passage. In that analysis we ran correlations across the three states and looked for clustering of types of groups and persons.

In the analysis to follow, we shall restrict ourselves only to the variable "influenced by." Our goal is to gauge the configuration of power around corrections. "Influenced by" appears a much better indicator than "have influenced" because it is likely to be more accurate. It is fairly clear to an individual whether someone has tried to influence him and if his mind and/or actions changed as a result. (This is most likely a conservative estimate of influence since respondents may not be very willing to admit that they have been influenced or perhaps even be aware of the fact that they have been influenced. Hence, the admitted level of influence is likely to be an underestimate of the full amount of influence transactions.)

For "have influenced" the individual in our data will know if he tried to influence, but, since he cannot look into his subject's mind, he would have to infer from other, less obvious cues, if indeed the person was influenced and if he was the person who did the influencing. This estimate is likely to be fraught with error which wipes out variability existing in the "real" patterns of influence. Recall that on tables 4–9 and 4–10, where the data for this analysis was presented, the "influenced by" column always showed more variance than the "have influenced" for a given state. In addition, for "have influenced," *systematic* variance across states will be covered up, since what variability exists will be more a function of the psyche of our respondents. This proposition too gains some support from our data. In the matrices on table 4–11 we noted that the correlations between the "influenced by" items were generally higher than the correlations between the "have influenced" items.

Table 4–13 shows the correlations across the three states for the percentages of respondents who claim to have been influenced by the twelve selected persons or groups. It is immediately apparent that the pattern here is more complicated than in table 4–6, where the reputational items were used. Apparently the picture is neater when respondents are asked to make summary judgments about influence than when we consider these more specific relationships, as in table 4–13. Nevertheless, there are some important similarities.

To begin, the correlations among the four party leaders of the legislature are extremely high and positive, as shown in the lower triangle of table 4–13. In states where people claim to have been influenced by one of the leaders they are also very likely to claim they have been influenced by the others. This supports our earlier findings based on summary reputations. Another parallel with the earlier data can be found by looking at which groups exercise influence associated with the governor. When the governor is said to influence people, so are the legislative corrections committees, the attorney-general, and the parole department (see upper triangle in table 4–13).

The corrections head is a good place to begin in pointing out where this matrix differs from the earlier matrix. While not particularly associated with the governor (r = .10), he is no longer in the legislative camp at all. His main allies are other criminal justice agencies, which suggests a third, somewhat independent force in state politics: the criminal justice bureaucracy. However, recall that most of these agencies seem powerful when the governor seem powerful, so the independence is far from complete. Hence, the role of the corrections head indicated in table 4–13 will have to remain a provocative mystery until we have more states to tabulate.

Another pattern that tends to blur the executive coalition are the strong links between the legislature's corrections committees and those of the four party leaders in the house and senate as shown in the rectangle of table 4–13. Apparently the legislative committees are influenced both by the executive and their party leaders, not a surprising finding.

In spite of the blurred findings provided by the correlations in table 4–13, the importance of these data should not be underestimated. First, the basic patterns found with the reputational items remain. This underscores the distinction between states dominated by the executive branch and those dominated by the legislative branch. Second, the credibility of our respondents and the validity of the questionnaire items are enhanced. In a sense the reliability of the data has been tested. Third, the fact that interesting, plausible patterns have appeared with only three states suggests that data on a larger state

Table 4–13. Correlations Among Groups in Levels of Having Been Influenced (N = 3 States)

Person/Group		1	2	3	4	5	6	7	8	9	10	11	12
Governor	1		-17	96	56	89	62	10	-28	05	23	03	-63
Citizens' Crime Commission	2			02	-48	56	74	90	-76	-99	-99	-99	-59
State Senate Corrections Comm.	3				78	71	36	-77	-55	38	50	32	-38
State House Corrections Comm.	4					12	-30	-77	-95	85	93	84	28
Attorney-General	5						91	55	19	-42	-25	-44	-92
Parole Dept.	6							85	58	-76	-63	-77	-99
Head of Corrections Dept.	7								-93	-99	-95	-99	-83
Police Chiefs	8									-97	-99	-96	-57
Democratic Leader in Senate	9										98	99	74
Republican Leader in Senate	10											98	61
Democratic Leader in House	11												76
Republican Leader in House	12												

Table 4–14.   Regressions of Influence and Influenced Scores on Elite Respondent Characteristics (N = 266)[a]

Respondent Characteristics	Knowledge Scores[b]		Contact Scores[b]	
A. *Position*[c]				
Corrections Officials	1.07	(.68)	1.44	(1.29)
State Elected Officials	2.45[f]	(3.18)	2.94[f]	(4.78)
Local Elected Officials	.73	(.21)	.88	(.32)
Criminal Court Judges	−.90	(.30)	−.27	(.03)
Prosecutors	.23	(.01)	−.59	(.11)
Police	.18	(.02)	.21	(.02)
Bar Assoc. & Public Defenders	−.62	(.13)	−.90	(.30)
Other Partisans	2.43	(2.20)	1.48	(.86)
B. *State*[d]				
Illinois	−.17	(.04)	−.29	(.12)
Florida	−.24	(.09)	−.14	(.00)
C. *Knowledge and Experience*[e]				
Visited Prisons	.51	(1.89)	−.17	(.23)
Met with Prisoners	.93	(1.35)	.95	(1.46)
Talked with Corrections Officials	.31	(.56)	.45	(1.19)
Estimated Recidivism	−.18	(1.08)	−.01	(.83)
Estimated Juvenile Costs	−.57	(1.94)	−.05	(1.40)
Estimated Adults Costs	−.01	(.03)	−.01	(.10)
Reads about Corrections	−.77	(.83)	−.42	(.26)
D. *Biographic Characteristics*				
Age (Years)	.00	(.00)	−.01	(.03)
Education	.64[f]	(3.14)	.45	(1.66)
E. *Regression Constant*	−3.3	(.90)	−.58	(.03)
R² =	.28[f]		.25[f]	
F =	2.03		1.89	

[a]Scores computed by summing respectively for each respondent the number of groups influenced and influenced by.
[b]Numbers in parentheses are t-values for regression coefficients.
[c]Omitted category is corrections rank and file personnel.
[d]Omitted state is Washington.
[e]See previous tables for definitions of these variables.
[f]Significance level of .01.

sample should be most fruitful. We should be able to find new patterns and enrich those indicated by our current sample of states.

ELITE VARIATION IN INFLUENCE

The influence attributions discussed in the previous section can also be used to differentiate among elite respondents. We can anticipate that some will claim to be quite influential across a rather wide range of the nineteen groups; others may attribute to themselves the more modest position of not having influenced any. The same range of variation may be anticipated with respect to having been influenced by the nineteen groups. Those who are seemingly influential among our respondents can be viewed as participating especially strongly in the networks of personal contacts that define decision-making involving corrections legislation and administrative practice.

Almost half (46 percent) of our respondents do not claim to have influenced any of the nineteen groups, although, on the average, 2.6 groups are claimed as the recipients of respondents' influence. This finding suggests that there are some respondents who claim to have influenced a large proportion of the groups; indeed, those who claimed to have influenced any groups make that claim for an average of 4.8 groups.

An "influence score" was computed for each respondent, summing the number of groups each respondent claimed to have influenced. This score was regressed on a number of respondent characteristics with results as shown in the left-hand column of table 4–14. Note that a very modest amount of variation is captured by the regression analysis, R^2 being +.28. Only two of the variables used in the regression seem especially important. Being a state elected official has a regression coefficient of 2.45, indicating that persons in that position influence about twice as many groups as the average elite. (The average number of groups influenced was 2.62). Elite educational attainment also affected their claims to influence, .64 additional groups being claimed for each educational level.

It appears that state elected officials are most likely to claim influence along with those who have better than average educational attainment. This finding parallels those concerning knowledge and contact (discussed in a previous section of this chapter). State elected officials and lawyers are those elite members who are most likely to be close in the network of contact and mutual influence surrounding legislative activities in general and concerning corrections in particular.

"Influence scores" were also calculated for each respondent by summing the number of groups who influenced the respondents. While this index might be thought of as an index of the willingness of respondents to be influenced by others, in fact the index turns out to be an alternative expression of being part of the communications network surrounding political decision-making. The correlation between influence and influenced scores is rather high, +.63, indicating that persons high in influencing others are likely to be high on the receiving end of influence relationships.

Fewer respondents (35 percent) claim not to have been influenced by anyone of the nineteen groups and the average number of groups from whom influence was claimed is 2.8. (For those who claimed to have been influenced by any group, the average number of such influencee groups is 4.4.) Being influenced is apparently a more common phenomenon than being an influencer.

Using the influenced score as a dependent variable, respondents characteristics account for a small 25 percent of the variance in these scores, (table 4–14). Only one respondent characteristic seems important. Once again state elected officials are more likely to claim to have been influenced as compared to the average elite respondent. No other characteristic reaches statistical significance, although educational attainment approaches conventional standards.

In sum, influence means to be a part of the decision making scene, with the state elected officials being apparently in a good position both to influence others and to be influenced in turn.

CONCLUSIONS

What are the potential policy implications of such findings? First, the data have shown that groups and individuals are not equally active in corrections matters. Further, there appears to be a division of authority so that across states some groups define corrections as their "turf" while others do not. The same groups are not equally active in all states, rather, each state often shows clusters of active groups peculiar to that state.

Second, states differ in the degree to which the configuration of influence is based on personal contact between actors. Some states appear to have rather "clubby" structures in which a large proportion of interested people are in touch with one another. Other states are either less politically integrated or coordinate activity through different techniques. One would suspect that the "clubby" states might be more efficient in bringing about corrections reform. Once several key members of the dominant coalition are sold on a given set of reforms they can more easily coordinate their efforts.

Third, states differ in the coalitions dominating corrections issues. Obviously, persons interested in lobbying should know which people can most easily implement their programs. To understand who supports which reforms is of little use without knowing which supporters have "clout."

Fourth, being a state elected official brings one far into the network of reciprocal influence that surrounds decision-making on the state level. (Indeed, it would be surprising if we found to the contrary.) Elite members who were especially well acquainted with powerful groups, had contacted them, and had either influenced their stands on corrections or been influenced by them tended to be state elected officials and the better educated among our respondents. Since being better educated in our sample means to have some training beyond the BA level, this probably means that state-level decision-making surrounding corrections is dominated by elected officials and lawyers.

Finally, it must be emphasized that much of this chapter, resting as it does on comparisons between states, should be regarded more as an example of what could be done with a large sample than a compelling analysis. The findings are most tentative since the relations on which they are based are statistically unstable. We would not suggest that this data alone has the strength from which sound policy recommendations can be made.

✳ *Chapter 5*

Power-Weighted Support
for Corrections Reform

Even in elections of public officials where the Supreme Court has mandated "one man, one vote," (sic) the Orwellian aphorism that "some are more equal than others" usually applies. Practical politicians have long known that some members of the public have far more influence on the voting plans of their peers than others. Social researchers as well have been able to identify likely influentials. These opinion leaders, frequently the foci of interpersonal networks, need to be given special consideration when the direction of public opinion trends is plotted, for influentials are the harbingers of opinion change.

In legislative bodies where lobbying, negotiations, and trading are normal practices, the differential importance of participants is magnified. As we have seen in the last chapter, it matters far more what the governor thinks about corrections than the views of usual rank-and-file probation officers. Because we had these considerations in mind in designing this study, one of its unusual features is that the data permit the measurement of the support for alternative futures and specific programs by opinions *weighted* by the importance of respondents. This procedure literally means that in computing the distribution of opinion on particular issues we count individual respondents more heavily if they are influentials and less heavily if they are not. The resulting distribution of opinions on a given issue is closer to what we believe to be the *effective elite opinion*, the opinion that is more likely to carry the day because it is closer to the opinions of those whose voices count the most.

The general idea of weighting public opinion by the importance of its sources is intuitively appealing to most practical politicians and to students of political life. The main obstacle is, of course, how to accomplish this weighting? There are several ways to proceed. Under ideal conditions one good solution would have been to rank respondents according to their political influence, and then to cross-tabulate this measure with support and opposition for various programs. Though not an especially sophisticated technique, it would permit one to gauge rather easily the kind of views held by more and less powerful individuals. However, there are two difficulties. First, the development of a ranking system is not easy. Recall that we have reputational measures, claims of being influenced and influencing others, measures of activity in corrections matters, and other material less obviously related to one's political power, though certainly relevant, such as, "Who do you know well enough to call on corrections matters?" Hence, there may be several different ways of conceptualizing and measuring influence and several ways of constructing scales and indices from these measures.

An additional problem is that cross-tabulation pays a high price for intuitive clarity. One must have enough cases in each cell from which to make stable estimates. For our three-state data, this is a severe limitation. For example, we know from earlier analyses that there are about a dozen groups in each state whom at least 25 percent of the sample label as either very important for bill passage or able to stop passage. Were this to be one of the categories in a ranking system of influence, a state-by-state comparison would be impossible (since only a small number of our respondents fall into those most influential groups) and even at the aggregate level the number of respondents that could be allocated to various levels of support and opposition (recall the "filtering" of respondents in the alternative future items) would be very small.

A more practical solution than breaking the sample into levels of political influence is to develop a weighting system that would by-pass cross-tabulations and give each respondent an individual weight proportionate to his influence. One could then use a variety of techniques to assess support and opposition and not be as concerned as much about the small sample. For example, there may be a sensible way of multiplying each response by some measure of each respondent's influence so that a governor's opinion, for example, might count five times that of a probation officer. However, though this weighting approach minimizes sample problems, one is still faced with the difficult task of developing appropriate weights.

In this chapter we have chosen a "solution" that should be viewed as a simplified example of the kind of approach that may be used to weight the importance of respondents in a larger study. It is not the best procedure that could be applied, but a useful first approximation and probably not too misleading. Once we weight the "importance" of each respondent, then the transformed data can be tabulated in a form exactly like the tables we presented earlier when analyzing support and oppositions for different corrections programs. At the very least, our technique will have intuitive meaning and the results should be easily understood.

Our weighting system is based on a questionnaire item asking which groups or persons the respondent influenced on corrections matters. (See chapter four for a detailed analysis of the item.)

Our weighting scheme is rather straightforward. We simply counted for each individual the number of people he claimed he could influence (including himself). For example, if a corrections head claimed he could influence four groups his weight in any further analysis was five.

In spite of this intuitive neatness, there are at least two problems with the technique. First, it is based on a claim of influence, and as we argued earlier, this measure is somewhat suspect. Second, the weight does not take account of the fact that influencing some people has a greater impact than influencing others. To influence a party leader in the state senate would indicate more power than influencing, say, a police chief. We considered employing a double weighting system in which each person's influence would be calculated by first counting how many people each respondent could influence and then passing over the data again and giving each person an influence score that was the sum of the influence scores of all the persons the respondent claimed to influence. For example, if the governor claimed he could influence ten people, then anyone who could influence the governor would get ten added to his influence score. This measure will not be used however. It presents several subtle complications such as counting the influence of some respondents redundantly (inflating their power).

Another obstacle in the way of such double weighting schemes in the context of this study is the heterogeneity within each of the nineteen groups. Thus, while we asked respondents how important was, for instance, the corrections committee in the lower house of the state legislature, such a group may contain up to a dozen persons. Hence the fact that a respondent claims to have influenced someone on that legislative committee may not mean very much if the representative in question was the least important member of the committee. In any case, some partial tests of double weighting indicated the single weighting approach gave quite similar results with less effort and better grounding.

The limitations of our weighting system have two substantive implications. First, the weights probably do not differentiate our respondents as much as their actual influence does. Powerful individuals are *underweighted* in our system. Consequently, the differences appearing between the weighted support for programs and the unweighted analysis presented earlier are probably underestimated. Second, we are at the mercy of our respondents' ability to assess accurately whom they can influence. Though it is hard to measure the direction and magnitude of errors that can creep into one's claims of power, it seems likely that the less powerful people will be more likely to overestimate their "clout" and the more powerful to err in the other direction. We also believe the less powerful people will be less informed about how power is really wielded "on the inside" and will consequently be less accurate about what impact they have really had. In addition, the common desire to feel important may cause respondents to consistently claim that they influence more people than they do in fact. The interaction of less realistic knowledge of their impact with the human desire to feel important may bias our weighting system in favor of "little people."

It is also appropriate to remind the reader of the previous chapter's analysis of the characteristics of elite respondents who were likely to claim more influence. High levels of influence (a greater number of groups) were claimed particularly by state elected officials and by the better educated. This analysis makes a lot of intuitive sense; those who are assigned the primary tasks of decision-making because of their committment to that task also should be those who are most likely to influence others. To be influenced and to influence others means to be close to the modes of the communications network that involve a given activity.

Of course, these results also indicate that the opinions of state elected officials will get particular high weightings in the computations of this chapter.

SUPPORT FOR "FUTURES"

Given these caveats, what do the data indicate? Table 5–1 shows weighted support levels for the punitive alternative future. The unweighted data showed that 78 percent of the sample were opposed; now, 84 percent of the sample oppose. The weighted analysis appar-

Table 5–1. Support for Punitive Alternative Future (Weighted and Unweighted)[a]

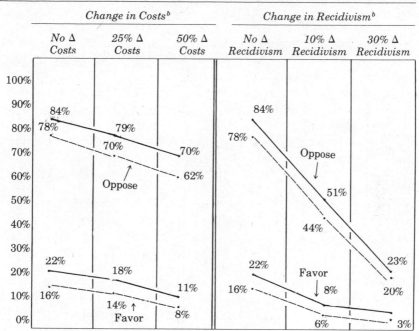

	Change in Costs[b]			*Change in Recidivism*[b]		
	No Δ Costs	*25% Δ Costs*	*50% Δ Costs*	*No Δ Recidivism*	*10% Δ Recidivism*	*30% Δ Recidivism*

[a]Dotted line graphs are unweighted support for punitive alternatives futures. Solid lines are weighted support measures.

[b]For those opposed Δ means *decrease* in costs or recidivism. For those in favor Δ means *increase* in costs or recidivism.

ently indicates more "progressive views" as the "effective" elite opinion. The reader should keep in mind that the weighting system used may underestimate the weights of more powerful respondents, and hence, we may be *underestimating* the progressiveness of *effective* elite opinions.

Though the opposition to the punitive future is larger, there is virtually no change in the impact of different conditions. The effects of changing rates of recidivism are still far greater than the effects of changing costs, and the "slopes" of the four lines are about the same as in the earlier material. In short, it appears that effective actors have about the same utilities for this future as the rest of the sample.

Table 5–2 shows support and opposition for the "rehabilitative" alternative future. Weighted responses are more similar to the unweighted data, both in the initial amount of support and in the impact of different project outcomes. However, it is worth noting that what

Table 5–2.   Support for Rehabilitative Alternative Future (Weighted and Unweighted)[a]

	Change in Costs[b]				*Change in Recidivism*[b]		
	No Δ Costs	*25% Δ Costs*	*50% Δ Costs*		*No Δ Recidivism*	*10% Δ Recidivism*	*30% Δ Recidivism*

Change in Costs line graph:

Favor (weighted): 86%, 80%, 69%
Favor (unweighted): 84%, 74%, 63%
Oppose (unweighted): 16%, 13%, 10%
Oppose (weighted): 14%, 12%, 8%

Change in Recidivism line graph:

Favor (weighted): 86%, 42%, 17%
Favor (unweighted): 84%, 38%, 12%
Oppose (unweighted): 16%, 8%, 12%
Oppose (weighted): 14%, 7%, 4%

[a] Dotted line graphs are unweighted support for "rehabilitative" alternative futures. Solid lines are weighted support measures.
[b] For those opposed Δ means *decrease* in costs or recidivism. For those in favor Δ means *increase* in costs or recidivism.

differences exist show the weighted sample again to be more "progressive."

Table 5–3 shows the support and opposition for the "supervised treatment" alternative future. Support has been increased considerably by weighting (especially since in the unweighted data support was already 79 percent). Eighty-eight percent of the weighted sample endorses this package involving various community treatment techniques. Again, the more powerful people appear more willing to try new approaches to corrections and remain more liberal as costs and recidivism increase.

Table 5–4 shows support and opposition for a variety of rather specific corrections practices. Compared to the earlier analysis with unweighted data, the message is very clear. The weighted sample is more "progressive" in *every case*. For example, while 48 percent favored capital punishment originally, now 36 percent support it. Fifty-

Table 5–3. Support for Supervised Treatment Alternative Future (Weighted and Unweighted)[a]

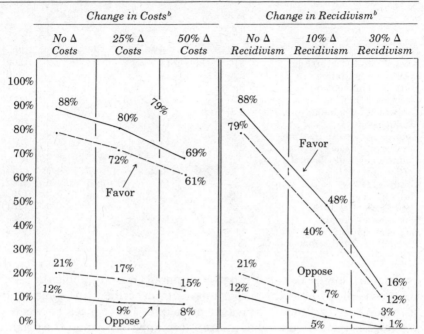

	Change in Costs[b]			*Change in Recidivism[b]*		
	No Δ Costs	*25% Δ Costs*	*50% Δ Costs*	*No Δ Recidivism*	*10% Δ Recidivism*	*30% Δ Recidivism*

[a] Dotted line graphs are unweighted support for "supervised treatment" alternative futures. Solid lines are weighted support measures.

[b] For those opposed Δ means *decrease* in costs or recidivism. For those in favor Δ means *increase* in costs or recidivism.

six percent originally favored prisoner self-government; the weighted sample shows 67 percent in support. Fifty-six percent originally favored weekend furloughs; now 70 percent are in favor. Such uniform effects for a transformed variable are quite rare in social science data. Further, its effects are probably underestimated.

If the findings of this chapter were to hold for a larger sample of states, there would be several important policy implications. First, those most in a position to affect corrections policy and program are considerably more willing to implement innovative, nontraditional practices than less influential actors. Massive majorities support virtually all the "progressive" programs that have been considered in our questionnaire. Hence, a simple poll that does not consider differential importance of respondents will *underestimate* substantially possibilities for change.

Second, as suggested originally by the unweighted data, differences

Table 5–4. Support for Changes in Correctional Practices (Weighted)

Corrections Proposals	Percent Oppose	Percent Neutral	Percent Favor	100% =
Death Penalty	56%	8	36	[252]
Abolish Mail Censorship	31%	11	58	[262]
Methodone Maintenance	23%	13	64	[246]
Solitary Confinement	69%	13	18	[252]
Vocational Training	3%	2	97	[265]
Corporal Punishment	81%	6	13	[259]
Conjugal Visits	20%	15	66	[253]
Counsel at Offense Hearings	24%	10	65	[258]
Counsel at Parole Hearings	21%	5	74	[261]
Counsel at Parole Revocation Hearings	7%	2	91	[264]
Group Therapy	1%	14	85	[262]
Halfway Houses	2%	3	96	[261]
Community Corrections	2%	3	94	[261]
Weekend Furloughs	20%	10	70	[257]
Self-Government	20%	13	67	[263]
Strengthen Guard's Power	67%	16	17	[248]

in support for corrections programs among our respondents become more visible when the programs are described in some detail. Everyone is for "good" things in principle. Differences between the unweighted and weighted data are more apparent when the practices assessed are more concrete. This suggests that proper judgments about the kinds of support and opposition for correctional programs must not only consider the differential influence of respondents, but also how concretely the alternatives are phrased. In addition, one may infer that the kinds of statements about corrections made in typical speeches may be rather poor indicators of the degree and type of opinion about treatment of offenders.

Finally, the political facts faced by our respondents may be heightened into a dilemma for the more powerful actors. Recall that our unweighted sample saw themselves far more ready to accept major change in corrections practices than the general public. Our weighted sample suggests that the more influential the respondent, the more he differs from this projection of public opinion. However, two qualifications must be added. First, we have not analyzed the weighted perceptions of projected support. It may be that more influential persons see the public (and other constituencies) as less traditional than indicated in the unweighted analysis. Were this the case, their political dilemma might not be as acute as it appears now. Second, in order to assess the reality of potential conflict between state leaders and the public one really needs a survey of the general population. There is no other systematic way of gauging where the public stands on corrections issues. Since the likelihood that state leaders will press for changes in their corrections system may well depend on the kinds of support and opposition reform proposals will generate, it seems crucial to have this complementary data.

※ *Chapter 6*

Reforms in the Treatment of Convicted Offenders[a]

In barest outlines, a corrections system is an organizational device that takes persons who have been convicted of crimes, administers sentences ordered by the courts, and then discharges them into civilian life when the sentences have been completed. Depending upon the specific state criminal codes involved and upon the courts, a corrections system has some discretion in the treatment of convicted offenders, the exact amount varying widely from state to state and case to case. Offenders may be sent to a minimum security prison or a maximum security prison; parole may be granted as quickly as possible or the maximum sentence imposed. Prison regimes may be arbitrary, capricious, and cruel, or they may be just, predictable, and as humane as imprisonment can be. In some way the punishment is supposed to "fit the crime," prison treatments are to maximize the possibility of rehabilitation, and society is to be protected from the recurrence of antisocial behavior.

To change a corrections system in its functioning means to make changes in the ways in which sentences are made, in the sentences themselves, and in the criteria used for discharging persons from the system. The decisions made by the courts and the corrections system are necessarily complicated. Convicted offenders vary in a wide variety of ways: offenses range in seriousness; extenuating circumstances may be present; an offender may have no previous record of convictions or he may have a considerable dossier; an offender may be a juvenile, a young adult, or mature. Changes in the corrections system may involve milder treatments for some types of offenders and not for others.

[a] With Thomas Laurent

In the criminal code some offenses may call for mandatory treatment provisions that involve the harshest possible treatment, while other offenses may carry a wide choice of treatments ranging from almost instant parole to lifetime incarceration. Two persons may agree on what changes ought to be made, but disagree upon which sorts of convicted offenders ought to be given the new treatments involved.

What we are trying to get at in this chapter is the meaning of reforms *in practice* to members of the elites in the three states at the level of what should be done with concrete specific convicted offenders. In some ideal sense, we would have liked to present to them concrete, possibly actual cases of convicted offenders, and ask each respondent what sort of corrections treatment ought to be accorded to each of the cases. Thus, we might have proceeded to summarize a number of trial records in order to present to a respondent a record upon which he could make a judgment on what he thought would be an appropriate treatment for that offender—whether he would grant an offender probation, assign him to a community treatment center, or sentence him to prison. It is not at all easy to put together a set of concrete cases that covers the full range of decisions the criminal justice system has to make. Each case tends to be somewhat idiosyncratic. It would be difficult to cover a wide variety of crimes and types of offenders in a set of cases that could be given easily to respondents and that could be analyzed in a sensible fashion.

We chose to put together hypothetical cases of convicted offenders. In these hypothetical cases, the characteristics of the offenders and the crimes of which they were convicted were systematically varied. Each hypothetical offender was described in a short vignette containing a brief description of the offender in terms of the crime of which he was convicted, his age, and his previous criminal record.

There are several advantages to hypothetical vignettes as opposed to concrete cases. First of all, in hypothetical cases it is possible to choose characteristics of the offenders to accentuate the salience of those characteristics in which one is particularly interested. In the world of concrete offenders, most have been convicted of a narrow variety of crimes, cluster heavily in the early years of adulthood, and have a narrow band of previous convictions. In a hypothetical world it is possible to provide wider ranges of offenses, previous records, age, and any other characteristic that might be considered as relevant.

Second, it is possible to produce sets of vignettes in which offender characteristics are unrelated to each other, so that the effects of differences in a particular characteristic can be separated from those with which it is ordinarily associated. For example, in the real world, young offenders tend to commit different crimes than older ones. Hence, it is difficult to separate out the effects of age from offense in the sentences that courts give to convicted offenders. In the fictitious world represented by our offender vignettes, older offenders and younger ones can be described as having been convicted of the same set of crimes. Because of this characteristic, we can separate the effects of offenders' ages and their offenses on the sentences deemed appropriate.

Finally, vignettes can be written so that certain detail can be omitted. The physical appearance of a specific offender for instance, may be important in the judgment of his particular case, but since the effects physical appearances are not likely to be directly affected by broad policy changes of the kind considered here, it may be best to ignore such factors. Consequently, two characteristics of possible relevance were deliberately omitted. We restricted ourselves to male offenders, mainly on the grounds that there are relatively few women in state prisons. Second, we did not specify the convicted offender's race, an individual characteristic that is also probably of considerable importance in the actual treatment of offenders. We were well aware of the criminal justice literature that makes the impact of race and class its central problematic, but were reluctant to raise this controversial issue and hence distract respondents from the assessment variables that for our purposes, were more relevant to *manifest* corrections policy.

These advantages of vignettes argued strongly for their use in this study. We needed some measure of the ways in which our respondents would treat individual offenders, a way in which the effects of various offender characteristics on those judgments could be assessed, and some way of sampling the judgments of respondents in order to assess each respondent's "traditional" or "progressive" leanings with respect to types of offenders.

The vignettes used in this study were formed out of the cross classification of the following characteristics:

1. Age of offender: Five ages were permitted: fifteen, nineteen, twenty-two, thirty-five, and fifty.

2. Previous record: Seven types of previous records were permitted: no previous record, only misdemeanors, one felony involving property, several felonies involving property, one felony involving persons, several felonies involving persons, and several felonies involving both persons and property.

3. Crime of which convicted: Forty crimes were chosen, varying in their seriousness and covering mainly offenses that are

common (Appendix A). "Seriousness" was
measured by a separate special survey conducted in Baltimore.

These three characteristics permit the writing of 1400 unique
vignettes, each bearing a unique description of a hypothetical convicted
offender.

In actuality, only 1160 of the 1400 possible combinations were used
in the study since there were some with very unusual, odd, or impossible combinations (e.g., thirty-five- and fifty-year-old men convicted of
"repeated running away from home," or fifteen-year-olds who were
convicted of "selling worthless stocks and bonds"). These anamolous
vignettes were deleted from the total vignette universe.

The remaining 1160 "sensible" vignettes were divided into twenty
samples of forty vignettes each. Each sample was chosen systematically from among the 1160 combinations in such a fashion as to insure
the statistical equivalence of the samples. Analysis of variance of the
"seriousness scores" of the crimes included in the samples showed that
the variations in such scores from sample to sample was consistent
with the hypothesis that they differed only by sampling error.

Each respondent was given two of the vignette samples in his
questionnaire or interview, one sample to be rated by him according to
the "treatment" he thought *desirable* and *appropriate* to the offender
described in each vignette and the other sample (a different sample
than the first) to be rated according to what were his impressions of the
typical treatments accorded to such offenders in his state. The samples
were administered to respondents randomly, i.e., each respondent had
the same probability of receiving each of the samples.

The respondent was asked to designate one of the nine treatments
listed below as appropriate to each offender vignette (or as typical
treatment accorded in his state):

1. Release under supervision to his local community for a period of up
    to one year.
2. Release under supervision to his local community for a period of
    one to five years.
3. Part-time confinement (nights and/or weekends) in a residential
    center in a local community for a period of up to one year.
4. Part-time confinement (nights and/or weekends) in a residential
    center in a local community for a period of up to one year.
5. Incarceration full time in a prison for up to one year.
6. Incarceration full time in a prison for one to five years.
7. Incarceration full time in a prison for more than five years.

8. Confinement in a mental hospital for treatment.
9. Referral to a medical facility for treatment.

The first seven "treatments" are designed to form a scale ranging from the least restraint on personal freedom to a maximum degree of restraint. At the outset we could not be at all sure whether the seven treatments did form such an ordinal scale, much less whether they could be treated as having equal intervals. Subsequent analysis indicated that respondents treated the response categories as if they formed an equal interval scale and hence the responses 1 through 7 are treated in the analysis as if they had equal interval properties.[b]

Obviously, treatments 8 and 9 cannot be treated as falling somewhere among the first seven. They will have to be treated separately. Because so few respondents used these ratings, we will simply ignore them, discarding the few responses of this sort that the respondents gave. In a larger sample, it may be possible to make a special analysis of these ratings and of the crimes to which they are considered appropriate.

The vignettes and their ratings can be handled in three ways. First, since each and every vignette in the total set of 1160 was rated by from three to twelve respondents, the modal number of respondents being between seven and nine, an *average* treatment rating can be computed for each vignette constituting an unbiased estimate of the average for the entire set of respondents. Since each respondent had an equal chance of rating each of the vignettes, the respondents who rated any one vignette may be considered a random subsample of the total sample, and hence, the average rating is an unbiased estimate of the average rating that the total sample would have given. These average vignette ratings (1160 in all) can be used to uncover the rating principles used collectively by the respondents in allocating offenders to desired (or typical) treatments.

Second, each respondent can be characterized by the *average* of the ratings he gave to the forty vignettes that appeared in his sample. This individual average rating can then be used as an indicator of the respondent's stringency-leniency in handling convicted offenders (in the case of the ratings of what he would consider to be desired treatments) and of his perceptions of the stringency-leniency of the corrections system in his state (in the case of his ratings of what he perceived to be the typical treatment in his state). These individual *average*

[b] The tests involved transforming the scores into a variety of forms (e.g., logarithms, power functions, etc.) and testing whether each transformation yielded in analysis better fitting results than the assumption of equal intervals. In no case, did any transformation produce closer fittings than the equal interval assumption.

ratings (266 in all) can then be analyzed to uncover the ways in which different kinds of respondents varied in their leniency-stringency towards the treatment of convicted offenders.

A third mode of analysis regards each separate rating as the basic unit, a procedure that makes it possible to relate characteristics of individual respondents to ratings. Under this procedure there are 10,640 observations, each consisting of a vignette that has been rated by an individual. This analysis provides much the same information as the first described above but in addition provides additional data on how differences among individual respondents affect their ratings.

All three modes of analysis are presented in this chapter to illustrate how these ratings can be handled. It should be noted that the first two modes are based on rather small numbers and expected to be somewhat fragile and, hence, likely to change in a larger sample of states from sampling fluctuations alone.

THE STRUCTURE OF COLLECTIVE JUDGMENTS ABOUT CONVICTED OFFENDERS

To each respondent the sample of vignettes he was given to rate must have seemed to be a hodge-podge collection of somewhat arbitrarily put together descriptions. Indeed, some of the respondents interviewed by the senior authors kept looking over the set of vignettes in an attempt to understand the principles underlying the selection of the particular combinations of offender characteristics that appeared. Of course, that is exactly what we wanted the respondents to experience so that it would be difficult for them to develop a set of self-conscious principles that would guide their selection of treatments for the vignettes. That is, if we systematically varied the combinations that appeared in each respondent's samples it might have been possible for them to decide consciously to vary treatments according to a weighting system that, for example, counted previous record half as much as the crime of which the offender was convicted. The fact that each sample was a chance combination of vignettes made it difficult for respondents to develop biasing response sets of this sort.

Yet, there is an underlying rationale to the judgments made by elite members concerning the convicted offenders described in the vignettes. The rationale can be uncovered by examining the mean ratings given to the vignettes and the regression of those averages on offender characteristics. The mean ratings may be taken as representing the total sample's collective judgments concerning either the treatment considered appropriate by the respondents or their perception of the typical treatment accorded to such offenders in their corrections system. The term "collective judgment" is used in this connection to express the fact that it is the *average rating* given to a vignette that is being predicted by the regression equation. Thus, the analysis does *not* tell us directly how individuals varied their judgments of vignettes according to the characteristics that went into the vignettes construction. It does tell us how the vignette characteristics affected the average (or collective) judgments of the sample of elite members interviewed.

The average rating given to vignettes in the "appropriate treatment" rating task was 4.08, a value corresponding to "part-time confinement in a residential center for a period of from one to five years." The standard deviation of the average ratings was 1.7, indicating that about two-thirds of all the appropriate treatment collective judgments fell between 2 and 6. When we consider that the crimes involved are deliberately chosen to range across a wide band of seriousness, and hence represent more crimes on the less serious side than would ordinarily be found among prison inmates, this relatively lenient average sentence is to be expected.

In contrast, the collective perception of "typical treatment" accorded to convicted offenders in their states is an average rating of 4.59, a half point higher on the scale than what was considered appropriate treatment collectively by the respondents, a point that is somewhere in between a sentence of part-time confinement for one to five years and incarceration for up to one year. The standard deviation of collective perceptions of typical treatment is 1.6, not appreciably different from that computed for desired treatments.

Collectively, our respondents were more lenient in the treatments they deemed *appropriate* and desired than they saw being *typically* accorded in their states' correction system. The pattern of differences is, of course, very much in line with the findings of previous chapters. Our elite respondents were more "progressive" in their views than they perceived their states' corrections practices to be.

Although there is some considerable risk in making such comparisons, it does *not* appear that the gap between the collective judgments of "appropriate" and "typical treatments" is as big as some of the differences respondents reported between themselves and their perceptions of groups in their states such as the general public and the police. Perhaps what the respondents are reporting is that the corrections system in its working is more progressive than one might have expected on the basis of the climate of state public opinion.

The multiple regression analysis of collective *typical* ratings is shown in table 6–1. In the upper panel of the table are zero-order

Table 6–1.   Regression Analysis of Average Typical Treatment Ratings for Convicted Offender Vignettes (N = 1160 Vignettes)

A. *Zero Order Correlations, Means and Standard Deviations:*

	Average Typical Ratings	Offender Age[a]	Previous Record[b]	Crime Seriousness[c]
Average Typical Ratings		.12	.36	.73
Offender Age			.07	.00
Previous Record				.00
Crime Seriousness				
Mean =	4.59	30.5	2.05	6.5
SD =	1.58	12.66	1.24	1.15

B. *Regression Statistics: Dependent Variable = Average Typical Treatment Ratings*

Vignette Characteristic	Unstandardized Regression Coefficients	Standardized Regression Coefficients	Significance
Crime Serious Score	.991	.725	p < .01
Previous Record	.450	.355	p < .01
Age	.012	.095	p < .01
Intercept =	−3.176		
R =	.815		
R² =	.665		p < .01

[a]Age entered as shown in vignettes (i.e., 15, 19, 22, 34 or 50).
[b]Previous Record coded as follows:

Record = 0
Misdemeanor = 1
One Property or Person Felony = 2
Several Property or Person Felonies = 3
Several Property *and* Person Felonies = 4

[c]Crime Seriousness Score obtained from Baltimore Survey (see appendix A).

correlation coefficients showing the pairwise interrelationships of average typical treatment ratings and the three vignette characteristics. The first row of correlations are findings, but the remaining correlation coefficients reflect the design of the vignettes. Thus, the coefficients of .00 between offender age and crime seriousness and previous record and crime seriousness merely reflect the fact that every age category used was associated equally often with almost every crime used in the vignettes. The fact the second- and third-row correlations are either zero or very small shows that the design of the study was successfully carried out.

Table 6–2 presents the same analysis for desired treatments. The

Table 6-2. Regression Analysis of Average Desired Treatment Ratings for Convicted Offender Vignettes (N = 1160 Vignettes)

A. *Zero Order Correlations, Means and Standard Deviations:*

	Average Typical Ratings	Offender Age	Previous Record	Crime Seriousness
Average Desired Ratings		.12	.40	.73
Offender Age			.07	.00
Previous Record				.00
Crime Seriousness				
Mean =	4.08	30.5	2.05	6.5
SD =	1.66	12.66	1.24	1.15

B. *Regression Statistics: Dependent Variable = Average Desired Treatment Ratings*

Vignette Characteristic	Unstandardized Regression Coefficients	Standardized Regression Coefficients	Significance
Crime Seriousness Score	1.05	.728	p < .01
Previous Record	.523	.391	p < .01
Age	.013	.096	p < .01
Intercept =	−4.249		
R =	.835		
R² =	.697		p < .01

Note: See table 6-1 for definitions of variables.

zero-order correlation coefficients in the second and third rows are identical to those in table 6–1, since they reflect the same design elements.

The bottom parts of tables 6–1 and 6–2 contain the regression statistics for typical and desired treatments. Note that the multiple correlation coefficients are quite high, .82 and .84, respectively, indicating that there is considerable structure to the collective judgments made by our respondents. Indeed, almost two-thirds of the variation in the average ratings can be accounted for by the characteristics that go into the construction of the vignettes. This result is hardly unanticipated. Since the only information we gave to the respondents are the characteristics that go into the construction of the vignettes, it is to be expected that this information should count very heavily in the ratings. We can also expect that the amount of unexplained variation will decline as the sample size is increased and as the numbers of respondents who contribute to each average increase correspondingly. At least some of the unexplained variance is due to sampling error incorporated into the average ratings, an error that can be anticipated to be relatively large, since samples that contribute to these ratings range in size from 2 to 8.

Since we are dealing with 1160 cases, the multiple correlation coefficients are statistically significant at astoundingly low probabilities. (We were not able to find a published table of the sampling distribution of F that contained probability values for the F values involved.)

The unstandardized regression coefficients shown in tables 6–1 and 6–2 indicate the weights to be applied to each of the characteristics that would produce the best estimate of the average rating based on the linear regression model. Thus, the equations for "typical" and "desired" collective judgments are:

$$\hat{Y}_{Typ} = -3.176 + .991X_1 + .450X_2 + .012X_3$$

$$\hat{Y}_{Des} = -4.249 + 1.05X_1 + .523X_2 + .013X_3$$

$\hat{Y}_{Typ}$ = estimated average score for "typical treatment"

$\hat{Y}_{Des}$ = estimated average score for "desired treatment"

where X_1 = Crime Seriousness Scores

$\quad\quad X_2$ = Previous Record (see table 6–1 for code used)

$\quad\quad X_3$ = Age of Offender (years)

For example, the estimated "typical" treatment score for a thirty-five-year-old offender who has been convicted of "beating up a spouse" (crime seriousness score of 5.8) and who has a record of one previous felony is 3.89 and the estimated "desired" treatment score is 3.34. The collective judgment of desired appropriate treatment would place the convicted offender in short-term (up to one year) part-time confinement arrangement, while the "typical" treatment would place the offender closer to longer term part-time confinement (one to five years).

A similar calculation for a convicted offender whose crime was rape (and who was also thirty-five and had a previous conviction record of one felony) yields an estimated incarceration score of 6.3 for the *typical* treatment in the three states and 5.9 for the *desired* treatment. The difference between these two estimates scores is primarily a matter of how many years of incarceration should the sentence be. The estimated typical treatment in a state puts the convicted offender away in a sentence that is close to five or more years in prison, while the desired treatment is from one to five years in prison.

The main difference between the two equations lies in the values computed for the intercepts. The typical ratings have a higher intercept than the desired ratings, indicating that by and large our respondents saw that the corrections systems of their states were treating convicted offenders correctly according to their crimes, ages, and previous records, but the respondents would like to see a more lenient treatment given to all offenders. The leniency is shown in the fact that the intercept value for the desired ratings is almost one scale value lower than the typical treatment.

The standardized regression coefficients provide a measure of the relative strengths of the three characteristics and indicate that for both "typical" and "desired" collective judgments, the "seriousness score" of the crime is clearly the most important characteristic, followed by previous record and age.[c] The last variable, age, is given a relatively minor role in both analyses. In short, collective judgments about treatment stress the seriousness of the crime most heavily and use characteristics of the offender as secondary criteria.

It is not at all easy to reconcile these findings with the approval our respondents have given in previous chapters to rehabilitation and community-based treatment "futures." However, both futures are vague on exactly how specific types of offenders are to be treated. The rehabilitation orientation stresses that offenders are to be retrained and subjected to therapeutic measures, but the specific retraining and rehabilitation measures to be applied to specific types of offenders certainly were not spelled out in our description of this future. The community-based corrections future also has the same vagueness concerning which offenders were to be incarcerated, released, or held in part-time confinement. Because of these ambiguities, it is impossible to confidently judge whether our respondents are collectively sentencing hypothetical offenders consistent with their overwhelming endorsement of either the rehabilitation or the community-based "futures." While on face value liberal pretensions appear to have been abandoned, it is difficult to be certain.

---

[c] Since the variances of the characteristics are unequal and quite unlike the variances of such characteristics in the real world of concrete convicted offenders, the standardized regression coefficients are to some degree dependent on the particularities of the way the vignettes were constructed. We had planned to run multiple regression analyses in the larger study in which these characteristics would be given distributions (by weighting) which would correspond more closely to the distributions of such characteristics in the "real world" of convicted offenders.

These analyses demonstrate that the collective judgments of the elite respondents are quite lawful. The average scores given to the vignettes by extremely small subsamples of respondents can be quite well accounted for by the characteristics that went into the construction of vignettes. Furthermore, we saw that the structure of judgments was quite similar for both "appropriate" treatments and perceived "typical" treatments, although the respondents on the average were more lenient in their treatments than they saw their corrections system typically behaving.

RESPONDENT DIFFERENCES IN THE TREATMENT OF CONVICTED OFFENDERS

The vignette ratings can also be used to characterize individual respondents. Since each of the twenty-nine samples administered to the respondents is a fair sample of the total set of vignettes (and, hence, statistically equivalent to each other), we can compute the average scores given by each respondent to the vignettes in his sample and use that score to characterize the respondent's leniency-stringency in treating convicted offenders. We can also compute the same average over the vignette sample rated according to his perception of the typical treatment accorded to convicted offenders in his state and use that average to measure his perceptions of the leniency-stringency of his state's corrections system.

These individual average scores can then be subjected to the same analytic technique employed in the first section of this chapter in order to uncover the sources of variation from individual to individual. Table 6–3 contains the results of regressing the individual mean ratings for desired and typical treatments on a variety of individual respondent characteristics. Note that because "positions" and "states" are dummy variables, the resulting b-coefficients are relative to respondents in the ommitted categories of "Other Partisans" and the state of Florida respectively. Thus the b-coefficient of 1.15 for prosecutors should be interpreted as a net increment of 1.15 points in treatment scores for prosecutors as compared to "Other Partisans" (i.e., state and other variables held constant). Since "Other Partisans" have been shown in previous analyses to be quite a liberal group on corrections issues, most of the coefficients for other positions are positive, indicating that ceteris paribus, the latter are more punitive in the kinds of treatments they want meted out to convicted offenders. Since our dependent is a 5 point scale, this increment cannot be easily dismissed.

Despite a few such coefficients, all that the individual respondent characteristics used do not account for much of the variation from

Table 6-3. Regression of Respondent Mean Desired and Mean Typical Ratings on Respondent Characteristics (N = 256)[a]

	Desired Ratings		*Typical Ratings*	
Respondent Characteristic	*b*	*T-value*	*b*	*T-value*
I: *Positions*[b]				
Prosecutors	1.15[d]	9.20	.84	.24
State Elected Officials	.78[d]	6.64	.08	.32
Local Elected Officials	.77[d]	4.60	.88[d]	2.89
Judges of Criminal Courts	1.09[d]	10.72	.12	.58
Police	.57[d]	2.95	−.50	−1.09
Bar Assoc. and Public Defenders	.60[d]	2.88	.41	.63
Corrections Officials	.28	.89	−.23	−.30
Corrections Rank and File	.32	.92	0.06	.14
II: *State*[c]				
Washington	−.24[d]	−2.06	−.09	−.16
Illinois	−.08	−.21	−.43[d]	−3.24
III: *Biography and Experience*				
Age	−.008	−1.11	−.009	−.74
Education	−.09	−1.52	−.04	−.16
Visited Prisons	.23	1.11	−.06	−.44
Met with Prisoners	−.01	−.50	.23	1.06
Talked with Prisoner Rep.	.68	.93	−.29	−.79
Intercept	4.10		5.27	
R^2 =	.10[d]		.06	

[a]Individual means are computed over the ratings of each respondent and hence represent the average of the treatments accorded by each respondent to typical and desired vignettes.
[b]Omitted category is "Other Partisans."
[c]Omitted state is Florida.
[d]$p < .05$.

individual to individual in the mean treatment ratings given in either the desired or typical ratings. Only 10 percent of the variance in individual means could be accounted for in the desired ratings, an amount that just barely reaches the conventional .05 statistical significance level. Even less variance in the individual means for typical ratings in accounted for (6 percent), an amount that does not succeed in getting over the .30 threshold.

Looking now at all the b-coefficients for desired ratings, we see that only the positions of the respondents make much difference. Prosecutors and judges would like to see convicted offenders have slightly more than a one point increment in severity of treatment. State and local elected officials are almost as punitive, adding about three-quarters of a point. Recall that these coefficients are all in comparison to "Other Partisans," ordinarily a very liberal group, which helps to explain why along with police, public defenders and influential members of the bar also have positive coefficients of about half a unit.

Only state elected officials and Illinois residents have regression coefficients that reach conventional levels of statistical significance in the regressions on typical treatment averages. The former believe that typical sentences are more severe, the latter believe they are less severe. Of course, since respondents were asked to report on what typically occurs within their states, we should expect to find a good deal of consensus among respondents and therefore little in the way of explained variance and few (if any) important b-coefficients.

In short, we find that respondents from a variety of positions, biographies, and experiences agree on what is going on within their present corrections system. There is a bit less agreement on the desired state of affairs, however. Compared to the liberal "Other Partisans," judges, prosecutors, elected officials on both the state and local levels, police, and parts of the legal profession more generally, would want to see more stringent treatment of criminals in their systems. All agree, nevertheless, that the desired state of affairs would be one in which less punitive sentences were routinely handed out to convicted offenders.

INTERACTION EFFECTS BETWEEN RESPONDENT AND VIGNETTE CHARACTERISTICS

We have now considered in some depth the ways in which characteristics of vignettes affect mean ratings and the ways in which respondent biography affects mean ratings. The next logical question is how, if at all, these two clusters of independent variables interact in the production of respondent assessments.

We will look at the typical treatment ratings first. Table 6–4 presents regression analyses computed separately within each of the three states. Note that the regressions were computed on the ratings received by individual vignettes since the numbers of respondents who rated each of the vignettes within each state were too small to compute average ratings within a state. The effect of using individual vignette ratings is to lower considerably the amount of variance explained. The regression coefficients, however, are unaffected; they are identical, except for rounding error, to those obtainable by using average ratings received by vignettes. (Also note that a somewhat more statistically efficient procedure which would have also routinely per-

Table 6–4. Regressions of Typical Vignette Ratings Within Each State on Vignette Characteristics

| | | *b-coefficients* | | | | |
State	Age	Crime Seriousness Score	Previous Record	Intercept	R^2	N
Florida	.007	.945[a]	.452[a]	−2.62	.35[a]	3754
Illinois	.017[a]	1.02[a]	.431[a]	−3.77	.38[a]	2484
Washington	.012[a]	1.02[a]	.467[a]	−3.88	.40[a]	3117

[a].05 significance for the null hypothesis that b coefficient equals zero.

mitted the equivalence of significance tests *across* equations could have been employed through the use of single equation models with interaction terms by state. However, this was discarded as unnecessarily cumbersome given the low priority we have given statistical inference. See J. Johnston's *Econometric Methods*, New York, McGraw Hill, 1972, Section 6.3)

The differences among the three states are far less than the overall similarities. Consistent with the overall patterns in table 6–1, elite respondents in each of the states report that their particular criminal justice system most emphasizes the seriousness of the crimes involved; next, the previous record of the convicted offenders; and least, the age of the offender. Within this overall similarity however, some small differences do appear. In Florida, the intercept value is shifted toward heavier sentencing, indicating that Florida respondents, as we could anticipate from earlier findings, report that their criminal justice system metes out tougher penalties. Floridians also report that the age of the offender is given a bit less attention in sentencing, as suggested by the fact that the b-coefficient for age is smaller by about one-half. Illinois and Washington may resemble each other more closely than any other pair, but even in this case, Washington respondents report that their system weighs previous records more heavily and age less heavily in giving out sentences. In short, there is little evidence for important interaction effects by state for the typical ratings, and other types of interactions for the typical ratings (not reported here) were even less interesting.

Interaction effects for desired ratings were also very small with differences by respondent position the only findings worth reporting in any detail. For table 6–5, we computed separate regressions of desired vignette ratings on vignette characteristics for each of the nine different positions. First of all, the amount of variance explained ranges

Table 6–5. Regression of Vignette Desired Ratings on Vignette Characteristics Within Each Position

Position			b-coefficients			
	Age	Crime Seriousness Score	Previous Record	Intercept	R^2	N
State Elected Officials	.014[a]	1.07[a]	.524[a]	−4.52	.45[a]	1501
Corrections Officials	.014[a]	1.03[a]	.534[a]	−4.68	.43[a]	1728
Corrections Rank and File	.016[a]	1.11[a]	.427[a]	−4.70	.44[a]	1245
Police	.007	1.14[a]	.429[a]	−4.68	.44[a]	1077
Criminal Court Judges	.010	1.10[a]	.538[a]	−4.38	.48[a]	1291
Prosecutors	.010	1.12[a]	.532[a]	−4.38	.49[a]	616
Bar and Public Defenders	.009	.97[a]	.544[a]	−3.97	.39[a]	764
Local Elected Officials	.009	1.06[a]	.398[a]	−4.08	.43[a]	835
Other Partisans	.012	.91[a]	.426[a]	−3.93	.36[a]	664

[a].05 significance.

from thirty-six percent (in the case of other partisans) to 49 percent in the case of prosecutors. Indeed, the two most heterogeneous groups, the other partisans and the bar association officials and public defenders, are the ones in which the smallest amounts of variance are explained. (We combined these two possibly quite dissimilar types of respondents mainly in order to get a large enough N to sustain separate analyses, reasoning that lawyers were more similar to each other regardless of their occupations than each would be to other groups. Apparently that may not be the case.)

Other differences among the groups center around the role in judgments to be played by the age of the respondent, with the first three groups in table 6–5 stressing that role slightly more than the last six groups. On the role played by criminal records, there appears to be similar disagreement, with state elected officials, corrections officials, criminal court judges, prosecutors, and bar association and public defenders putting a bit more emphasis on previous records than the other groups.

In summary, there is little evidence of important interaction effects between respondent characteristics and vignette characteristics for either the typical or desired treatments. This conclusion survived a variety of different analytical procedures both in the variables considered and various weighting schemes for measures whose scales could not be simply assumed to possess equal interval properties. For example, we regressed previous record on mean vignette rating and then used the resulting regression coefficients to construct a new scale for previous record. In later analyses, this refinement yielded trivial improvements and was thus discarded.

SUMMARY

This chapter has attempted to take the study of desired prison reform from the level of abstractly phrased programs and specific prison reforms to the level of what should be done with specific convicted offenders. Our respondents by and large endorsed a system of sentencing that was less harsh than they saw their present criminal justice system pursuing. In that sense, our elite respondents—including those in the criminal justice system as well as outside—were for more lenient in the treatment of criminal offenders and more likely to endorse the use of means other than incarceration in conventional prisons.

The elites were also in favor of a system of allocating sentences that weighted most heavily the seriousness of the crime for which an offender was convicted and then the previous record of the offender. The weight attached to an offender's age favored the young slightly, although some would not put any weight on this factor at all.

In contrast to the powerful effects of vignette characteristics, respondent biography played a very small role. While differences consistent with earlier chapters did in fact appear, they reflected by and large surprising homogeniety. In other words, earlier differences among respondents at a more abstract level, in part dissolved in the face of actual sentencing options. While prosecutors, for example, were still more punitive than high level corrections officials, the practical implications of this disparity are not nearly as striking as disputes over more theoretical issues. Hence, the rhetoric surrounding corrections reform may typically be very misleading.

In short, the analysis presented in this chapter broadly support the results of previous chapters. Generally, the elite would like to see less harsh treatment meted out to convicted offenders than they believe the present system provides. However, a liberalization of the criminal justice system receives far more than lip service on the level of abstractly presented reforms. Actual sentencing decisions reveal a more traditional posture, perhaps because of strictures existing within current corrections systems. In other words, liberals and conservatives may have had their ideal preferences constrained by a reality in which many desirable options were simply not available. There were, for example, very few community-based corrections facilities in 1973. Alternatively, questions about more abstract principles and hypothetical reforms may encourage respondents to reveal their more ideological side and thus produce a more polarized picture. In any case, were political compromises to be attempted at a more concrete, specific level of discourse, there would seem considerable consensus on which to build modest reforms.

Chapter 7

Summary and Conclusions

Since World War II, as the crime rates have climbed ever higher and as we have increasingly learned about illegal activities at the highest levels of our society, more and more questions are being asked about the purposes and the functioning of our criminal justice system. The solutions proposed are varied, ranging from an affirmation of quite traditional procedures to a radical reconstruction. From all viewpoints, however, there is little support for the present system—or nonsystem. As far as prisons are concerned, almost all agree that they have failed. Prisons do not rehabilitate prisoners, by themselves probably do not deter would-be criminals, nor do they function very well as purely custodial institutions.

The time for reform is at hand. The main problem is: What should the changes be? What should the prisons attempt to do? How should they achieve those goals, once specified? The research described in the previous chapters should be seen as one of many attempts to gauge the depths of dissatisfactions with our prisons, to measure the potential for change, and the directions in which change should go. The research concentrated on political elites in a sample of states, operating on the assumption that the balances of sentiments within such elites are good leading indicators of the changes that would most likely occur at least over the short run.

The research is best viewed as having two purposes. First, it was designed to test whether it was possible to reach members of state political elites and to measure their receptivity to corrections reform. Second, the research was to add to substantive knowledge on the climate of acceptance for specific types of corrections changes, namely a series of graduated forms of treatment ranging from more widespread use of parole through community-based part-time confinement to full-time incarceration in traditional prisons.

How well the first purpose of the research was fulfilled we leave to the reader to judge. Our own appraisal is that we have demonstrated that it is not only possible to reach members of state political elites with personal interviews but that their responses are reasonable and interpretable.

The goal of assessing the potential for corrections reform we also believe to be fulfilled in the body of this monograph. Nothing seems clearer (to us) than that in 1973 the political elites of Florida, Illinois, and Washington personally endorsed more diversified treatment of convicted offenders in a wider variety of institutions, with stronger emphasis on rehabilitation. Beyond this overall characterization of the substantive import of our findings, there are interesting subtleties of detail.

The political elites we studied are far from a random sample of the population of their states. They are well educated, middle-aged, upper middle class in income, and almost entirely white and male. These characteristics predispose them to be articulate and well-informed, but within the range of practices we considered, do not by themselves signal any particular correctional philosophy. Their positions, either within state governments or within the organizations they represent, provide them with considerably better than average knowledge about, and acquaintance with, the corrections system. Large proportions have visited state prisons, met corrections officials and prisoners, and have intimate knowledge of how corrections legislation and administrative practices in their states are formed and carried through.

The elite view of how decisions are made about corrections is one in which the governor, portions of the state legislatures, and corrections officials play key roles in the initiation of changes and in seeing such changes through to enactment. There is a hint in our data that some states may be ruled by a legislative coalition centering around the appropriate committees in each house and the majority party leaders and that others may be more dominated by an executive coalition centering around the governor and heads of state agencies that run the corrections systems.

In each state, the major groups that can influence both the course of corrections reform and the respondents themselves are state elected officials and the appointed heads of corrections agencies. However, the reader is cautioned that these findings may be descriptive only when no especially controversial proposals are actively on the state agendas. In short, this may be what decision-making is like for relatively routine adjustments in the corrections system; major changes that attract a great deal of public and partisan attention might produce quite different power and influence configurations.[1] For example, it may be that local and state police have greater influence when capital punishment is considered since they may speak for one segment of a polarized public.

As a group, the political elites are quite liberal in their ideas of the directions that changes in the corrections should go. They subscribe to the view that a critical goal of corrections is to rehabilitate offenders, and they reject the belief that prisons should only punish criminals and render offenders incapable of inflicting further harm on the public. Thus, in the future prisons should place still greater emphasis on rehabilitation with community-based corrections is a desirable way to provide a series of gradated treatments. Such opinions are held rather strongly and apparently do not deteriorate easily in the face of providing additional funds to run such institutions.

Elite preferences run counter to their assessments of current corrections performance. They see their prisons as doing less than a satisfactory job, as beset with the variety of problems ranging from lack of public support to insufficient rehabilitative programs.

Elite views of the future also contradict what they perceive to be the views of the general public. The state publics are seen as endorsing punitive and custodial functions for the correction system, rejecting community-based corrections reforms, and endorsing a future for prisons that would emphasize imprisonment as punishment.

There is also a certain amount of pluralistic ignorance among the elite. They tend to see their colleagues as less liberal on corrections than they themselves were in answering our questionnaires. Perhaps the perception of a hostile public opinion restrains them from openly revealing their liberal views. Whatever the cause, it is apparent that elites do not realize the extent to which, as a group, elites are liberal.

Although as a group liberalism prevails, there are differences within the elite. "Other partisans" (a category that includes the ACLU and other groups interested in providing more civil rights to prisoners) tend to be the most liberal among the state elites. At the more conservative extreme, state and local police, prosecutors, and judges tend to be conservative, especially on issues that would provide wider civil rights to prisoners and increase the leniency of sentences.

State elected officials and appointed corrections officials tend to fall somewhere between the extreme liberalism of the ACLU and the conservatism of local police chiefs, although clearly still on the liberal side. If we also consider that these groups play an extremely central role in the initiation and implementation of change, then the prospect for liberalization of state corrections is apparently quite good. Indeed, when we weight opinions by the reputed power of respondents, the proportion who give the liberal responses to a wide variety of questions increases, further bolstering the view that the climate for change in the liberalizing direction is quite favorable.

The liberalism of the elites does not rest only on endorsement of rather global slogans (e.g., community-based corrections reforms) but also on the endorsement of very specific reforms within prisons and on the treatment of individual convicted offenders. Few elites supported restoration of physical punishment, strengthening the powers of guards, or reinstatement capital punishment. Rather, the elites were generally in favor of extending more civil rights to prisoners and increasing support for attempts at rehabilitation.

The measurement of preferred treatments for convicted offenders was based on a new technique that could support a sophisticated analysis of the principles that underlay judgments in complex cases. Analyses performed showed that elite members thought the major factor that should govern the punishment of convicted offenders was the seriousness of his offense, supplemented somewhat by the offender's previous record. On these two points both liberals and conservatives agreed. In other words, conservatives would not be as lenient as their liberal counterparts in the *kinds of sentences* they would like to see handed out, but were similar in the *kinds of criminals* to whom they would hand out stiffer or more lenient sentences.

All elites saw their present corrections systems as handing out sentences that were harsher than desirable, evidencing once again a preference for more differentiated treatment of convicted offenders.

All told, the climate for liberal reforms appeared in the early part of 1973 to be very favorable. Each of the state's elites were dissatisfied with their prisons and endorsed both a philosophy of liberal change and the content of such perspectives.

That was the situation in Florida, Illinois, and Washington in the first three months of 1973. In retrospect, taking into account more recent alterations in the general climate surrounding our criminal justice systems, we may have intervened at a point of liberal ascendancy, emphasizing lenient treatment and the rehabilitation of criminals. The climate has shifted since that time. For one thing, it has become increasingly clear that rehabilitative measures, at the level of intensity that have been implemented in our prisons, simply do not work. Scores of evaluative studies have shown that efforts to rehabilitate prisoners do not produce any signs that prisoners so treated fare any better when returned to civil status. Second, there has been a revival of interest in emphasizing the deterrence functions of imprisonment, a philosophy that attributes the recent rise in the crime rate to the fact that punishment is neither sure, swift, nor uniform. Third, the civil rights enthusiasts have come to understand that such rehabilitative measures as indeterminate sentences—especially in the absence of effective rehabilitative programs—result in prisoners being subjected to arbitrarily varying sentences, a sign of injustice itself.

We cannot know how much these new currents of corrections criticisms have reached the state elites, and how much those elites may have changed in response. This last point obviously rests on how strongly the liberal convictions of 1973 were held. If the liberal climate of 1973 was mainly a shallow reflection of what were the then current "in" criticisms of the criminal justice system, then we can expect that some of the elites have changed to mirror the new fashionable views. On the other hand, if the liberalism of the elites is a reflection of the generally more liberal stances of the better-educated, public affairs oriented citizens and public officials, the 1973 climate may still persist.

We are inclined to believe that there has been no lessening of elite criticisms of their corrections system; little has changed in the last three years to support any revisions in negative assessments. We are also inclined to believe that we would find more skepticism expressed toward rehabilitation; some of the relevant findings of social scientists must have percolated out through the society. We also believe that the deterrence philosophy has not yet won the status of a majority philosophy; there is still far too much disagreement among professionals to ensure widespread diffusion throughout the better educated levels of our society. In sum, we would predict that if our study were to be repeated in 1977, state political elites would find their prison systems falling far short of perfection; and they would endorse a future for their prison systems that emphasized rehabilitation (but not as strongly) and a more differentiated system of treatment of offenders according to the crimes they had committed.

※ *Appendix A*

Measuring the Seriousness of Crimes

The crime seriousness scores were generated in order to help solve the problem of which offenses to use in the construction of the offender vignettes used in the last chapter.[1] Ideally, one would like to choose crimes that varied in some dimension closely related to how seriously our society regarded offenses. This view rests upon the assumption that there is some large degree of agreement among members of our society about at least the rank ordering of offenses and possibly also about the absolute position of offenses along a continuum ranging from the most serious to the trivial. There are several seemingly reasonable ways of constructing this ordering of offenses. For example, one might have used the actual sentences given to persons convicted of a variety of crimes to rank those offenses, following the assumption that the more serious the offense, the more heavy the punishment meted out in the courts. Alternatively, we might have examined criminal statutes and ranged offenses according to the punishments provided. Either of these ways of proceeding obviously rests on the assumption that the statutes or the judicial procedures reflect more or less accurately the consensus in our society on the seriousness of crime. Furthermore, the assembling of criminal statutes for a variety of states and the statistics on sentencing variations for convicted offenders is by no means an easy task, especially in the brief period of time we had to design the study.

We decided to proceed more directly to devise "crime seriousness" measures by measuring consensus on these matters in the society at large. The crime seriousness scores essentially were generated by a sample survey launched in Baltimore among the city's adult population. The scores used in constructing the vignettes and in the analysis of the vignettes represent the average "seriousness ratings" given to each offense by a sample of two hundred adults in the city of Baltimore.[2]

The choice of Baltimore is obviously one of convenience bolstered by the expectation that there would be relatively so little disagreement among subgroups in that city (as defined by the socio-economic status, educational attainment, race, and sex) that one could safely generalize those results to other parts of the United States with quite different population mixtures. Obviously, regional differences generated by "cultural" variations along regional lines could not be measured in this fashion. In the last respect, it is clear that the results of our survey are flawed to some unknown degree. Balancing convenience and cost against a possible loss in generalizability, we made the reasonable (to us) choice of Baltimore, a choice that is to some degree vindicated by the analysis presented later in this chapter.

THE DESIGN OF THE BALTIMORE STUDY

The universe sampled was the adult (eighteen and over) population of Baltimore City. In order to pick the sample, census tracts in the city were divided into three strata: those whose population was 90 percent or more white in 1970, those whose population was 90 percent or more black in 1970, and the remaining census tracts whose proportion black was more than 10 percent and less than 90 percent. Since there are only a handful of tracts in this last category and they would present special problems in interviewing, they were droped from further consideration. Within each of the first two strata we divided the census tracts into thirds according to the median income of households in each tract as of 1970. Within each of the six thirds so defined (one set of thirds for each race) we picked census tracts at random. One census tract was picked within each largely black stratum, anticipating that we would have more difficulty obtaining interviews among blacks than among whites. Within each of the census tracts so chosen we picked three to eight blocks, depending upon the number of interviews desired and the number of tracts within that stratum. Within each block, professional trained interviewers from Sidney Hollander and Associates chose available male and female adult respondents until their quotas for total number of interviews and for equal numbers of each sex were fulfilled.[3] Interviewers were instructed to divide their interviewing time equally between daytime hours and nighttime or weekend hours in order to insure that persons working during the day would not be slighted. When there was no one at home in a dwelling unit or when no one eligible by virtue of age or sex was available in a dwelling unit, the interviewer proceeded to another dwelling unit. No callbacks were made to dwelling units where no one appeared to be at home and no callbacks were made to obtain interviews with potentially eligible respondents who were not at home at the time of the initial contact.

Quotas were fixed to obtain 125 interviews with whites and 75 interviews with blacks, and 100 interviews with males and 100 interviews with females. Within each race the fifty-fifty sex quota was maintained.

The sampling plan outlined above was used mainly to cut down on costs of callbacks, under the assumption that respondents shared widely in societal consensus on the seriousness of crime. The block quota system employed, while obviously not fulfilling the requirements of the best sampling plans, does spread the interviewing effort around considerably better than alternative plans calling only for quotas on sex and race. The biases of the sampling plan employed are well known, with young males, households without children and very active persons generally being less likely to be interviewed under such plans.[4] Of course, whether or not a potential bias is *in fact* a bias that influences the findings is problematic in each particular case, dependent entirely on the correlation between the potentially biasing factors and the phenomena under study.

The core of the interview administered to the sample of Baltimore respondents was a rating task in which respondents were asked to judge the "seriousness" of a list of eighty offenses. Two lists of eighty offenses were employed in which twenty were common to both lists and sixty were different in each list. Thus, a total of 140 offenses were rated by the Baltimore sample, although each respondent rated only eighty. The offenses to be rated were picked by the authors by expanding the *Uniform Crime Report* listing by adding specific acts (e.g., "burglary" became "breaking and entering a house stealing a transistor radio") and by adding offenses not normally reported, especially white-collar crimes and crimes that are in the process (at least in some states) of decriminalization. In addition to the ratings of the eighty crimes, each respondent was asked questions concerning perceptions of the crime problem in Baltimore and such "background" identifying variables as age, occupation of household head, and educational attainment. Each interview lasted about half an hour on the average.

The main body of the interview consisted of a card-sorting task in which the respondent sorted eighty IBM cards, each containing a short description of an offense, into a box containing nine slots, each slot corresponding to a level of crime seriousness. Respondents were instructed to place cards containing descriptions of crimes they considered to be most serious in the slot labelled "9" and crimes which were least serious in the slot labelled "1" with crimes of intermediate seriousness being placed closer or further away from those two poles depending on the respondent's perceptions of seriousness.[5] There was no attempt in the interview to define for the respondent what was meant by "seriousness."

Each card contained a crime description and punches indicating a code for the crime described on the card and a code for the respondent. Interviewers placed each sorted card into envelopes labelled with the slot number from which the card came. Computer programs were developed to automatically mark each card with the number of the slot into which it was sorted and to create a record for each sorted card. This tape became the basic data tape from which the analysis described in this chapter is based. This technique considerably shortened interviewing time and reduced the interviewer error involved in recording responses. It also made it possible to produce tabulated results within a day after the interviewing had been completed.

Interviewing was conducted in the first two weeks of November 1972.

Interviewers reported that most respondents were able to perform the rating task. Indeed, most of the crimes were rated by most of the respondents. The survey design called for 16,000 ratings (200 respondents each rating 80 crimes) and 15,521—or 97 percent—were finally obtained. The distribution of ratings given tended to be more dense on the high serious end of the nine-point scale. Indeed, the most popular rating was "9" with the lower rating being less popular in almost inverse relationship to size. The average rating given to all the crimes was 6.27, indicating that the typical crime was placed more often on the serious rather than the less serious side.

THE CRIME RATINGS

Table A–1 shows the average ratings received by the 140 offenses, with the offenses arranged in rank order. A word of caution should be sounded with respect to this rank order: The differences between adjacent crimes are not ordinarily statistically significant. A typical standard error for a score is between .1 and .3. Most crimes in adjacent standard ranks differ in the third decimal place. Thus, the offense with rank 1 is not statistically significantly different from the next five crimes.

There are few surprises in the ratings shown in table A–1. Crimes against persons, especially murder, receive very high seriousness

Table A-1.   Average Seriousness Ratings Given to 140 Offenses in Baltimore Survey (N is at least 100)

Scores have a theoretical range of 9 (most serious) to 1 (least serious).

Rank	Crime	Mean	Variance
1.	Planned killing of a policeman	8.474	2.002
2.	Planned killing of a person for a fee	8.406	2.749
[a]3.	Selling heroin	8.293	2.658
[a]4.	Forcible rape after breaking into a home	8.241[b]	2.266
5.	Impulsive killing of a policeman	8.214	3.077
[a]6.	Planned killing of a spouse	8.113[b]	3.276
7.	Planned killing of an acquaintance	8.093	3.273
8.	Hijacking an airplane	8.072	2.776
[a]9.	Armed robbery of a bank	8.021	2.020
10.	Selling LSD	7.949	3.048
11.	Assault with a gun on a policeman	7.938	3.225
12.	Kidnapping for ransom	7.930	3.844
13.	Forcible rape of a stranger in a park	7.909	3.737
14.	Killing someone after an argument over a business transaction	7.898	3.536
15.	Assassination of a public official	7.888	5.400
[a]16.	Killing someone during a serious argument	7.867	3.663
[a]17.	Making sexual advances to young children	7.861	3.741
18.	Assault with a gun on a stranger	7.847[b]	2.172
[a]19.	Impulsive killing of a spouse	7.835	3.952
20.	Impulsive killing of a stranger	7.821[b]	3.429
21.	Forcible rape of a neighbor	7.778	3.726
22.	Impulsive killing of an acquaintance	7.717	4.205
[a]23.	Deliberately starting a fire which results in a death	7.707	4.189
[c]24.	Assault with a gun on a stranger	7.662	2.976
25.	Manufacturing and selling drugs known to be harmful to users	7.653	3.280
26.	Knowingly selling contaminated food which results in a death	7.596	5.202
[a]27.	Armed robbery of a company payroll	7.577	3.080
[a]28.	Using heroin	7.520	4.871
29.	Assault with a gun on an acquaintance	7.505	3.482
30.	Armed holdup of a taxi driver	7.505	3.336
[a]31.	Beating up a child	7.490	3.840
[a]32.	Armed robbery of a neighborhood druggist	7.487[b]	3.221
33.	Causing auto accident death while driving when drunk	7.455	3.904
34.	Selling secret documents to a foreign government	7.423[b]	5.722
35.	Armed street holdup stealing $200 cash	7.414	3.633
[a]36.	Killing someone in a bar-room free-for-all	7.392	4.637
37.	Deliberately staging a fire in an occupied building	7.347	5.177

Table A–1.   Continued

Rank	Crime	Mean	Variance
[a]38.	Assault with a gun on a spouse	7.323	4.650
39.	Armed robbery of a supermarket	7.313	3.911
40.	Assault with a gun in the course of a riot	7.245	3.218
41.	Armed hijacking of a truck	7.198	3.866
42.	Deserting to the enemy in time of war	7.194	4.673
[a]43.	Armed street holdup stealing $25 in cash	7.165	4.431
44.	Armed robbery of an armored truck	7.163	5.210
45.	Spying for a foreign government	7.135	7.024
46.	Killing a pedestrian while exceeding the speed limit	7.122	3.964
47.	Seduction of a minor	7.021	5.729
48.	Beating up a policeman	7.020	5.734
49.	Selling marijuana	6.969[b]	7.216
50.	Father-daughter incest	6.959	7.112
[a]51.	Causing the death of an employee by neglecting to repair machinery	6.918	4.556
52.	Breaking and entering a bank	6.908	4.641
[a]53.	Mugging and stealing $25 in cash	6.873[b]	5.305
54.	Selling pep pills	6.867	5.683
[a]55.	Cashing stolen payroll checks	6.827	4.784
56.	Mugging and stealing $200 cash	6.796	5.051
57.	Causing the death of a tenant by neglecting to repair heating plant	6.704	6.314
58.	Killing spouse's lover after catching them together	6.691	7.695
59.	Blackmail	6.663	7.715
60.	Advocating overthrow of the government	6.663	7.715
[a]61.	Neglecting to care for own children	6.660	6.988
62.	Forcible rape of a former spouse	6.653	6.394
[a]63.	Manufacturing and selling autos known to be dangerously defective	6.604	5.968
[a]64.	Beating up a stranger	6.604	5.379
65.	Using LSD	6.557	7.479
66.	Driving while drunk	6.545	6.006
67.	Practicing medicine without a license	6.500[b]	6.908
[a]68.	Burglary of a home stealing a color TV set	6.440[b]	5.048
69.	Knowingly passing counterfeit money	6.392	5.220
70.	Beating up someone in a riot	6.368	5.788
71.	Performing illegal abortions	6.330	7.723
[a]72.	Passing worthless checks for more than $500	6.309	5.119
73.	A public official accepting bribes in return for favors	6.240	6.467
74.	Employee embezzling company funds	6.207[b]	5.030
[a]75.	Knowlingly selling stolen stocks and bonds	6.138[b]	4.960
76.	Refusing to obey lawful order of a policeman	6.118[b]	5.806
[a]77.	Burglary of a home stealing a portable transister radio	6.115[b]	5.871
[a]78.	Theft of a car for the purpose of resale	6.093[b]	5.085
79.	Knowingly selling defective used cars as completely safe	6.093	5.023

Table A-1. Continued

Rank	Crime	Mean	Variance
[a]80.	Burglary of an appliance store stealing several TV sets	6.062	5.371
81.	Looting goods in a riot	6.043	5.052
82.	Knowingly selling stolen goods	6.021	4.463
83.	Leaving the scene of an accident	5.949	6.620
84.	Printing counterfeit $10 bills	5.948	6.820
85.	Shoplifting a diamond ring from a jewelry store	5.939	6.820
86.	Mother-son incest	5.907	9.189
87.	Theft of a car for joy-riding	5.876	6.047
88.	Intimidating a witness in a court case	5.853	4.850
89.	Brother-sister incest	5.825	8.709
[a]90.	Knowingly selling worthless stocks as valuable investments	5.821	5.021
[a]91.	Beating up a spouse	5.796	7.051
92.	Selling liquor to minors	5.789	7.572
[a]93.	Burglary of a factory stealing machine	5.7	5.317
94.	Using stolen credit cards	5.750	5.832
95.	Using pep pills	5.656	9.5.2
96.	Joining a riot	5.656	6.750
97.	Lending money at illegal interest rates	5.653	5.775
98.	Knowingly buying stolen goods	5.596	5.794
99.	Refusal to serve when drafted in peace	5.535	8.864
[a]100.	Resisting arrest	5.449	6.271
101.	Impersonating a policeman	5.449	7.405
102.	Using false identification to obtain goods from a store	5.438	6.628
103.	Bribing a public official to obtain favors	5.394	6.198
[a]104.	Passing worthless checks involving less than $100	5.339[b]	5.921
105.	Desertion from military service in peacetime	5.323	7.526
[a]106.	Under-reporting income on income tax returns	5.305	6.321
107.	Willfully neglecting to file income tax returns	5.157[b]	6.470
[a]108.	Soliciting for prostitution	5.144	7.687
109.	Proposing homosexual practices to an adult	5.140	9.361
110.	Overcharging on repairs to automobiles	5.135	6.455
[a]111.	Shoplifting a dress from a department store	5.070	6.308
[a]112.	Beating up an acquaintance	5.032	5.644
113.	Driving while license is suspended	5.031	7.988
114.	Pouring paint over someone's car	4.938	7.449
115.	Shoplifting a pair of shoes from a shoe store	4.990	6.781
116.	Overcharging for credit in selling goods	4.970	6.213
[a]117.	Shoplifting a carton of cigarettes from a supermarket	4.969	6.793
118.	Smuggling goods to avoid paying import duties	4.918	5.618
119.	Killing a suspected burglar in home	4.868[b]	8.930
120.	False claims of dependents on income tax return	4.832	6.801
[a]121.	Knowingly using inaccurate scales in weighing meat for sale	4.786	5.902
122.	Refusal to make essential repairs to rental property	4.781	6.678

Table A–1.   Continued

Rank	Crime	Mean	Variance
123.	Engaging in male homosexual acts with consenting adults	4.736	9.396
124.	Engaging in female homosexual acts with consenting adults	4.729	9.042
125.	Breaking a plate glass window in a shop	4.653	6.697
126.	Fixing prices of a consumer product like gasoline	4.629	6.069
127.	Fixing prices of machines sold to businesses	4.619	6.218
128.	Selling pornographic magazines	4.526	6.218
129.	Shoplifting a book in a bookstore	4.424[b]	6.551
130.	Repeated refusal to obey parents	4.411	9.074
131.	Joining a prohibited demonstration	4.323	6.486
132.	False advertising of headache remedy	4.083	7.972
133.	Refusal to pay alimony	4.063	6.670
134.	Refusal to pay parking fines	3.583[b]	6.475
[a]135.	Disturbing the peace	3.779	7.174
136.	Repeated truancy	3.573	7.658
[a]137.	Repeated running away from home	3.571[b]	6.342
138.	Loitering in public places	3.375	8.111
139.	Refusal to answer census-taker	3.105	7.329
140.	Being drunk in public places	2.849	6.021

[a]Used in vignettes.

[b]Crimes rated by all members (200) of the Baltimore sample.

[c]This offense was inadvertently repeated (see crime rank No. 18), indicating that differences in scores as much as .185 can be obtained by sheer replication.

ratings. Crimes against property which involve no action against persons are rated significantly lower, and at the end of the list are offenses that are often classified as misdemeanors, e.g., "disturbing the peace," or "being drunk in public places."

Although the general ordering of the crimes is in line with common sense expectations, it is still interesting to note where some particular offenses fall. For example, crimes involving action taken against police officers are almost always regarded as more serious than similar actions taken against strangers or persons known to the offender. Another tendency is for crimes involving persons known to the offender to be regarded as less serious than crimes committed against strangers. Apparently our respondents feel that in the former cases, the fact that the victim is known to the offender may indicate that the offense was, in some sense, understandable and possibly justified. Finally, it may be noted that "white-collar" crimes (e.g., embezzlement, price gouging, etc.) and "crimes without victims" (e.g., homosexuality) are not regarded as particularly serious offenses.

Crimes used in the vignettes analyzed in previous chapters have been noted. They were chosen both to represent frequent offenses for which adult prisoners were incarcerated and to represent the full range of scores in the distribution of table A–1.

THE QUESTION OF CONSENSUS

The usefulness of the crime seriousness ratings rests very heavily on the extent to which significant subgroups in the general population agree with each other on how seriously these crimes should be regarded. Obviously, if there is considerable disagreement, then the seriousness ratings are mainly a matter of individual preference, conditioned perhaps by subcultural norms, but certainly not a matter of generalized social norms.

It is easier to assert that there should be consensus than it is to devise a suitable standard against which a given degree of consensus should be measured. In short, how much agreement constitutes consensus? In part the answer depends on what device is used to measure consensus. In this section we use correlations to measure consensus, a statistical device that provides a measure of the agreement between two arrays of data, in this case, sets of ratings generated by significant subgroups of the sample interviewed. In part, the answer to the question of how much agreement constitutes consensus is an arbitrary decision: We are going to apply the standard that the correlation among subgroups should meet the requirements of a "reliable test." That is, if a "test" is to be regarded as reliable, we ordinarily expect that alternative forms of the test or that test-retest correlations be .70 or more.

The correlations between major divisions of the Baltimore sample are shown in table A–2. All the correlations in that table meet the "reliability" requirement, the correlation between blacks and whites being +.89, between males and females, +94, and between the better educated and the less well educated, +.89. It is important to under-

Table A–2. Correlations Among Average Crime Ratings for Major Subgroups: Race, Sex, and Educational Attainment

Subgroups	Correlation	N = [a]
Blacks and Whites	.89	(100)
Males and Females	.94	(100)
Less than High School Graduation and High School Graduation or Better	.89	(96—104)

[a]In this context N denotes the number of respondents who rated each of the crimes. Note that for twenty of the crimes shown in table A-1 all respondents (200) contributed to the ratings. Hence N refers to the number who rated all but common twenty crimes.

stand what these coefficients mean: they indicate that, knowing the scores given by one group, the scores given by the other group can be fairly well predicted. A correlation of +.89 indicates that such predictions can be made with a high degree of accuracy.

Another way of looking at consensus is to consider the regression equation that is the "best" straight line that can be fitted to the array of the average ratings given by a pair of groups. The regression equations for race and sex groups are shown below.

Regression Equation for Blacks and Whites:

$$\hat{Y}_{Wh} = -.39 +.998X_{Bl}$$

Regression Equation for Males and Females:

$$\hat{Y}_{Male} = -.80 +1.059X_{Fem}$$

In short, blacks, on the average, tend to rate each crime as more serious than whites by .4 units, and females tend to rate crimes more serious by .8 units. The overall agreement between the races and the sexes rests largely on agreement about the relative seriousness of crimes, with blacks and females regarding all crimes as more serious than their counterpart groups. In the case of females the difference in overall seriousness amounts to almost one scale unit of seriousness.

A large variety of sample subgroups can be envisaged as of potential interest. But with so small a total sample, it is not possible to do more than compare a few of the more complex subgroup combinations than would be possible with larger samples. In table A–3 correlations are shown among subgroups that are defined by the cross classification of sex, race, and educational attainment, creating eight subgroups in all.

Note that the number of persons in each subgroup considered in table A–3 who contribute individual ratings to the averages that go into the comparisons is rather small. For example, the average ratings for relatively well educated black males are based on samples of seven and eight.[a] The largest subgroup size (18 or 19) can be found for white males of lesser educational attainment.

Given the small number of ratings on which these averages were computed, the correlations among the subgroups must be considered

[a] Recall that half of the respondents rated 120 of the crimes, the crimes being rated by any individual being a function of which alternate form of the questionnaire was received by the respondent. Twenty of the crimes were rated by all respondents and hence for those crimes twice the number of ratings are available for these subgroups (see table A-4).

Table A–3. Correlations Among Subgroup Means Computed for All 140 Crimes: Race, Educational Attainment, and Sex Subgroups

| | | Subgroup | | | | | | | | |
| | | Less Than High School Graduation | | | | High School Graduation or Better | | | | Overall Sample |
		Black Females (1)	White Females (2)	Black Males (3)	White Males (4)	Black Females (5)	White Females (6)	Black Males (7)	White Males (8)	
Less Than High School Graduate	Bl Fem (1)		.76	.70	.77	.74	.75	.78	.74	.86
	Wh Fem (2)			.61	.83	.76	.78	.77	.77	.88
	Bl Male (3)				.66	.65	.67	.63	.65	.77
	Wh Male (4)					.73	.79	.79	.79	.90
High School Graduate or Better	Bl Fem (5)						.78	.80	.74	.86
	Wh Fem (6)							.83	.93	.94
	Bl Male (7)								.84	.90
	Wh Male (8)									.93
	N =	[9]	[14]	[16–17]	[18–19]	[9–10]	[17]	[7–8]	[18]	[100]

159

quite high. The lowest correlation is +.61 and the highest +.94, and the average of all the correlations among subgroups is +.75.

Note that it is poorly educated black males who disagree most with the other subgroups in the sample, only one of the correlations involving this subgroup being as high as +.70.

In the last column of table A–3 the correlations of each subgroup's ratings with the overall sample ratings are given. Note that these correlations are rather high, above +.86 in every case, except for poorly educated black males. In short, the eight subgroups defined by race, educational attainment, and sex do not vary much from the ratings given by the total sample.

The correlations in table A–3 were computed over the 140 crimes. For a small subgroup of twenty crimes (marked by a "b" in table A–1) all respondents contributed to the ratings and hence by considering this subgroup alone, as in table A–4, we can essentially double the number of ratings.[a]

Note that doubling the number of ratings going into each subgroup average seriousness ratings considerably raises the correlation (table A–4 as compared with table A–3). Only four of the twenty-eight correlations are below +.80, and two of these are just barely below (+.79) that criterion. The range of correlations is from +.75 to +.96, averaging .86. Furthermore, the correlations of the subgroup ratings with the ratings of the total sample are all above +.88.

The data presented in table A–3 and table A–4 amount to a finding that there is considerable consensus within the sample of respondents. In short, the subgroups formed by the cross-classification of race, sex, and educational attainment agree with each other on the relative seriousness of the 140 crimes presented to them.

The overall agreement among subgroups tends to obscure the individual differences in crime seriousness ratings. In part, these individual differences arise out of disagreement with the general ordering of crimes given by the total sample, and in part they represent "error" in the sense of misunderstanding of the rating task, actual mistakes made by an individual in placing a card, etc. These latter individual differences tend to be ironed out by computing averages within a subgroup.

To obtain a measure of the degree to which individual respondents agreed with each other, a correlation was computed for each respon-

[a] These twenty crimes were chosen using our intuition to represent a "spread" in seriousness. Indeed, the average seriousness of the first twenty crimes is 6.24, which compares very favorably with the average seriousness of all 120, 6.27, with comparable standard deviations of 1.39 and 1.30 respectively. In short, these twenty crimes can be regarded as a reasonable subsample of the full 140 crimes.

Table A–4. Correlations Among Subgroup Average Crime Seriousness Ratings for First Twenty Crimes (Rated by All Respondents)

| | Subgroup | | | | | | | | |
| | Less Than High School Graduation | | | | High School Graduation or Better | | | | Overall Sample |
	Black Females (1)	White Females (2)	Black Males (3)	White Males (4)	Black Females (5)	White Females (6)	Black Males (7)	White Males (8)	
Less Than High School Graudate — Bl Fem (1)		.86	.87	.91	.88	.85	.87	.87	.93
Wh Fem (2)			.75	.88	.82	.89	.79	.84	.91
Bl Male (3)				.85	.83	.79	.78	.82	.88
Wh Male (4)					.87	.95	.87	.95	.98
High School Graduate or Better — Bl Fem (5)						.84	.85	.81	.91
Wh Fem (6)							.89	.96	.97
Bl Male (7)								.91	.93
Wh Male (8)									.97
N =	[18]	[28]	[23]	[27]	[19]	[34]	[15]	[36]	[200]

dent between the respondent's individual ratings and the average ratings given by the entire sample. One hundred and ninety-five out of the 200 (98 percent) of the correlation coefficients computed were positive, covering a range from −.78 to +.86, with an average correlation of +.54. Four out of the five negative correlations were smaller (in absolute size) than .10. The single high negative correlation (−.78) most likely resulted from either the respondent reversing the meaning of the scale or an error on the part of the interviewer in placing the sorted cards in the correct envelopes.

In short, even on the individual level where we can expect to find idiosyncratic factors at work, there is a considerable amount of agreement between individuals and the total sample. Indeed, given the amount of intergroup consensus, it would be surprising (if not arithmetically impossible) to find otherwise.

The data presented on the amount of consensus on the crime ratings are quite encouraging, in our view. There is more than a minimally acceptable amount of agreement among significant subgroups of the population. Hence, the crime ratings can be used as a measure of the extent to which our society regards crimes as serious.

The forty crimes in the construction of the offender vignettes can be viewed as a subsample of the forty crimes studied in our Baltimore survey. The question can be raised concerning the amount of consensus over these particular forty crimes; specifically, whether the generally favorable evidence for the total 140 crimes can also cover the subsample used in the vignettes.

The evidence on this question is shown in table A–5, where the correlations among subgroups are computed for the forty crimes used in the offender vignettes. In general, the correlations in table A–5 are higher than those shown in table A–3, averaging .77. However, the correlations involving the poorly educated black males do not share as strongly in the general consensus over the seriousness of the crimes and in the offender vignettes. It is difficult to provide an explanation for this pattern. Inspection of the residuals for the regression of the overall mean sources on the average scores for poorly educated black males suggests that this group tends to regard crimes against the person as considerably less serious than the total sample. For example, "beating up an acquaintance" is regarded as considerably less serious by the members of this group than one would expect from the scores given by the total sample.

Examining the correlations in the last column of table A–5, we are somewhat reassured to note that these correlations are quite high, and even the correlation involving poorly educated black males is +.72. The majority of the correlations in this column are over .9, indicating

Table A–5. Correlations Among Subgroup Means Computed for Forty Crimes Used in Construction of Offender Vignettes: Race, Educational Attainment, and Sex Subgroups

| | | Subgroup | | | | | | | | |
| | | Less Than High School Graduation | | | | High School Graduation or Better | | | | Overall Sample |
		Black Females (1)	White Females (2)	Black Males (3)	White Males (4)	Black Females (5)	White Females (6)	Black Males (7)	White Males (8)	
Less Than High School Graduate	Bl Fem (1)		.87	.73	.88	.76	.83	.87	.82	.91
	Wh Fem (2)			.55	.87	.80	.88	.86	.84	.92
	Bl Male (3)				.67	.57	.60	.66	.59	.72
	Wh Male (4)					.78	.88	.85	.86	.95
High School Graduate or Better	Bl Fem (5)						.84	.83	.83	.88
	Wh Fem (6)							.86	.95	.96
	Bl Male (7)								.88	.93
	Wh Male (8)									.95
	N =	[9]	[14]	[16–17]	[18–19]	[9–10]	[17]	[7–8]	[18]	[100]

that on these forty crimes, subgroups tend to agree very closely with each other and with the total sample on relative seriousness. Perhaps more important, the pattern of correlations in table A–5 is similar to those in earlier tables where the total set of 140 crimes were considered.

The forty crimes used in constructing the offender vignettes are also representative in the sense of having a mean (6.4) which is close to that of the mean of the total set of 140 crimes (6.3), and standard error (1.9) which is only slightly larger than that of total crime sample (1.1). In short, the sample chosen is reasonably representative of the full 140 crimes.

WHAT IS SERIOUSNESS?

In asking the respondent to rate crimes, we did not specify what we meant by "seriousness." Nor did we ask respondents what they meant by their ratings. Obviously, respondents imparted some meaning to the term "seriousness," a meaning shared sufficiently with others to produce the degree of consensus manifested.

We may never know precisely what our respondents had in mind when they placed each card bearing a description of an offense in a slot representing their subjective judgments about seriousness. However, we can reconstruct some of the principles that guided their placements by examining the way in which characteristics of the crimes being rated influenced the ratings given to those crimes. We shall see in this section that a very crude crime classification system can account for a rather large amount of the variation from crime to crime in the average ratings given.

The crime classification system employed was developed ad hoc by Rossi and applied by two research assistants to each of the crimes. The system consists of the following binary judgments applied to each of the offenses:

1. Crimes Against the Person I: murder, manslaughter
2. Crime Against the Person II: assault, rape and incest
3. Crime Against the Person III: all other crimes involving actual or threatened personal injury exclusive of those shown above
4. Crimes Involving Property I: cases in which the value of goods involved was more than $25
5. Crimes Involving Property II: all other crimes involving property
6. Selling Illegal Drugs: heroin, LSD, marijuana, pep pills
7. "White-Collar Crimes": embezzlement, income tax cheating, fraudulent business practices, etc.

8. "Victimless" Crimes: prostitution, homosexuality, etc.
9. Subversion (Crimes Against the State): desertion, spying for enemy, etc.
10. Crimes Against Policemen:
11. Crimes Against Order: loitering, disturbing the peace, etc.

Each of the crimes listed in table A–1 was given a code indicating the researchers' combined judgment whether it had one or more of the characteristics listed above. For example, "planned killing of a policeman" was coded "10000000010," indicating that the crime involved murder and was directed against a policeman. Although most of the crimes fell into only one of the categories distinguished above, a considerable minority were classified, as in the example given, as fitting more than one category.

Using the codes as dummy variables, a multiple regression was run using the mean crime seriousness rating as the dependent variable. The results are shown in table A–6. In this table, the unstandardized regression coefficients are shown for each of the eleven binary (or "dummy") variables listed above. These coefficients have a very specific meaning representing the estimated increment in average rating received by a crime with those characteristics. The increment is given in relation to crimes that have none of the characteristics represented in the eleven binary variables, i.e., crimes that would be coded "00000000000," the estimated score for which is given by the intercept

Table A–6. Regression Analysis of Crime Characteristics and Mean Seriousness Ratings for 140 Crimes

Dummy Variable	Unstandardized Regression Coefficient
1. Persons Crime I	1.92[a]
2. Persons Crime II	1.73[a]
3. Persons Crime III	1.12[a]
4. Property Crime I	.76[a]
5. Property Crime II	−.31
6. Drug Selling	1.82[a]
7. White-Collar Crimes	−.09
8. Victimless Crimes	.17
9. Subversion	.62[a]
10. Crime Against Police	.40
11. Crime Against Order	−1.92[a]
Intercept = 5.45	
R = .824[a]	
R^2 = .68[a]	

[a]Statistical significance at .05 level.

value, 5.45. Thus a crime involving a homicide is estimated by the regression equation to receive the score of 7.37 (1.92 + 5.45), and a crime involving the homicide of a policeman receives an estimated score of 7.77 (1.92 + .40 + 5.45).

The extent to which the eleven characteristics "account" for the mean seriousness scores given to the crimes is measured by the multiple correlation coefficient, .824, indicating that a relatively large amount (68 percent) of the variation from crime to crime in average seriousness can be accounted for by these characteristics. This value is in part dependent on the particular mix of crimes in the set of 140, a different set—for example, containing more crimes against property—would generate a smaller or larger correlation coefficient. It is unlikely, however, that the coefficient would decline or increase by very much.

The interpretation that can be placed upon these regression coefficients is that they represent the way in which respondents "typically" reacted to the characteristics of the crimes in question. Under this interpretation, it is clear that crimes against persons and drug selling are regarded as especially heinous, whereas crimes involving only property are not markedly different from the base crimes. At the opposite side, crimes "against order" are not viewed as particularly serious, as indicated by the large negative regression coefficient for the eleventh variable.

Some characteristics that we thought would play a role in the collective ratings of seriousness turned out to have regression coefficients that were not statistically significantly different from zero: white-collar crimes and "victimless crimes" are not marked by especially different collective judgments than the base crimes. Indeed, if we remove these dummy variables from the regression, we do not change the correlation coefficient by any significant degree.

The findings of this section can be summarized in two statements. First, it is clear that collectively[a] respondents were reacting to rather simple characteristics of the crimes they rated, as indicated by the fact that these eleven binary variables can account for so much of the variation in the mean ratings given. Second, crimes against persons

---

[a] The term "collective judgments" has been used throughout this section to indicate that we have been treating *average* ratings given by the entire sample and *not* ratings given by individuals. We can anticipate that an individual level of analysis in which we try to predict the reactions of individuals to crime seriousness on the basis of the characteristics of crimes may turn out to be quite different. At minimum, we can expect that the total amount of variation of "explained" will be considerably less since individual idiosyncrasies ironed out by the use of averages would have a chance to appear in the data. At maximum, we might find that the judgment processes require quite a different equation, although that does seem unlikely.

and illegal drug selling are seen as especially serious offenses, as compared with crimes against property.

SUBGROUP VARIATION IN MEAN SERIOUSNESS RATINGS

In an earlier section of this chapter, we examined the amount of agreement among subgroups of the sample defined by cross-classifying race, sex, and educational attainment. Although there was considerable agreement on the relative seriousness of crimes, there can still be differences among subgroups in the extent to which they consider the *entire set* of crimes to be more or less serious. This is the question to which this section will be devoted. In other words, do racial groups, males and females and persons who differ with respect to education, occupation, and age react differently to the total set of crimes presented to them?

In order to pursue this line of analysis we computed mean seriousness ratings for each of the crimes for each of the subgroups we wanted to distinguish. For example, in studying the effects of age, sex, and race simultaneously, the sample was divided into eight subgroups on the basis of the cross-classification of these three characteristics. (The sample size is too small to allow finer than dichotomous distinctions in age, occupation, or education, as the N's in table A–3 illustrate for the case of education.) Average ratings were computed for each of the 140 crimes, leading to a total of 1120 average seriousness ratings (8 subgroups times 140 crimes). Regression analyses were then run using subgroup membership as a dummy variable along with the characteristics of the crime, coded as shown in the previous section, omitting codes for "white-collar" and "victimless crimes."

The results of an analysis using age, race, and sex to define the subgroups is shown in table A–7. Note that the regression coefficients in that table have exactly the same meaning as shown in table A–6: that is, the coefficients represent the estimated increment (or decrement) that a crime receives when it is rated by members of a subgroup or, in the case of the coefficients for crime characteristics, when it has each of the characteristics in question. Thus, the coefficient .68 shown for young black females indicates that a crime receives .68 of a unit more when it is rated by a young black female, holding the characteristics of the crime constant. The base against which the increment (or decrement) is compared is more complicated in this case; it is the estimated rating given by older white males[a] rating crimes which have

---

[a] White males of higher status (older age, higher occupation, and higher education).

Table A–7.   Regression of Subgroup and Crime Characteristics on Mean Crime Ratings: Age, Sex, and Race Subgroup Characteristics

	Dummy Variable			*Unstandardized Regression Coefficient*
	Age	*Race*	*Sex*	
Subgroup Identification	Young	B	F	.68[a]
	Young	W	F	.73[a]
	Young	B	M	.79[a]
	Young	W	M	.12
	Old	B	F	.91[a]
	Old	W	F	.87[a]
	Old	B	M	1.00[a]
Crime Characteristics	Crimes Against Persons I			1.93[a]
	Crimes Against Persons II			1.78[a]
	Crimes Against Persons III			1.12[a]
	Property Crimes I			.75[a]
	Property Crimes II			−.09
	Illegal Drug Selling			2.08[a]
	Subversion			.56[a]
	Crime Against Police			.40[a]
	Crime Against Order			−1.65[a]

Intercept = 4.85
R = .76[a]

Note: Young age is defined as less than forty-five.
[a]Statistical significance at .05 level.

none of the characteristics shown in the table, and is designated in table A–7 as the intercept.

Note that each of the subgroups distinguished in table A–7 adds an increment to the average crime ratings (as compared with the base). In short, being black, female, or younger leads to a generally higher seriousness rating over all the crimes regardless of their characteristics. The amount of the increment varies, being least (and statistically insignificant) for young white males and greatest (1.00) for older black males.

The correlation coefficient at the bottom of table A–7 measures the extent to which the combination of subgroup characteristics and crime

in every analysis in this chapter have been taken as the base against which the other subgroups would be compared, a decision that was made on the basis of the high level of agreement between upper status males and the overall average ratings given by the sample.

characteristics "accounts" for the total variation among the 1120 average crime seriousness ratings. The correlation is fairly large, .76, indicating that about 58 percent of the variance among mean ratings is "accounted" for.[a] However, most of the variation among ratings is accounted for by the characteristics of the crime being rated (52 percent) with only a small amount of the variation (6 percent) being contributed by subgroup characteristics. In short, age, sex, and race count, but not for very much. (The analysis upon which this last statement is based is not shown here.)

Similar findings can be found for subgroups defined by educational attainment and the prestige rating of the occupation of the head of the house (a reasonable measure of socio-economic status). These findings are shown in tables A–8 and A–9. Persons coming from lower socio-economic level households have average seriousness ratings higher than those of higher status in this respect. Similarly, lower educated respondents generate seriousness averages higher than those of the better educated.

Although it is difficult to make precise judgments in this respect, it does appear that of all the characteristics considered, educational attainment seems to make the most difference. That is to say, race, sex, age, socio-economic status, and education all make a difference, but educational attainment seems to make a slightly greater difference. However, none of these subgroup characteristics account for very much of the total variation between average crime ratings, compared to the overarching influence of the characteristics of the crime being rated.

We turn to a last subgroup characteristic, this time one based on experience with crime as a victim. Our respondents were asked whether or not they or members of their households had been victims of any crime during the year (1972) of the survey.[b] Using the answers to this question, subgroups were formed based on whether or not the household had been victimized.

The findings of the subsequent regression analysis are shown in table A–10 and appear to be rather inconclusive. Some of the victimized groups regard crimes as more serious than their nonvic-

---

[a] Note that this is a smaller correlation than obtains for the crime characteristics alone (table A-6). In large part, this difference can be explained by the small number of ratings that go into each of the averages in table A-7 and hence the greater amount of "error" in the average ratings. All of the averages in table A-6 are computed for 100 or more respondents while some of the averages in table A-7 are computed over seven respondents, and the largest group is fifteen.

[b] Professional victimization researchers will find that our method for measuring victimization is far from adequate for any purposes other than very crude measurement. Obviously, we were not trying to estimate the extent of victimization in Baltimore, but mainly trying to get at an experiential component in crime seriousness ratings.

Table A–8.   Regression of Subgroup and Crime Characteristics on Mean Crime Ratings: Prestige of Occupation of Head of House, Race, and Sex

	Dummy Variable			Unstandardized Regression Coefficient
	Occupational Prestige	Race	Sex	
Subgroup	Low	B	F	.90[a]
Identification	Low	W	F	.89[a]
	Low	B	M	.86[a]
	Low	W	M	−.06
	High	B	F	.24[a]
	High	W	F	.65[a]
	High	B	M	.66[a]
Crime	Crimes Against Persons I			1.88[a]
Characteristics	Crimes Against Persons II			1.77[a]
	Crimes Against Persons III			1.13[a]
	Property Crimes I			.72[a]
	Property Crimes II			.12
	Illegal Drug Selling			2.13[a]
	Subversion			.60[a]
	Crime Against Police			.46[a]
	Crime Against Order			−1.60[a]

Intercept = 4.93
R = .75[a]

Note: Low Occupational Prestige is defined as NORC Prestige score of 36.3 or less.
[a]Statistical significance at .05 level.

timized counterparts, but some do not. Indeed, since the regression coefficients in the bottom three subgroups tend to be slightly higher than the top three subgroups. one might infer that being victimized leads to a slightly lower collective view of the seriousness of crimes in general.

The findings of this section indicate that subgroup characteristics do make some difference in the overall ratings of crime seriousness, but not much of a difference. Indeed, if we look at the regression coefficients for subgroups in tables A–7 through A–10, we find that the largest is 1.27 and the average is .45 (computed without regard to sign), indicating that varying the mixture of subgroups will not affect the vignette average ratings by very much. In other words, if all the raters were composed of the average subgroup, the ratings shown in table A–1 would vary at maximum by less than half a unit on the rating scale.

The implications of these findings are quite important. Because

Table A–9. Regression of Subgroup and Crime Characteristics on Mean Crime Ratings: Education, Sex, and Race Subgroup Characteristics

	Dummy Variable			*Unstandardized Regression Coefficient*
	Education	*Race*	*Sex*	
Subgroup	Low	B	F	.99[a]
Identification	Low	W	F	1.02[a]
	Low	B	M	1.27[a]
	Low	W	M	.08
	High	B	F	.61[a]
	High	W	F	.68[a]
	High	B	M	.27[a]
Crime	Crimes Against Persons I			1.92[a]
Characteristics	Crimes Against Persons II			1.81[a]
	Crimes Against Persons III			1.13[a]
	Property Crimes I			.77[a]
	Property Crimes II			−.07
	Illegal Drug Selling			2.18[a]
	Subversion			.56[a]
	Crime Against Police			.45[a]
	Crime Against Order			−1.66[a]

Intercept = 4.84
R = .76[a]

Note: Low Education is defined as less than high school graduation.
[a]Indicates statistical significance at .05 level.

subgroups vary so little from each other, the fact that our sample is not a representative one does not appear to be a fatal flaw. For example, our Baltimore sample is 37 percent black, more than twice the national percentage for the United States as a whole. However, since blacks add as a group .8 to the average seriousness score, this over-representation adds on to the scores of seriousness only .3 if we weight blacks according to national racial proportions. Furthermore, since blacks tend to agree quite closely with whites (r = .89) on the relative ordering of scores, the scores may be inflated slightly (.3) by the overrepresentation of blacks, but the resulting scores may still be used with little error to order crimes according to their seriousness.

CONCLUSIONS

The purpose of this appendix was to explore the extent to which the use of crime seriousness ratings in the construction of offender vignettes

Table A–10.   Regression of Subgroup and Crime Characteristics on Mean Crime Ratings: Victimization, Sex, and Race Subgroup Characteristics

	Dummy Variable			Unstandardized Regression Coefficient
	Victimized	*Race*	*Sex*	
Subgroup	Yes	B	F	.34[a]
Identification	Yes	W	F	.85[a]
	Yes	B	M	.39[a]
	Yes	W	M	−.17
	No	B	F	.75[a]
	No	W	F	.70[a]
	No	B	M	.88[a]
Crime	Crimes Against Persons I			2.04[a]
Characteristics	Crimes Against Persons II			1.91[a]
	Crimes Against Persons III			1.21[a]
	Property Crimes I			.77[a]
	Property Crimes II			−.06
	Illegal Drug Selling			2.04[a]
	Subversion			.61
	Crime Against Police			.47[a]
	Crime Against Order			−1.81[a]

Intercept = 4.88
R = .73[a]

Note: Victimization status is determined on the basis of an item in the questionnaire asking the respondent whether the respondent or any member of his household had been the victim of any crime in the previous year.
[a]Statistical significance at .05 level.

was justified. We believe that the findings displayed in this chapter do support their use.

The major prop for the use of crime seriousness ratings is the rather large amount of consensus that can be found among subgroups of our sample about the relative seriousness of the 140 crimes. By and large, the correlations between the mean ratings given by any reasonable subgroup and any other subgroup exceeds the usual standards for reliability in psychometric measurement.

The second line of reasoning is based upon the finding that a very crude classification of the characteristics of the crimes can account for much of the variation in the average ratings given to them. In contrast, the characteristics of individual raters did little more. By and large, the ratings are generated by the normative consensus that is characteristic of both sexes, socio-economic levels, races, and educational attainment levels.

It appears that ratings of crime seriousness are relatively invariant over significant subgroups, at least in the range of variation that we were able to observe in our Baltimore sample. Whether the invariance extends to time, region, and place is a matter for further research to probe.

The Pilot Study Questionnaire

The questionnaire that follows is in all essentials equivalent to the personal interview version, the main differences being question wordings changed to reflect the personal interview situation.

Note that Section V contains two of the twenty-nine samples of offender vignettes.

THE JOHNS HOPKINS UNIVERSITY

AND

NORTHWESTERN UNIVERSITY

STABILITY AND CHANGE
IN STATE CORRECTIONS SYSTEMS

Conducted Under a Grant From the
National Institute of Criminal Justice and Law Enforcement
of the Law Enforcement Assistance Administration

Peter H. Rossi, Ph.D., The Johns Hopkins University

Richard A. Berk, Ph.D., Northwestern University

Co-Principal Investigators

Survey Conducted by

Audits and Surveys, Inc.
One Park Avenue
New York, New York 10016

177

STATISTICAL CONTROL NUMBER

A-11	A-12	A-13	A-14	A-15	A-16	A-17	A-18

INSTRUCTIONS

Most of the questions can be answered by circling the number corresponding to the answer which comes **closest to your opinion or knowledge.**

FOR EXAMPLE:

Have you ever served on a jury in a criminal case?

 1. Yes

2. No

Please use the alternative answers we have provided even if they do not fit perfectly with what your own opinion or knowledge may be. If you want to modify your answer by writing in an explanation of your choice, please do so in a space close to the question involved.

Some of the questions ask that you write in your answer. Please give as full an answer as you can. If you don't have enough space for your answer, please write in the margins of the questionnaire.

All responses will be held in complete confidence. No one besides the research personnel will see your answers. Please mail the completed questionnaire to Audits & Surveys, Inc., using the stamped envelope provided for that purpose. If you have any questions about the survey—its purposes or whatever—please call us collect.

Peter H. Rossi: (301) 336-3300, Ext. 1272
Richard A. Berk: (312) 492-5342

Section I

The first few questions ask about your general assessment of the corrections system in your state

1. What do you see as the major strengths of your state's correctional system?
(A19-20)

_____
_____
_____
_____
_____
_____

2. From your point of view, are there any major problems facing the state's correctional system at this time?
(A-21)

   1. No

(A22-23)   2. Yes — what are they?

_____
_____
_____
_____
_____

3. Overall, how well do you think the state corrections system is doing in meeting problems it is facing?
(A24)

   1. Very Well

   2. Adequately

   3. So-so

   4. Inadequately

   5. Very Poorly

   6. Does not Apply

   9. Don't Know

4. State corrections systems usually consist of a number of parts. Each may be doing its particular job well or poorly. Please circle how well you think each of the following corrections components are doing in this state.

		Very Well	Ade-quately	So-So	Inade-quately	Very Poorly	No Such Institution In This State	Don't Know
(A25)	a. Juvenile Institutions and Reformatories	1	2	3	4	5	6	9
(A26)	b. Adult Men's Prisons	1	2	3	4	5	6	9
(A27)	c. Parole Board	1	2	3	4	5	6	9
(A28)	d. Parole Department	1	2	3	4	5	6	9
(A29)	e. Probation Department	1	2	3	4	5	6	9
(A30)	f. Community Treatment Facilities	1	2	3	4	5	6	9

5. In the preceding question, you made an overall
(A31)   assessment of the state's **adult men's prisons.** Such assessments are sometimes difficult to make, and one may not be completely confident about the judgment. How sure are you about your judgment about adult prisons?

1. Absolutely Certain

2. Very Sure

3. Fairly Sure

4. Somewhat Unsure

5. Not Sure at All

9. Don't Know

6. You also made an overall assessment of the state's
(A32)   **juvenile institutions and reformatories.** How sure are you of that assessment?

1. Absolutely Certain

2. Very Sure

3. Fairly Sure

4. Somewhat Unsure

5. Not Sure at All

6. Not Applicable (For example: No juvenile institutions in your state)

9. Don't Know

2

7. Some state corrections systems are having problems nowadays. As you read the following list of prison conditions, please indicate whether for your state you consider each to be a very serious problem, a moderately serious problem, a minor problem, or no problem at all.

		Very Serious	Moderately Serious	Minor Problem	Not A Problem	Don't Know
(A33) a.	Overcrowding	1	2	3	4	9
(A34) b.	Inadequate financial support	1	2	3	4	9
(A35) c.	Poorly trained guards	1	2	3	4	9
(A36) d.	Antiquated buildings	1	2	3	4	9
(A37) e.	Violence among prisoners	1	2	3	4	9
(A38) f.	Racial antagonism among prisoners	1	2	3	4	9
(A39) g.	Inadequate vocational training	1	2	3	4	9
(A40) h.	Inadequate psychiatric counseling	1	2	3	4	9
(A41) i.	Prisoner uprisings against prison conditions	1	2	3	4	9
(A42) j.	Public apathy about prisons	1	2	3	4	9
(A43) k.	Court interference in prison administration	1	2	3	4	9
(A44) l.	Harsh treatment by prison guards	1	2	3	4	9
(A45) m.	Lack of adequate security	1	2	3	4	9
(A46) n.	Homosexuality among prisoners	1	2	3	4	9
(A47) o.	Drug use among prisoners	1	2	3	4	9
(A48) p.	A high proportion of hardened offenders	1	2	3	4	9
(A49) q.	Inadequately trained prison administrators	1	2	3	4	9

8. Are there any problems faced by the corrections system in this state which were not listed?

(A50)   1.   No

(A51-52)   2.   Yes — What are those problems?_____

_____
_____
_____
_____

Section II

Next, we're interested in knowing how much contact you've had personally with various parts of your state's corrections system.

9.   How often have you visited any of the state's prison
(A53)   facilities?

    1.   My job requires that I visit prisons regularly (For example: prison warden, lawyer, etc.)

    2.   Never

    3.   Once

    4.   A Few Times

    5.   Many Times

10.   Have you ever talked to corrections officials or
(A54)   personnel about the problems of your state's corrections system?

    1.   No

    2.   Yes — How often? (circle one below)
        2. Once
        3. A Few Times
        4. Many Times

11.   When you come across articles in newspapers about
(A55)   criminal justice or corrections issues, how interested are you in reading them?

    1.   Very Interested

    2.   Somewhat Interested

    3.   Not Very Interested

    4.   Not at all Interested

    5.   Never come across articles like that

12.   Have you ever met with a group of prisoners, or
(A56)   ex-prisoners about problems of corrections institutions?

    1.   No

    2.   Yes

4

13.   We are also interested in learning about the prisons in your state. For example, as far as you know, are there . . .

		Yes	No	Don't Know
(A57) a.	Separate facilities for juvenile and adult offenders?	1	2	9
(A58) b.	Are most prisoners in your state released on parole before the end of their sentence?	1	2	9
(A59) c.	Are there counseling programs for prisoners conducted within prisons?	1	2	9
(A60) d.	Special treatment programs for imprisoned drug addicts?	1	2	9
(A61) e.	Vocational training programs for prisoners?	1	2	9
(A62) f.	Employment opportunities for prisoners in prison industries?	1	2	9
(A63) g.	Community based programs? (such as work release or part time prison)	1	2	9

(A64-65)
14.   As far as you know, about what proportion of released prisoners are tried and convicted of new offenses after release?

    ☐ Proportion (e.g., 10%, 70%, etc.)

    9 Don't Know

(A66-67)
15.   As far as you know, what does it cost your state per year to keep an adult offender in a state prison?

    ☐ Amount per year, approximately

    9 Don't Know

(A68-69)
16.   As far as you know, what does it cost your state per year to keep a juvenile offender in juvenile corrections facilities?

    ☐ Amount per year, approximately

    8 Does not apply

    9 Don't know

Section III

17. Below is a list of programs for corrections systems. Some of these programs are currently used in some states, and some may be introduced in the near future.

START
CARD
B

In Part A below please indicate whether each program is currently employed in your state.

Then, in Part B, please indicate whether you think implementation of each program would be better, make no difference, or be for the worse.

		Part A Is this a practice in your state?				Part B Do you think this practice would be for the better, make no difference, or be for the worse?			
		Yes	No	Don't Know		Better	Same	Worse	Don't Know
(B19) a.	Consolidation of jails and prisons under one state corrections agency with the elimination of locally-run jails	1	2	9		1	2	3	9 (B25)
(B20) b.	Longer required sentences for most crimes, and substantial reduction in opportunities for probation and parole	1	2	9		1	2	3	9 (B26)
(B21) c.	Community-based corrections for some offenders involving confinement evenings and weekends and freedom during the day to pursue normal occupations	1	2	9		1	2	3	9 (B27)
(B22) d.	Shorter, more flexible sentences for most offenders with a higher probability of granting parole	1	2	9		1	2	3	9 (B28)
(B23) e.	Probation and parole supervision consolidated in a single agency independent of the courts and prison systems	1	2	9		1	2	3	9 (B29)
(B24) f.	Increased use of sentences in which the offender must do some kind of work that benefits the offender's victim or larger society	1	2	9		1	2	3	9 (B30)

Section IV

18. State corrections systems could have a number of different goals. We are interested in your **personal assessment** of the importance for society of the goals listed below.

Circle the priority you would personally give to each goal.

	GOAL	HIGHEST PRIORITY	HIGH	IMPORTANT	USEFUL BUT NOT IMPORTANT	NEITHER USEFUL OR IMPORTANT	COUNTER-PRODUCTIVE
(B31) a.	Deterring crime by showing potential offenders the serious consequences for them of committing a criminal offense.	1	2	3	4	5	6
(B32) b.	Protecting the public by removing offenders from the community where they might commit additional crimes	1	2	3	4	5	6
(B33) c.	Administering punishment to offenders as retribution to society for the crimes committed	1	2	3	4	5	6
(B34) d.	Rehabilitating offenders so that they might pursue non-criminal lives.	1	2	3	4	5	6

19. What priorities do you think the **general public** in this state would give to these same goals?

Circle the priority you believe the general public would give to each goal .

	GOAL	HIGHEST PRIORITY	HIGH	IMPORTANT	USEFUL BUT NOT IMPORTANT	NEITHER USEFUL OR IMPORTANT	COUNTER-PRODUCTIVE	DON'T KNOW
(B35) a.	Dettering crime by showing potential offenders the serious consequences for them of committing a criminal offense.	1	2	3	4	5	6	9
(B36) b.	Protecting the public by removing offenders from the community where they might commit additional crimes	1	2	3	4	5	6	9
(B37) c.	Administering punishment to offenders as retribution to society for the crimes committed	1	2	3	4	5	6	9
(B38) d.	Rehabilitating offenders so that they might pursue non-criminal lives.	1	2	3	4	5	6	9

6

| START CARD H | (H11) (H12) | (H13) (H14) | (H15) (H16) | 2 3 (H17) (H18) | SECTION V |

20. As you know, there are many different ways a corrections system can treat convicted offenders. Below is a list of nine such alternative dispositions. Please read the nine alternatives carefully.

ALTERNATIVE DISPOSITIONS FOR CONVICTED OFFENDERS

1. **Release under supervision** to his local community for a period of **up to one year.**

2. **Release under supervision** to his local community for a period of **1 to 5 years.**

3. **Part-time confinement** (nights and/or weekends) in a **residential center** in a local community for a period of **up to one year.**

4. **Part-time confinement** (nights and/or weekends) in a **residential center** in a local community for a period of from **1 to 5 years.**

5. **Incarceration full-time** in a **prison** for up to one year.

6. **Incarceration full-time** in a **prison** for **one to five years.**

7. **Incarceration full-time** in a **prison** for **more than five years.**

8. **Confinement in a mental hospital for treatment.**

9. **Referral to a medical facility for treatment.**

The next few pages contain brief descriptions of convicted offenders. We would like you to . . .

Glance over the list of different types of offenses and offenders included.

Then, read each carefully and **circle a number**—1 to 9—in each row corresponding to the treatment **you think** ought to be given to each offender.

In cases where the offender description may include a wide range of people, select an appropriate treatment for the typical offender within that range.

We are interested in **your opinion**, regardless of what correctional treatment may be common in your state.

CIRCLE TYPE OF TREATMENT YOU THINK APPROPRIATE

		Release under Supervision		Part-Time Confinement		Prison			Mental Hospital	Medical Facility
		up to 1 yr.	1-5 yrs.	up to 1 yr.	1-5 yrs.	up to 1 yr.	1-5 yrs.	5+ yrs.		
(H19) 1	50 year old male, with a prior record of **several** felony convictions for crimes against **persons**, is found guilty of **killing someone in a bar room free-for-all.**	1	2	3	4	5	6	7	8	9
(H20) 2.	35 year old male, with a prior record of **several** felony convictions for crimes against **persons**, is found guilty of **beating up his spouse.**	1	2	3	4	5	6	7	8	9
(H21) 3.	15 year old male, with a prior record of **one** felony conviction for a crime against **property**, is found guilty of **using heroin.**	1	2	3	4	5	6	7	8	9
(H22) 4.	50 year old male, with **no** prior record, is found guilty of **impulsive killing of his spouse.**	1	2	3	4	5	6	7	8	9
(H23) 5.	22 year old male, with a prior record of convictions for **misdemeanors**, is found guilty of **shoplifting a dress from a department store.**	1	2	3	4	5	6	7	8	9
(H24) 6.	19 year old male, with a prior record of **several** felony convictions for crimes against **persons**, is found guilty of **planned killing of his spouse.**	1	2	3	4	5	6	7	8	9
(H25) 7.	50 year old male, with a prior record of convictions for **misdemeanors**, is found guilty of **burglary of a factory, stealing machine tools.**	1	2	3	4	5	6	7	8	9

		Release under Supervision up to 1 yr. 1-5 yrs.		Part-Time Confinement up to 1 yr. 1-5 yrs.		Prison up to 1 yr. 1-5 yrs. 5+ yrs.			Mental Hospital	Medical Facility
(H26) 8.	22 year old male, with **no** prior record, is found guilty of **knowingly selling worthless stocks.**	1	2	3	4	5	6	7	8	9
(H27) 9.	22 year old male, with a prior record of **several** felony convictions for crimes against **property,** is found guilty of **selling heroin.**	1	2	3	4	5	6	7	8	9
(H28) 10.	50 year old male, with a prior record of convictions for **misdemeanors,** is found guilty of **armed robbery of a bank.**	1	2	3	4	5	6	7	8	9
(H29) 11.	19 year old male, with a prior record of **several** felony convictions for crimes against **persons,** is found guilty of **passing worthless checks involving less than $100.**	1	2	3	4	5	6	7	8	9
(H30) 12.	22 year old male, with a prior record of **several** felony convictions for crimes against **persons,** is found guilty of **deliberately starting a fire which results in someone's death.**	1	2	3	4	5	6	7	8	9
(H31) 13.	35 year old male, with a prior record of **several** felony convictions for crimes against **persons,** is found guilty of **beating up a stranger.**	1	2	3	4	5	6	7	8	9
(H32) 14.	35 year old male, with a prior record of **several** felony convictions for crimes against **persons,** is found guilty of **armed robbery of a neighborhood druggist.**	1	2	3	4	5	6	7	8	9
(H33) 15.	22 year old male, with **no** prior record, is found guilty of **passing worthless checks involving less than $100.**	1	2	3	4	5	6	7	8	9
(H34) 16.	50 year old male, with a prior record of convictions for **misdemeanors,** is found guilty of **resisting arrest.**	1	2	3	4	5	6	7	8	9
(H35) 17.	22 year old male, with a prior record of **one** felony conviction for a crime against **persons,** is found guilty of **selling heroin.**	1	2	3	4	5	6	7	8	9
(H36) 18.	22 year old male, with **no** prior record, is found guilty of **beating up a stranger.**	1	2	3	4	5	6	7	8	9
(H37) 19.	19 year old male, with a prior record of **several** felony convictions for crimes against **property,** is found guilty of **soliciting for prostitution.**	1	2	3	4	5	6	7	8	9

		Release under Supervision up to 1 yr. 1-5 yrs.		Part-Time Confinement up to 1 yr. 1-5 yrs.		Prison up to 1 yr. 1-5 yrs. 5+ yrs.			Mental Hospital	Medical Facility
	20.	19 year old male, with a prior record of **one** felony conviction for a crime against **property**, is found guilty of **passing worthless checks for more than $100.**	1	2	3	4	5	6	7	8	9
(H39)	21.	22 year old male, with a prior record of **one** felony conviction for a crime against **persons,** is found guilty of **beating up an acquaintance.**	1	2	3	4	5	6	7	8	9
(H40)	22.	19 year old male, with a prior record of **one** felony conviction for a crime against **persons,** is found guilty of **shoplifting a carton of cigarettes from a supermarket.**	1	2	3	4	5	6	7	8	9
(H41)	23.	35 year old male, with a prior record of convictions for **misdemeanors,** is found guilty of **manufacturing and selling autos** known to be dangerously defective.	1	2	3	4	5	6	7	8	9
(H42)	24.	22 year old male, with a prior record of **several** felony convictions for crimes against **persons,** is found guilty of **causing the death of an employee by neglecting to repair machinery.**	1	2	3	4	5	6	7	8	9
(H43)	25.	15 year old male, with a prior record of convictions for **misdemeanors,** is found guilty of **armed robbery of a bank.**	1	2	3	4	5	6	7	8	9
(H44)	26.	22 year old male, with a prior record of **several** felony convictions for crimes against **persons,** is found guilty of **theft of a car for the purpose of resale.**	1	2	3	4	5	6	7	8	9
(H45)	27.	35 year old male, with a prior record of **several** felony convictions for crimes against **property,** is found guilty of **beating up an acquaintance.**	1	2	3	4	5	6	7	8	9
(H46)	28.	19 year old male, with a prior record of **several** felony convictions for crimes against **persons,** is found guilty of **beating up his spouse.**	1	2	3	4	5	6	7	8	9
(H47)	29.	35 year old male, with a prior record of convictions for **misdemeanors,** is found guilty of **theft of a car for the purpose of resale.**	1	2	3	4	5	6	7	8	9
(H48)	30.	22 year old male, with a prior record of **one** felony conviction for a crime against **property,** is found guilty of **armed robbery of a bank.**	1	2	3	4	5	6	7	8	9
(H49)	31.	22 year old male, with a prior record of **one** felony conviction for a crime against **persons,** is found guilty of **using heroin.**	1	2	3	4	5	6	7	8	9

		Release under Supervision up to 1 yr. 1-5 yrs.		Part-Time Confinement up to 1 yr. 1-5 yrs.		Prison up to 1 yr. 1-5 yrs. 5+ yrs.			Mental Hospital	Medical Facility
(H50)	32.	22 year old male, with no prior record, is found guilty of killing someone in a bar room free-for-all.	1	2	3	4	5	6	7	8	9
(H51)	33.	50 year old male, with a prior record of convictions for misdemeanors, is found guilty of impulsive killing of his spouse.	1	2	3	4	5	6	7	8	9
(H52)	34.	15 year old male, with no prior record, is found guilty of shoplifting a carton of cigarettes from a supermarket.	1	2	3	4	5	6	7	8	9
(H53)	35.	22 year old male, with a prior record of one felony conviction for a crime against property, is found guilty of using heroin.	1	2	3	4	5	6	7	8	9
(H54)	36.	50 year old male, with a prior record of convictions for misdemeanors, is found guilty of planned killing of his spouse.	1	2	3	4	5	6	7	8	9
(H55)	37.	22 year old male, with a prior record of one felony conviction for a crime against persons, is found guilty of burglary of a home, stealing a color TV set.	1	2	3	4	5	6	7	8	9
(H56)	38.	50 year old male, with a prior record of several felony convictions for crimes against persons, is found guilty of soliciting for prostitution.	1	2	3	4	5	6	7	8	9
(H57)	39.	19 year old male, with a prior record of several felony convictions for crimes against property, is found guilty of beating up a stranger.	1	2	3	4	5	6	7	8	9
(H58)	40.	22 year old male, with a prior record of convictions for misdemeanors, is found guilty of killing someone during a serious argument.	1	2	3	4	5	6	7	8	9

21. In cases where addictive drug use was a contributing factor in a felony, would you employ different corrections treatments than if drug use were not involved?

    1.   No
    2.   Yes—in what way?

22. In cases where habitual alcohol use was a contributing factor in a felony, would you employ different corrections treatments than if alcohol were not involved?

    1.   No
    2.   Yes—in what way?

START
CARD
J

23. Now we would like to know how convicted offenders are **usually treated in this state.** Using the **same set** of correctional treatments as before we would like you to . . .

Read each of the descriptions of offenses and offenders below and **circle a number**—1 to 9—corresponding to the treatment that is **usually given** to such offenders in this state.

We are interested in your impressions as well as precise knowledge. If you are not sure how a particular type of offender would be treated in this state, make an educated guess.

ALTERNATIVE DISPOSITIONS FOR CONVICTED OFFENDERS

1. **Release under supervision** to his local community for a period of **up to one year.**

2. **Release under supervision** to his local community for a period of **1 to 5 years.**

3. **Part-time confinement** (nights and/or weekends) in a **residential center** in a local community for a period of **up to one year.**

4. **Part-time confinement** (nights and/or weekends) in a **residential center** in a local community for a period of from **1 to 5 years.**

5. **Incarceration full-time** in a **prison** for up to **one year.**

6. **Incarceration full-time** in a **prison** for **one to five years.**

7. **Incarceration full-time** in a **prison** for more than **five years.**

8. **Confinement in a mental hospital for treatment.**

9. **Referral to a medical facility for treatment.**

CIRCLE TYPE OF TREATMENT TYPICALLY GIVEN IN THIS STATE

		Release under Supervision up to 1 yr.	1-5 yrs.	Part-Time Confinement up to 1 yr.	1-5 yrs.	Prison up to 1 yr.	1-5 yrs.	5+ yrs.	Mental Hospital	Medical Facility
(J19)	1.	19 year old male, with a prior record of convictions for **misdemeanors,** is found guilty of **mugging, and stealing $25 in cash.** → 1	2	3	4	5	6	7	8	9
(J20)	2.	22 year old male, with a prior record of **several** felony convictions for crimes against **persons and property,** is found guilty of **beating up an acquaintance.** → 1	2	3	4	5	6	7	8	9
(J21)	3.	22 year old male, with a prior record of **several** felony convictions for crimes against **persons,** is found guilty of **cashing stolen payroll checks.** → 1	2	3	4	5	6	7	8	9
(J22)	4.	35 year old male, with a prior record of one felony conviction for a crime against **property,** is found guilty of **armed robbery of a neighborhood druggist.** → 1	2	3	4	5	6	7	8	9
(J23)	5.	50 year old male, with a prior record of one felony conviction for a crime against **property,** is found guilty of **disturbing the peace.** → 1	2	3	4	5	6	7	8	9
(J24)	6.	35 year old male, with a prior record of one felony conviction for a crime against **property,** is found guilty of **neglecting to care for his own children.** → 1	2	3	4	5	6	7	8	9
(J25)	7.	19 year old male, with a prior record of one felony conviction for a crime against **persons,** is found guilty of **soliciting for prostitution.** → 1	2	3	4	5	6	7	8	9

	Release under Supervision up to 1 yr. 1-5 yrs.		Part-Time Confinement up to 1 yr. 1-5 yrs.		Prison up to 1 yr. 1-5 yrs. 5+ yrs.			Mental Hospital	Medical Facility
(J26) 8. 35 year old male, with a prior record of one felony conviction for a crime against property, is found guilty of **beating up a stranger.**	1	2	3	4	5	6	7	8	9
(J27) 9. 19 year old male, with a prior record of **several** felony convictions for crimes against **persons,** is found guilty of **resisting arrest.**	1	2	3	4	5	6	7	8	9
(J28) 10. 35 year old male, with a prior record of **one** felony conviction for a crime against **persons,** is found guilty of **passing worthless checks for more than $500.**	1	2	3	4	5	6	7	8	9
(J29) 11. 19 year old male, with a prior record of **one** felony conviction for a crime against **property,** is found guilty of **passing worthless checks involving less than $100.**	1	2	3	4	5	6	7	8	9
(J30) 12. 50 year old male, with a prior record of **several** felony convictions for crimes against **persons and property,** is found guilty of **passing worthless checks involving less than $100.**	1	2	3	4	5	6	7	8	9
(J31) 13. 19 year old male, with **no** prior record, is found guilty of **armed robbery of a company payroll.**	1	2	3	4	5	6	7	8	9
(J32) 14. 35 year old male, with a prior record of **one** felony conviction for a crime against **property,** is found guilty of **burglary of a factory, stealing machine tools.**	1	2	3	4	5	6	7	8	9
(J33) 15. 50 year old male, with **no** prior record, is found guilty of **resisting arrest.**	1	2	3	4	5	6	7	8	9
(J34) 16. 50 year old male, with a prior record of **several** felony convictions for crimes against **persons,** is found guilty of **killing someone during a serious argument.**	1	2	3	4	5	6	7	8	9
(J35) 17. 22 year old male, with a prior record of **several** felony convictions for crimes against **persons and property,** is found guilty of **shoplifting a carton of cigarettes from a supermarket.**	1	2	3	4	5	6	7	8	9
(J36) 18. 19 year old male, with a prior record of **one** felony conviction for a crime against **persons,** is found guilty of **armed robbery of a bank.**	1	2	3	4	5	6	7	8	9
(J37) 19. 19 year old male, with a prior record of **one** felony conviction for a crime against **property,** is found guilty of **planned killing of his spouse.**	1	2	3	4	5	6	7	8	9

	Release under Supervision up to 1 yr.	1-5 yrs.	Part-Time Confinement up to 1 yr.	1-5 yrs.	Prison up to 1 yr.	1-5 yrs.	5+ yrs.	Mental Hospital	Medical Facility
20. 22 year old male, with **no** prior record, is found guilty of **killing someone during a serious argument.**	1	2	3	4	5	6	7	8	9
(J39) 21. 35 year old male, with a prior record of convictions for **misdemeanors**, is found guilty of **causing the death of an employee by neglecting to repair machinery.**	1	2	3	4	5	6	7	8	9
(J40) 22. 19 year old male, with **no** prior record, is found guilty of **killing someone in a bar room free-for-all.**	1	2	3	4	5	6	7	8	9
(J41) 23. 35 year old male, with a prior record of **one** felony conviction for a crime against **persons**, is found guilty of **burglary of a factory, stealing machine tools.**	1	2	3	4	5	6	7	8	9
(J42) 24. 22 year old male, with a prior record of **one** felony conviction for a crime against **property**, is found guilty of **Impulsive killing of his spouse.**	1	2	3	4	5	6	7	8	9
'43) 25. 35 year old male, with **no** prior record, is found guilty of **impulsive killing of his spouse.**	1	2	3	4	5	6	7	8	9
(J44) 26. 22 year old male, with **no** prior record, is found guilty of **burglary of a factory, stealing machine tools.**	1	2	3	4	5	6	7	8	9
(J45) 27. 50 year old male, with a prior record of **one** felony conviction for a crime against **property**, is found guilty of **causing the death of an employee by neglecting to repair machinery.**	1	2	3	4	5	6	7	8	9
(J46) 28. 35 year old male, with a prior record of convictions for **misdemeanors**, is found guilty of **burglary of a home, stealing a portable transistor radio.**	1	2	3	4	5	6	7	8	9
(J47) 29. 22 year old male, with a prior record of **several** felony convictions for crimes against **persons**, is found guilty of **armed robbery of a company payroll.**	1	2	3	4	5	6	7	8	9
(J48) 30. 50 year old male, with a prior record of **one** felony conviction for a crime against **persons**, is found guilty of **beating up his spouse.**	1	2	3	4	5	6	7	8	9
(J49) 31. 50 year old male, with a prior record of **several** felony convictions for crimes against **property**, is found guilty of **burglary of a factory, stealing machine tools.**	1	2	3	4	5	6	7	8	9

		Release under Supervision up to 1 yr.	1-5 yrs.	Part-Time Confinement up to 1 yr.	1-5 yrs.	Prison up to 1 yr.	1-5 yrs.	5+ yrs.	Mental Hospital	Medical Facility
(J50) 32.	50 year old male, with a prior record of **one** felony conviction for a crime against **persons,** is found guilty of **assault with a gun on his spouse.**	1	2	3	4	5	6	7	8	9
(J51) 33.	22 year old male, with **no** prior record, is found guilty of **passing worthless checks for more than $500.**	1	2	3	4	5	6	7	8	9
(J52) 34.	50 year old male, with a prior record of one felony conviction for a crime against **property,** is found guilty of **burglary of a home, stealing a color TV set.**	1	2	3	4	5	6	7	8	9
(J53) 35.	19 year old male, with a prior record of convictions for **misdemeanors,** is found guilty of **killing someone during a serious argument.**	1	2	3	4	5	6	7	8	9
(J54) 36.	19 year old male, with a prior record of **several** felony convictions for crimes against **persons,** is found guilty of **armed robbery of a bank.**	1	2	3	4	5	6	7	8	9
(J55) 37.	35 year old male, with a prior record of **several** felony convictions for crimes against **persons,** is found guilty of **burglary of a home, stealing a portable transistor radio.**	1	2	3	4	5	6	7	8	9
(J56) 38.	19 year old male, with a prior record of **one** felony conviction for a crime against **persons,** is found guilty of **deliberately starting a fire which results in someone's death.**	1	2	3	4	5	6	7	8	9
(J57) 39.	50 year old male, with a prior record of convictions for **misdemeanors,** is found guilty of **cashing stolen payroll checks.**	1	2	3	4	5	6	7	8	9
(J58) 40.	15 year old male, with a prior record of convictions for **misdemeanors,** is found guilty of **armed robbery of a company payroll.**	1	2	3	4	5	6	7	8	9

24. In cases where addictive drug use was a contributing factor in a felony, are there typically different corrections treatments than if no drug use were involved?
    1. No
    2. Yes—in what way?

25. In cases where habitual use of alcohol was a contributing factor in a felony, are there typically different corrections treatments than if no use of alcohol were involved?
    1. No
    2. Yes—in what way?

SECTION VI

In this next few pages, you will find descriptions of how corrections systems might look in the future if some of the changes currently being proposed actually come about.

We are interested in getting your views on several of these alternative models.

26. Some people are advocating a general tightening up of our corrections system in which convicted offenders would be given fixed sentences based on the type of offense. Paroles and pardons would be given to just a small percentage of the offenders. Under this proposed alternative most offenders would serve out their full sentence in traditional prisons.

Assuming that it could be shown that these changes would lead to **no increase** in the costs of handling offenders and **no increase** in the rate of repeat offenders among those released, would you favor or oppose changes leading in this direction for this state?

Circle whether you favor or oppose the changes and then answer the four additional questions immediately below your choice.

(B39)

	1 FAVOR					**2 OPPOSE**			
	(Go to A-D Immediately Below)					(Go to E-H Immediately Below)			
	Yes, Still Favor	No, Now Oppose	Don't Know				Yes, Still Oppose	No, Now Favor	Don't Know
(B40) A. Suppose it could be shown that these changes would lead to a **25% increase in costs,** would you still be in favor?	1	2	9		E. Suppose it could be shown that these changes would lead to a **25% decrease in costs** would you still be opposed?	1	2	9	(B44)
(B41) B. How about a **50% increase in costs,** would you still be in favor?	1	2	9		F. How about a **50% decrease in cost,** would you still be opposed?	1	2	9	(B45)
(B42) C. Suppose it could be shown that these changes would lead to a **10% increase in repeat offenders,** would you still be in favor?	1	2	9		G. Suppose it could be shown that these changes would lead to a **10% decrease in repeat offenders,** would you still be opposed?	1	2	9	(B46)
D. How about a **30% increase in repeat offenders** would you still be in favor?	1	2	9		H. How about a **30% decrease in repeat offenders,** would you still be opposed?	1	2	9	(B47)

15

27. How likely do you think it is that the corrections system in this state will move in a direction like the one described above (in
(B48)   Question 26)?

1.   Very Likely

2.   It's a Possibility

3.   Unlikely

9.   Don't Know

28. In this state how much support to you think there would be among the groups listed below for such changes?

			Strong Support	Some Support	Neutral	Some Opposition	Strong Opposition	Don't Know
(B49)	a.	The General Public	1	2	3	4	5	9
(B50)	b.	State Legislators	1	2	3	4	5	9
(B51)	c.	State Courts	1	2	3	4	5	9
(B52)	d.	The Police	1	2	3	4	5	9
(B53)	e.	Corrections Officials	1	2	3	4	5	9
(B54)	f.	Citizens' Rights or Civil Liberties Organizations	1	2	3	4	5	9

29. If you were to actively **SUPPORT** changes like these
(B55)   would your support make any difference for your work
IN THE FUTURE? Would it improve your prospects,
worsen your prospects, or not matter much one way or
the other?

1.   Improve Prospects

2.   Worsen Prospects

3.   Not Matter

9.   Don't Know

31. Suppose such changes actually came about, would it
(B57)   make your **CURRENT WORK** harder, easier, or not
matter much one way or the other?

1.   Harder

2.   Easier

3.   Not Matter

9.   Don't Know

30. If you were to actively **OPPOSE** changes like these
(B56)   would your opposition make any difference for your
work **IN THE FUTURE?** Would it improve your
prospects, worsen your prospects, or not matter much
one way or the other?

1.   Improve Prospects

2.   Worsen Prospects

3.   Not Matter

9.   Don't Know

32. Suppose such changes came about. Would it make any
(B58)   differences for your work **IN THE FUTURE?** Would it
improve your prospects, worsen your prospects, or not
matter much one way or the other?

1.   Improve Prospects

2.   Worsen Prospects

3.   Not Matter

9.   Don't Know

16

33. Another set of proposals advocates a corrections system in which all convicted offenders would be given sentences of unspecified length. The major emphasis would be on rehabilitation through Job training, group and individual psychiatric counseling and other rehabilitation measures. Under this proposed alternative, most prisoners would be released on parole when they have improved enough to take a normal place in the community.

Assuming that it could be shown that these changes would lead to **no increase** in the costs of handling offenders and **no increase** in the rate of repeat offenders among those released, would you favor or oppose changes in this direction for this state?

Circle whether you favor or oppose these changes and then answer the four additional questions immediately below your choice.

<table>
<tr><td>(B59)</td><td colspan="4">**1 FAVOR** ↓
(Go to A-D Immediately Below)</td><td></td><td colspan="4">**2 OPPOSE** ↓
(Go to E-H Immediately Below)</td><td></td></tr>
<tr><td></td><td></td><td>Yes,
Still
Favor</td><td>No,
Now
Oppose</td><td>Don't
Know</td><td></td><td></td><td>Yes,
Still
Oppose</td><td>No,
Now
Favor</td><td>Don't
Know</td><td></td></tr>
<tr><td>(B60)</td><td>A. Suppose it could be shown that these changes would lead to a **25% increase in costs**, would you still be in favor?</td><td>1</td><td>2</td><td>9</td><td>E.</td><td>Suppose it could be shown that these changes would lead to a **25% decrease in costs**, would you still be opposed?</td><td>1</td><td>2</td><td>9</td><td>(B64)</td></tr>
<tr><td>(B61)</td><td>B. How about a **50% increase in costs**, would you still be in favor?</td><td>1</td><td>2</td><td>9</td><td>F.</td><td>How about a **50% decrease in costs**, would you still be opposed?</td><td>1</td><td>2</td><td>9</td><td>(B65)</td></tr>
<tr><td>(B62)</td><td>C. Suppose it could be shown that these changes would lead to a **10% increase in repeat offenders**, would you still be in favor?</td><td>1</td><td>2</td><td>9</td><td>G.</td><td>Suppose it could be shown that these changes would lead to a **10% decrease in repeat offenders**, would you still be opposed?</td><td>1</td><td>2</td><td>9</td><td>(B66)</td></tr>
<tr><td>(B63)</td><td>D. How about a **30% increase in repeat offenders**, would you still be in favor?</td><td>1</td><td>2</td><td>9</td><td>H.</td><td>How about a **30% decrease in repeat offenders**, would you still be opposed?</td><td>1</td><td>2</td><td>9</td><td>(B67)</td></tr>
</table>

34. How likely do you think it is that the corrections system in this state will move in a direction like the one described in
(B68) Question 33?

        1.   Very Likely   3.   Unlikely

        2.   It's a Possibility   9.   Don't Know

17

35. In this state how much support do you think there would be among the groups listed below for such changes?

		Strong Support	Some Support	Neutral	Some Opposition	Strong Opposition	Don't Know
(B69) a.	The General Public	1	2	3	4	5	9
(B70) b.	State Legislators	1	2	3	4	5	9
(B71) c.	State Courts	1	2	3	4	5	9
(B72) d.	The Police	1	2	3	4	5	9
(B73) e.	Corrections Officials	1	2	3	4	5	9
(B74) f.	Citizen's Rights or Civil Liberties Organizations	1	2	3	4	5	9

36. (B75) If you were to actively **SUPPORT** changes like these, would your support make any difference for your work **IN THE FUTURE?** Would it improve your prospects, worsen your prospects, or not matter much one way or the other?

1. Improve prospects
2. Worsen prospects
3. Not Matter
9. Don't Know

37. (B76) If you were to actively **OPPOSE** changes like these, would your opposition make any difference for your work **IN THE FUTURE?** Would it improve your prospects, worsen your prospects, or not matter much one way or the other?

1. Improve Prospects
2. Worsen Prospects
3. Not Matter
9. Don't Know

38. (B77) Suppose such changes actually came about, would it make your **CURRENT WORK** harder, easier, or not matter much one way or the other?

1. Harder
2. Easier
3. Not Matter
9. Don't Know

39. (B78) Suppose such changes came about. Would it make any difference for your work **IN THE FUTURE?** Would it improve your prospects, worsen your prospects, or not matter much one way or the other?

1. Improve Prospects
2. Worsen Prospects
3. Not Matter
9. Don't Know

18

40. Still another set of proposals would design a corrections system in which incarceration would be a treatment given only to a very small minority of offenders, such as habitual felons, and persons who had committed particularly serious crimes. Under this system, most offenders would be released under supervision to their local communities or committed to part-time confinement in community based corrections centers. Offenders would be released from supervision or part-time confinement as soon as they showed successful re-adjustment to the community.

START
9 7

Assuming that it could be shown that these changes would lead to **no increase** in the costs of handling offenders and **no increase** in the rate of repeat offenders among the released, would you favor or oppose changes in this direction for this state?

Circle whether you favor or oppose these changes and then answer the 4 additional questions immediately below your choice.

(C19)

	1 FAVOR (Go to A-D Immediately Below)			**2 OPPOSE** (Go to E-H Immediately Below)		
	Yes, Still Favor	No, Now Oppose	Don't Know	Yes, Still Oppose	No, Now Favor	Don't Know
(C20) A. Suppose it could be shown that these changes would lead to a **25% increase in costs,** would you still be in favor?	1	2	9	E. Suppose it could be shown that these changes would lead to a **25% decrease in costs,** would you still be opposed?	1	2	9	(C24)
(C21) B. How about a **50% increase in costs,** would you still be in favor?	1	2	9	F. How about a **50% decrease in costs,** would you still be opposed?	1	2	9	(C25)
(C22) C. Suppose it could be shown that these changes would lead to a **10% increase in repeat offenders,** would you still be in favor?	1	2	9	G. Suppose it could be shown that these changes would lead to a **10% decrease in repeat offenders,** would you still be opposed?	1	2	9	(C26)
(C23) D. How about a **30% increase in repeat offenders** would you still be in favor?	1	2	9	H. How about a **30% decrease in repeat offenders,** would you still be opposed?	1	2	9	(C27)

(C28) 41. How likely do you think it is that the corrections system in this state will move in a direction like the one described in Question 40?

1. Very Likely   3. Unlikely

2. It's a Possibility   9. Don't Know

19

42. In this state how much support do you think there would be among the groups listed below for such changes?

		Strong Support	Some Support	Neutral	Some Opposition	Strong Opposition	Don't Know
(C29) a.	The General Public	1	2	3	4	5	9
(C30) b.	State Legislators	1	2	3	4	5	9
(C31) c.	State Courts	1	2	3	4	5	9
(C32) d.	The Police	1	2	3	4	5	9
(C33) e.	Corrections Officials	1	2	3	4	5	9
(C34) f.	Citizen's Rights or Civil Liberties Organizations	1	2	3	4	5	9
(C35) g.	People who live in neighborhoods where community treatment centers might be located	1	2	3	4	5	9

43. (C36) If you were to actively **SUPPORT** changes like these would your support make any difference for your work **IN THE FUTURE?** Would it improve your prospects, worsen your prospects, or not matter much one way or the other?

1. Improve Prospects

2. Worsen Prospects

3. Not Matter

9. Don't Know

45. (C38) Suppose such changes actually came about, would it make your **CURRENT WORK** harder, easier, or not matter much one way or the other?

1. Harder

2. Easier

3. Not Matter

9. Don't Know

44. (C37) If you were to actively **OPPOSE** changes like these would your opposition make any difference for your work **IN THE FUTURE?** Would it improve your prospects, worsen your prospects, or not matter much one way or the other?

1. Improve Prospects

2. Worsen Prospects

3. Not Matter

9. Don't Know

46. (C39) Suppose such changes came about. Would it make any difference for your work **IN THE FUTURE?** Would it improve your prospects, worsen your prospects, or not matter much one way or the other?

1. Improve Prospects

2. Worsen Prospects

3. Not Matter

9. Don't Know

20

47. A great many specific changes in corrections are being proposed currently. Some involve new ideas on offender treatment and some are revisions of current or even once-abandoned practices. As you read the following list of proposals, please indicate whether you would generally favor, oppose, or take a neutral position on each **FOR YOUR STATE.**

		Oppose	Neutral	Favor	Don't Know
(C40) a.	Re-instatement of the death penalty for habitual felons who commit serious crimes.	1	2	3	9
(C41) b.	Abolition of censorship of prisoners' mail.	1	2	3	9
(C42) c.	Provision of methadone maintenance programs in prison.	1	2	3	9
(C43) d.	Greater use of solitary confinement for offenses committed in prison.	1	2	3	9
(C44) e.	Increased emphasis on vocational training that has a close relationship to outside employment possibilities.	1	2	3	9
(C45) f.	Greater use of corporal punishment for offenses committed in prisons.	1	2	3	9
(C46) g.	Permitting visits by prisoners spouses for sexual purposes.	1	2	3	9
(C47) h.	Allowing prisoners to be represented by counsel in prison offense hearings.	1	2	3	9
(C48) i.	Allowing prisoners to be represented by counsel at parole hearings.	1	2	3	9
(C49) j.	Allowing parolees to be represented by counsel at parole revocation hearings.	1	2	3	9
(C50) k.	Greater use of group therapy for prisoners.	1	2	3	9
(C51) l.	Greater use of half-way houses for prisoners awaiting full release.	1	2	3	9
(C52) m.	Greater use of community corrections centers for part-time confinement of some offenders.	1	2	3	9
(C53) n.	Routinely granting weekend furloughs so that many prisoners could periodically visit their communities.	1	2	3	9
(C54) o.	Allowing prisoner participation in prison self-government.	1	2	3	9
(C55) p.	Strengthening the powers of prison guards in disciplining prisoners.	1	2	3	9

SECTION VII

48. States vary in the ways in which legislation affecting the corrections system is brought to the legislature and enacted. In some states there are many groups and individuals who participate actively, and in others there are only a few key groups and persons involved.

On the page immediately to your right you will find a list of some of the people and groups who are sometimes active in corrections legislation in some states.

The columns in the facing page are for recording your answers to each question asked below. Circle your answers.

Read over the list first. If there are any groups or persons who are important in corrections policy in your state whom we left out, please write in the names on the blank lines (20-24) on the bottom of the list.

a. For each group, circle the number under "a" corresponding to **HOW ACTIVE** that group is in corrections policy making and legislation.

b. If you wanted to get a piece of corrections legislation through the state legislature, which of these groups or individuals would it be very important to **GET ON YOUR SIDE**. Please indicate these crucial allies by circling appropriate numbers in column "b".

c. Whose **OPPOSITION** could make it impossible or very difficult to get corrections legislation passed? Circle your answers in column "c."

d. Are there any of these groups in which you **KNOW SOME OF THE KEY MEMBERS** well enough to call them about something concerning corrections issues? Please circle your answers in column "d."

e. Have you ever **CONTACTED** any of these individuals or group members about corrections issues? Please indicate which in column "e."

f. For which groups or individuals, if any, do **YOU** feel you have **SIGNIFICANT INFLUENCE** on the positions **THEY** take? Please indicate this in column "f."

g. Which of the groups or individuals, if any, do you feel have **SIGNIFICANT INFLUENCE** on the positions **YOU** take? Please indicate this in column "g."

22

		(C56-79) a. How Active?				START CARD D (D19-42) b. Essen- tial for Aid	(D43-66) c. Can Stop a Pro- posal	START CARD E (E19-42) d. Know Members?	(E43-66) e. Have Con- tacted?	START CARD F (F19-42) f. Have Influ- enced?	(F43-66) g. Been Influ- enced by?
		Plays no Role	Rarely Active	Some- times Active	Always Active						
1.	Governor	1	2	3	4	1	1	1	1	1	1
2.	Citizens' Crime Commission	1	2	3	4	1	1	1	1	1	1
3.	Democratic Leader in State Senate (upper hse.)	1	2	3	4	1	1	1	1	1	1
4.	Republican Leader in State Senate (upper hse.)	1	2	3	4	1	1	1	1	1	1
5.	Democratic Leader in State House (lower hse.)	1	2	3	4	1	1	1	1	1	1
6.	Republican Leader in State House (lower hse.)	1	2	3	4	1	1	1	1	1	1
7.	State Senate Corrections Comm.	1	2	3	4	1	1	1	1	1	1
8.	State House Corrections Comm.	1	2	3	4	1	1	1	1	1	1
9.	LEAA State Planning Agency	1	2	3	4	1	1	1	1	1	1
10.	Head of State Corrections Dept.	1	2	3	4	1	1	1	1	1	1
11.	State Attorney- General	1	2	3	4	1	1	1	1	1	1
12.	State Bar Assoc.	1	2	3	4	1	1	1	1	1	1
13.	Police Chiefs of Large Police Depts.	1	2	3	4	1	1	1	1	1	1
14.	American Civil Liberties Union (ACLU)	1	2	3	4	1	1	1	1	1	1
15.	State Parole Dept. and Staff	1	2	3	4	1	1	1	1	1	1
16.	Ex-Offenders Org.	1	2	3	4	1	1	1	1	1	1
17.	Associations of Corrections Pers.	1	2	3	4	1	1	1	1	1	1
18.	Prominent Crim. Lawyers in State	1	2	3	4	1	1	1	1	1	1
19.	Assocs. of Police Personnel	1	2	3	4	1	1	1	1	1	1
20.	___	1	2	3	4	1	1	1	1	1	1
21.	___	1	2	3	4	1	1	1	1	1	1
22.	___	1	2	3	4	1	1	1	1	1	1
23.	___	1	2	3	4	1	1	1	1	1	1
24.	___	1	2	3	4	1	1	1	1	1	1

23

START
CARD
G

49. People involved with corrections sometimes vary in
(G19) their degree of participation in the formation of
corrections policy. Would you consider yourself to
be . . .

   1. A KEY PERSON, someone whose views are
sought and usually taken into account
before decisions are made

   2. An IMPORTANT PERSON, someone whose
views are often paid attention to

   3. An INTERESTED PARTICIPANT, someone
who usually tries to make his views
on corrections known

   4. An INTERESTED BYSTANDER, someone
who is concerned about what is done in
the field of corrections, but who rarely
has any influence over what happens

   5. NOT MUCH OF A PARTICIPANT in the
corrections policy process

   9. Don't Know

50. Have you ever testified before legislative committees or
(G20) state commissions on issues related to corrections?
(Circle as many as apply)

   1. No

   2. Yes, Legislative Committees

   3. Yes, Official State Commissions on Crime and/or
Corrections

51. Have you or any member of your household been
victimized by a crime in the last five years?

(G21) 1. No

(G22) 2. Yes.

    a. how many times? _____

(G23)   b. In general, do you think justice was
done in the(se) case(s)?

       1. No

       2. Yes

Section VIII

Now, a few questions about your background . . .

52. How old are you? [   ]
(G24-25)
      Years (round to nearest birthday)

53. What is your sex?
(G26)
    1. Male   2. Female

24

54. What is your race or ethnic background?
(G27)

   1. White

   2. Black (Negro)

   3. Oriental

   4. Spanish-speaking

   5. Other

55. What is your educational background?
(G28)

   1. Elementary School or Less (8 years or less)

   2. Some High School

   3. High School Graduate

   4. Some College

   5. College Graduate

   6. Advanced professional or academic degree
(Law School, Medicine, Social Work, Ph.D.)

56. When you were sixteen, what was your father's
(G29-30) occupation?

_____

57. Did your education include courses or internship
(G31-37) experiences in corrections, criminology, police science,
criminal law or penology or some other courses directly
related to corrections? (Circle as many as apply)

   1. None

   2. Corrections

   3. Criminology

   4. Police Science

   5. Criminal Law

   6. Penology

   7. Some Other Related Course (SPECIFY)

58. Have you ever held jobs as a police officer, judge,
(G38-44) probation officer, criminal lawyer, prison guard, prison
official, or some other job connected directly with
corrections? (Circle as many as apply)

   1. Never held any such jobs

   2. Police Officer

   3. Judge

   4. Probation Officer

   5. Criminal Lawyer

   6. Prison Official

   7. Some Other Related Job (SPECIFY)

_____

That is the end of the questionnaire. Thank you for your
help.

Notes

CHAPTER 1

1. Norman C. Miller, for example, in a recent *Wall Street Journal* article ("Does It Matter Who is Elected President? Many People Say No," 2 February 1976, p. 1) summarizes numerous studies to argue: "A grim array of polling evidence indicates that alienation and cynicism toward politics and government have become pervasive. . . ." He also quotes Irving Crespi of the Gallup Organization: "If this trend persists, it is within the realm of possibility that the U.S. will in the near future experience its greatest crisis in confidence since 1933."

2. See, for example: Gene Kassebaum, David Ward and Daniel Wilner, *Prison Treatment and Parole Survival: An Empirical Assessment* (New York: John Wiley and Sons, 1971); Walter C. Baily, "Correction Outcomes: An Evaluation of 100 Reports", *Journal of Criminal Law, Criminology and Police Science*, 52, no. 2 (1966); Douglas Lipton, Robert Martinson and Judith Wilks, *The Effectiveness of Correctional Treatment: A Survey of Treatment Evaluation Studies* (New York: Praeger, 1975).

3. See, for example: Jacqueline Cohen, Kenneth Fields, Michael Lettre, Richard Stafford and Claire Walker, "Implementation of the JUSSIM Model in a Criminal Justice Planning Agency," *Journal of Research on Crime and Delinquency*, July 1973.

4. See, for example: Franklin E. Zimring and Gordon J. Hawkins, *Deterrence* (Chicago: University of Chicago Press, 1974); Jack P. Gibbs, *Crime, Punishment and Deterrence* (New York: Elesevier, 1975).

5. There has been extensive academic research on these issues. See, for example: Rose Giallombardo, *Society of Women: A Study of a Women's Prison* (New York: John Wiley, 1966); John Irwin and Donald R. Cressey, "Thieves, Convicts and Inmate Culture," *Social Problems* 10 (Fall, 1962); Gresham M.

Sykes, *Society of Captives* (Princeton: Princeton University Press, 1958); Stanton Wheeler, "Socialization in Correctional Communities," *American Sociological Review* 26 (October, 1961); Thomas P. Wilson, "Patterns of Management and Adaptation to Organizational Roles: A Study of Prison Inmates," *American Journal of Sociology* 74 (September, 1968). But perhaps more compelling is material coming from prisoners themselves. See, for example: George Jackson, *Soledad Brother: The Prison Letters of George Jackson* (New York: Coward-McCann, 1970); Angela Y. Davis, *If They Come in the Morning* (New York: Signet Books, 1971); Eldridge Cleaver, *Soul On Ice* (New York: McGraw Hill, 1968).

6. *The Crime of Punishment* (New York: Viking, 1966).

7. Vernon Fox, "Prison Reform and Cost-Benefit Analysis" in *Criminal Justice Research*, Emilio Viano, ed., (Lexington, Mass.: Lexington Books, 1975), pp. 198–99.

8. See, for example, Benedict S. Alper, *Prisons Inside-Out: Alternatives in Correctional Reform* (Cambridge, Mass.: Ballinger Publishing Company, 1974).

9. See, for example, John P. Conrad, "Corrections and Simple Justice," *Journal of Criminal Law and Criminology* 64, no. 2 (1973).

10. See, for example, Norval Morris, "The Future of Imprisonment: Toward a Punitive Philosophy," *Michigan Law Review* 72 (1974); David J. Rothman, "Decarcerating Prisoners and Patients," *Civil Liberties Review* 1, no. 1 (1973); and David Fogel, *We are the Living Proof* (Cincinnati: W.H. Anderson, 1976).

11. *Ideology and Crime* (New York: Columbia University Press, 1966).

12. Andrew Rutherford, "Youth Corrections in Massachusetts," The Academy for Contemporary Problems, Columbus, Ohio, 1973.

13. The corrections recommendations studied were taken from a working draft of the Task Force on Corrections of the National Advisory Commission on Criminal Justice Standards and Goals. The draft was made available to us by the staff of the National Institute of Criminal Justice and Law Enforcement.

14. The model is a very general one, variants of which have been employed in the study of voting behavior (See Angus Campbell et al., *The American Voter*, New York: John Wiley and Sons, 1960), in the study of legislative rollcall votes (Duncan MacRae, Jr., *Issues and Parties in Legislative Voting*, New York: Harper and Sons, 1970), and in the study of local community decision-making (Peter H. Rossi, "Community Decision Making," *Administrative Science Quarterly* 1, March 1957).

15. Essentially a sample survey of the general population in Baltimore in which 140 offenses were rated according to seriousness. This survey is described in greater detail in appendix A.

16. The population data cited are as of December 31, 1970. Source: *National Prisoner Statistics: Prisoners in State and Federal Institutions of Adult Felons, 1968, 1969, 1970*, tables 10C and 11C (Washington, D.C.: U.S. Department of Justice, Bureau of Prisons, #47, April 1972).

17. The selection of the final sample and the three states to be used in the first phase of the study was undertaken in consultation with staff members of

the National Institute on Law Enforcement and Criminal Justice of the Law Enforcement Assistance Administration.

18. There was little in the way of published literature to aid in obtaining information on the typical composition of the partisan group. We were much helped by the pioneering study of Professor Heinz on the politics of criminal law policy in Illinois (see "Legislative Politics and the Criminal Law," *Northwestern University Law Review* 64, no. 3 (July–August 1969).

19. The assembly of these lists was in the able hands of Sally Zulver and Larry Kaagan, who became expert in extracting names and addresses from sometimes unwilling and suspicious sources.

20. We are especially indebted to Mr. Dexter Neadle and Mr. Nagesh Gupta of Audits and Surveys, who were in charge of shepherding the study into the field.

CHAPTER 2

1. There is, of course, a vast and pessimistic literature expressing critical views of corrections on which any of these parties might draw. Some of the more comprehensive and telling critiques include: Walter C. Bailey, "Corrections Outcomes: An Evaluation of 100 Reports," *Journal of Criminal Law, Criminology and Police Science* 57:2 (1966); Jessica Mitford, *Kind and Unusual Punishment* (New York: Knopf, 1973); Benedict S. Alper, *Prisons Inside-Out* (Cambridge, Mass.: Ballinger, 1974); Douglas Lipton, Robert Martinson and Judith Wilks, *The Effectiveness of Correctional Treatment: A Survey of Treatment Evaluation Studies* (New York: Praeger, 1975).

2. For a devastating critique of the actions of parole boards, see Robert K. Kastenmeir and Howard C. Eglit, "Parole Release Decision-Making: Rehabilitation, Expertise and the Demise of Mythology," *American University Law Review*, 22, no. 3 (Spring 1973), pp. 477–525.

3. For an interesting review of recent attempts to affect juvenile delinquency, see Stevens H. Clark, "Juvenile Offender Programs and Delinquency Prevention," *Crime and Delinquency Literature* 6 (1974), pp. 377–99.

4. See for example, David J. Rothman, "Decarcerating Prisoners and Patients," *The Civil Liberties Review* 1, no. 1 (1973), pp. 8–30.

5. The items in question are 13a through 13b in the questionnaire shown in appendix B. Another item that did not discriminate well among elite members asked how interested they were in articles on criminal justice or corrections issues that appeared in newspaper or magazines: 87 percent claimed to be "very interested" in such articles, and only one respondent claimed to be "not very interested."

6. However, the cost estimates are well within the range of estimates from other jurisdictions. See, for example, Jacqueline Cohen, Kenneth Fields, Michel Lettre, Richard Stafford, and Claire Walker, "Implementation of the JUSSIM Model in a Criminal Justice Planning Agency," *Journal of Research on Crime and Delinquency*, July 1973, pp. 117–31.

7. These tables represent "distilled" models in which only variables with

unique contributions over 1 percent are included. While this seat-of-the-pants stepwise procedure makes one vulnerable to Type I errors, in our case, the "full" models suggest identical substantive interpretations. Moreover, if one wants to take the significance tests seriously, the 1 percent criterion clearly errs in the direction of including unimportant effects. The reader may also notice much smaller Ns for these models. This results in part from the index construction in which respondents failing to answer *any* index component were dropped from the analysis.

CHAPTER 3

1. For an especially provocative discussion of many of these issues see Norval Morris, "The Future of Imprisonment: Toward a Punitive Philosophy," *Michigan Law Review* 72 (1974), pp. 1161–80.
2. Norval Morris, "The Future of Imprisonment: Toward a Punitive Philosophy," *Michigan Law Review* 72 (1974), pp. 1161.
3. See for example, John P. Conrad, "Corrections and Simple Justice," *Journal of Criminal Law and Criminology* 64, no. 2 (1973), pp. 208–217.

CHAPTER 4

1. Regressions were run with both "essential support" and "veto power" as dependent variables. As one would expect from the high correlation (.95) reported between these two measures, results of the regressions were only marginally different from each other. In neither case were the regressions significantly different from zero.

CHAPTER 7

1. This distinction cannot be overemphasized. See, for example Richard A. Berk, Selma Lesser and Harold Brackman, *The Measure of Justice: An Empirical Study of the Changing Criminal Law,* New York, Academic Press, 1977.

APPENDIX A

1. A shortened version of this appendix appears as "The Seriousness of Crime: Normative Structure and Individual Differences," *American Sociological Review* 39: 224–237 (April 1974). In addition to the current authors, Emily Waite and Christine Bose, participated as co-authors in that article.
2. Our survey is patterned in a general way after the pioneering work of M. Wolfgang and T. Sellin's *The Measurement of Juvenile Delinquency* (New York: John Wiley, 1964), differing from it mainly in the method used and in being applied to a more heterogeneous population.
3. Sidney Hollander and Associates is a reputable Baltimore market research firm maintaining an exceptionally good interviewing staff. We are

especially appreciative of the efforts made by Mary Lee Considine and Ruby Creighton to complete the assignment within record time.

4. Seymour Sudman *Reducing the Cost of Surveys* (Chicago: Aldine Press, 1967).

5. The actual wording of the question soliciting ratings was as follows: "Criminal law covers a very large number of different kinds of crimes. Some are considered to be very serious acts and others are not so serious. We are interested in your opinions about how serious you think different crimes are. We have made up descriptions of different kinds of crimes. Here is one of the descriptions of crimes. (Interviewer hands card to respondent.) Please put the card in the slot labelled number 9 if you think that this crime is among the most serious crimes. Put the card in slot number 1 if you think that the crime described on the card is among the least serious. If the crime described on the card fits somewhere in between the most serious and the least serious, put it in a slot in between 9 and 1 depending on how serious the crime is in your opinion."

About the Authors

Richard A. Berk is a Professor of Sociology at the University of California at Santa Barbara. He has published widely in the fields on collective behavior and evaluation research in such journals as the *American Sociological Review, Sociological Methods and Research, Social Problems,* and *Social Science Research.* He is also co-editor with Howard Freeman of *Evaluation Quarterly* and an associate editor of the *American Sociological Review.* Other research related to the study report in this monograph includes *The Measure of Justice: An Empirical Study of the Changing Criminal Law,* co-authored with Selma Lesser and Harold Brackman. (Academic Press, 1977).

Peter H. Rossi is Professor of Sociology and Director of the Social and Demographic Research Institute of the University of Massachusetts at Amherst. He has taught Sociology at Harvard, The University of Chicago and Johns Hopkins. From 1960 to 1967 he was Director of the National Opinion Research Center at The University of Chicago. His recent books include *Reforming Public Welfare* and *The Roots of Urban Discontent* as well as *Evaluating Social Programs.* He has published more than 80 articles in scholarly and professional publications and has served as the elected Secretary of the American Sociological Association.

365.7
B512

105494

DEMCO